FREUD, PROUST AND LACAN

Theory as fiction

MALCOLM BOWIE

CAMBRIDGE UNIVERSITY PRESS

Cambridge
New York Port Chester
Melbourne Sydney

Published by the Press Syndicate of the University of Cambridge
The Pitt Building, Trumpington Street, Cambridge CB2 1RP
40 West 20th Street, New York, NY 10011-4211, USA
10 Stamford Road, Oakleigh, Melbourne 3166, Australia

First published 1987
First paperback edition 1988
Reprinted 1988, 1990

Printed in Great Britain at
the University Press, Cambridge

British Library cataloguing in publication data

Bowie, Malcolm
Freud, Proust and Lacan: theory as fiction.
1. Freud, Sigmund 2. Lacan, Jacques
3. Proust, Marcel 4. Literature – Philosophy
I. Title
801 PN45

Library of Congress cataloguing-in-publication data

Bowie, Malcolm.
Freud, Proust, and Lacan: theory as fiction.
1. Proust, Marcel, 1871–1922 – Knowledge – Psychology.
2. Freud, Sigmund, 1856–1939 – Influence. 3. Lacan, Jacques, 1901–1981 – Influence. 4. Psychoanalysis and literature. I. Title.
PQ2631.R63Z545254 1987 843′.912 86–12928

ISBN 0 521 25614 3 hardback
ISBN 0 521 27588 1 paperback

leeds
metropolitan
university

Leeds Metropolitan University
17 0386954 1

ille fugit per quae fuerat loca saepe secutus,
heu! famulos fugit ipse suos. clamare libebat:
'Actaeon ego sum: dominum cognoscite vestrum!'
verba animo desunt; resonat latratibus aether.

He fled, where he had himself so often pursued his quarry, fled, alas, before his own faithful hounds. He longed to cry out: 'I am Actaeon! Don't you know your own master?' but the words he wanted to utter would not come – the air echoed with barking.

Ovid: *Metamorphoses*

in welche Zukunft sollte Erinnerung da noch eingehen?

Hermann Broch: *Der Tod des Vergil*

what was the future towards which remembrance must go?

The Death of Virgil

Contents

Illustrations

Acknowledgements

Earlier versions of these papers were read to university and psychoanalytic audiences in Britain and the United States. Chapter Two was originally an inaugural lecture delivered at Queen Mary College in the University of London and published as a pamphlet by the College. Chapter Four, which was my contribution to *Structuralism and Since* (ed. John Sturrock, Oxford University Press, 1979), has been revised and partially updated, although only those very pressed for time will now read it in preference to the fine full-length studies of Bice Benvenuto and Roger Kennedy (*The Works of Jacques Lacan*, Free Association Books, 1986) and Ellie Ragland-Sullivan (*Jacques Lacan and the Philosophy of Psychoanalysis*, Croom Helm and the University of Illinois, 1986). I am grateful for invitations to address the British Psycho-Analytical Society, the British Comparative Literature Association, the Society for French Studies, the Oxford Psycho-Analytical Forum, the Cambridge Modern Language Society, the Cultural Centre for Freudian Studies and Research and the Modern Critical Theory Group, to conduct seminars at the Tavistock Clinic and to write on psychoanalysis and related topics for *The Listener*, *Romance Studies*, *Paragraph* and BBC Radio 3. I should like to thank all the editors and publishers concerned for permission to reprint material that originally appeared in their pages, and the Accademia in Venice and the National Gallery of Scotland in Edinburgh for permission to reproduce paintings by Carpaccio and Titian.

I am indebted in specific ways to the following friends, colleagues and former pupils (among many others), and remember numerous individual acts of kindness even as I turn their names into a bare alphabetical list: Leo Bersani, Andrew Brown, Bernard Burgoyne, Ann Caesar, Kate Ford, John Forrester, Nigel Glendinning, Clive Gordon, Jackie Harris, Peter Hildebrand, Denis Hollier, Patrick Humphrey, Brett Kahr, Darian Leader, Giulio Lepschy, Hyam Maccoby, Terry Moore, Dinora Pines, Chris Prendergast, David Lee Rubin, David Shepheard, Riccardo Steiner, Corbet Stewart, John Sturrock, Malcolm Thompson, Tony Thorlby, Iain White, Margaret Whitford. Two debts deserve special mention: to the French Department at Berkeley for inviting me to a Visiting Professorship at a time when this book was beginning to take its final shape; to Alison Finch, whose trenchant and complex views on the matters discussed here made her a splendid interlocutor throughout the period of its composition. Alison, this book is for you.

Notes on texts and translations

FREUD

My quotations are taken from *The Standard Edition of the Complete Psychological Works* (translated from the German under the general editorship of James Strachey, 24 vols, The Hogarth Press and the Institute of Psycho-Analysis, 1953–74), although in the case of certain problematic terms and expressions Freud's original German is also given (from *Gesammelte Werke*, edited by Anna Freud and others, 18 vols, London, Imago Publishing, 1940–52 (Vols 1–17) and Frankfurt am Main, Fischer Verlag, 1968 (Vol. 18)). Volume and page references to the Standard Edition are given in my main text. References in the main text and notes to the *Gesammelte Werke* are preceded by the initials *GW*.

The quality of the translations in the Standard Edition is nowadays a topic for vigorous discussion among Freud scholars, and an entirely new translation is regularly called for. Readers of Freud in English wishing to acquaint themselves with the main deficiencies alleged against the Standard Edition are referred to Peter Gay's *Freud, Jews and Other Germans*, Bruno Bettelheim's *Freud and Man's Soul* and Samuel Weber's *The Legend of Freud*. For Gay, the English translators have made Freud 'both more prolix and more genteel than he really was' (41 n.); for Bettelheim, they have given Freud's writing a false veneer of positivistic science, and an unfortunate remoteness from ordinary usage, by their choice of such words as *id*, *ego*, *superego*, *cathexis* and *parapraxis* to translate readily comprehensible German terms and by their removal of the word 'soul' (*Seele*) and its cognates from Freud's accounts of the inward life of human beings; for Weber, they have gone to work with the familiar normalising assumption that Freud's 'original' text knew what it was talking about, whereas the German texts of Freud are 'a privileged theater in which the questions and struggles of psychoanalytical thinking play themselves out' (xvii). Invaluable guidance for those wishing to pursue Freud's technical terms in their passage from German to English, French, Italian, Spanish and Portuguese is to be found in Jean Laplanche and J.-B. Pontalis, *The Language of Psycho-Analysis*.

The following works are referred to in text and notes in the abbreviated form given in brackets: *Letters of Sigmund Freud, 1873–1939*, ed. Ernst L. Freud (*Letters*); *The Complete Letters of Sigmund Freud to Wilhelm Fliess, 1887–1904*, trans. and ed. Jeffrey Moussaieff Masson (Freud/Fliess); *The Origins of Psycho-Analysis. Letters to Wilhelm Fliess*, ed. Marie Bonaparte, Anna Freud, Ernst Kris (*Origins*); Ernest Jones, *Sigmund Freud. Life and Work* (J + volume number).

PROUST

I have used the Pléiade edition of *A la recherche du temps perdu* (3 vols edited by Pierre Clarac and André Ferré, Gallimard, 1954) and refer to it by volume number and page in my main text, except where repeated reference to the third volume is made – in which cases the volume number is omitted. An English translation of each quoted passage will be found in the Notes. These translations have been taken from the C.K. Scott Moncrieff version, *Remembrance of Things Past*, as revised by Terence Kilmartin (3 vols, Chatto and Windus, 1981). Page references are provided after each English extract; volume numbers are as for the Pléiade edition.

LACAN

Page numbers appearing without other indication in my main text refer to *Écrits* (Seuil, 1966). Quotations from the five volumes of Lacan's *Séminaire* that have appeared so far are identified by volume number and page, and those from his other works by short title and page. An English translation of each quoted passage will be found in the Notes. These translations have been taken from Alan Sheridan's *Écrits. A Selection* (Tavistock Publications, 1977) and *The Four Fundamental Concepts of Psycho-Analysis* (The Hogarth Press and the Institute of Psycho-Analysis, 1977), and from Jeffrey Mehlman's 'Seminar on "The Purloined Letter"', in *French Freud: Structural Studies in Psychoanalysis* (*Yale French Studies*, No. 48, ed. Mehlman, 1972). Where no other indication is given, page references for Lacan in English are to *Écrits. A Selection*. Translations not followed by a page reference are my own.

Other works by Proust, Freud and Lacan, and works by other authors, are referred to by short title in my main text and notes. Fuller details are to be found in my List of Works Cited.

Introduction

Nous vivions une lutte mortelle en échafaudant des théories

Luis Buñuel: *Mon dernier soupir*

We lived through a life-and-death struggle constructing theories

My Last Breath

Beethoven ends the first movement of his Opus 127 quartet with bold simplicity, by handing a single phrase from voice to voice. The phrase has by now contributed fully to a condensed sonata argument and nothing further need be expected of it. Yet in Beethoven's coda the phrase finds a rapturous afterlife. It becomes at last identical to itself, reiterative of itself, and leaves behind all but an attenuated echo of the thematic material with which it had previously been contrasted. After the pleasures of discussion, the still keener pleasures of self-repetition. I have often found myself wishing that repetition in the human sciences were as gratifying and as intellectually stringent as these closing bars, and that our learned institutions, as they handed phrases from voice to voice – across continents and across oceans –, could find Beethovenian ways of placing repetition in the service of the public good. But no. We have no Beethoven to compose us or to rescue the discourse of our human scientists from redundancy and babble.

My own unease in writing about Freud, Proust and Lacan springs not just from a chronic sense of the already-said but from an acute sense that features of their work with which I have been especially concerned have already been well described and well analysed. In what follows I shall speak about theory and about desire; about theories of desire and the desires of theorists; about theories held to be fictions and about a work of fiction thus classified by libraries and bookshops – Proust's *A la recherche du temps perdu* – that has as a main theme the pains and pleasures of the theorising mind. But 'desire', 'theory' and 'fiction', with or without their defensive quotation marks, turn to dullness even as I outline my agenda.

Powerful confluential currents within European and American culture have made 'desire' in particular into a major conceptual nostrum of the age, a terminological tribute paid by the bourgeoisie to its own purportedly new and self-aware sexuality. One current, which could be called that of 'high' desire, runs from Hegel through Kierkegaard, Darwin and Nietzsche to Sartre, Foucault and Deleuze/Guattari. The other, 'low' in that it more plainly concerns itself with the solicitations of the lower body but 'high' in its turn in so far as it abstractly schematises and taxonomises upon human sexual conduct, runs from Sade through Krafft-Ebing, Havelock Ellis and Weininger to Kinsey and

Masters/Johnson. Desire as it is now often described is the cosmological principle of our secular age. It is our *natura naturans*: it moves the stars in their courses, plumps the hazel shells, causes tumescence in mammalian sexual organs and, thanks to its inexhaustible capacity for displacement and sublimation, is the vitalising agent in art, science, religion, business, economics, politics and international relations. Under earlier metaphysical dispensations, desire had many names: it was eros and agape; it was love, lust, appetite, gluttony, cupidity, concupiscence, covetousness, ambition; it was need, wish, urge, impulse; it was hankering, longing, yearning, yen. The names of desire changed as its objects changed, and desires directed towards objects of a suprapersonal or supraterrestrial kind were distinguished by a special nomenclature from mere instinctual agitations. Nowadays this untidy multitude of forces is often perceived as a single force, and the welter of names is often casually condensed into a single name.

Although this picture of a unitary Desire bears little resemblance to any one of Freud's successive pictures of the instinctual life, it is psychoanalysis above all other conceptual systems of the century that has made the new cosmology possible. For Freud's *Three Essays on the Theory of Sexuality* (1905) were the first text of importance to belong equally to the two traditions that I have sketched: here was desire both high and low under discussion by a writer who was by turns systematist and dialectician in the organisation of his observational data; and here, beyond mere differences of theoretical style, was the incipient spectacle of the desiring One, the all-pervading and all-propelling energy of the human world, the force that infiltrated and activated the structures of analytic intellect no less completely than those of erectile tissue. Freud himself always drew back from this vision in building his theories of instinct: after a few oceanic moments of release, the psychologist had no choice but to return to classifying science and responsible citizenhood, both of which required that there should be more instincts than one. Desire was of necessity subdivisible, and Freud in many of his moral pronouncements readily sided with its upper, socialised division against its lower, merely self-gratifying one: the very etymology of the term 'sublimation', he told his curiosity-seeking hearers in the *Introductory Lectures*,[1] offered support, as he himself did, to this generally accepted valuation (XVI, 345). But, despite Freud's disclaimers, his seeming lesson to a numerous following of libido-liberators and campus orgasmicists was that desire was indeed all we could ever know on earth and the answer, already perfectly available to us, to all unanswered questions. And as is usual for any thinker of monumental stature, Freud has had an empowering effect not only upon these simplifying publicists and upon his creative successors but upon generations of brilliant adversaries. For many of these adversaries the 'question of desire' that Freud asked is still the crucial question of the century, Freud's deficiency being merely that he mis-posed and mis-answered it.

Let us remember briefly three celebrated recent cases. Deleuze and Guattari in their double diatribe on 'capitalism and schizophrenia' – *L'Anti-Œdipe* and *Mille Plateaux* – grant psychoanalysis extraordinary privileges: it is the necessary enemy, anathematised over a thousand exuberant pages; its allegedly unilinear logic of explanation is that without which their own multilinear, 'rhizomatic' logic cannot be, and cannot be understood; its enslaving unconscious is their own potentiating unconscious waiting to be born. Foucault, in his *Histoire de la sexualité*, historicises psychoanalysis, criticises what he claims to be its notion of an invariant 'sexuality' subject only to a changing array of repressive mechanisms in its passage through history, and uses psychoanalytic concepts only in extreme dilution.[2] Yet he plots the vicissitudes of the sexual instincts within culture in ways that Freud alone had made thinkable: it was by way of Freud's *Three Essays* that sexuality as combined cultural process and product became available to historical reconstruction of the kind that Foucault attempts. Feminism, in its central attacks on the phallocratic idiom of much psychoanalytic thought, insistently repeats the questions that such thought presents itself as having solved – is desire one or many? is sexual difference indelibly inscribed in nature? what are the moral and political consequences of dedifferentiating or redistributing sexual kinds? – as if the rehearsal of these questions were an inescapable prelude to the creation and execution of a coherent political programme.[3] In each of these cases, compellingly original work has been done, fuelled by Freud or by the rejection of Freud. But such work, ritualised in the writings of innumerable opportunistic imitators, has given desire a wider currency than any one concept is ever likely to deserve. The imitators have turned a once provocative set of insights into an obliging semi-theoretical *ritornello* and, removing their study of human instinct more readily than Freud ever did from the sphere of social and political actuality, have discovered in 'desire' a readily marketable metaphysical gadget.

The recent fortunes of 'theory' and 'fiction' have been somewhat more encouraging. For although yesterday's scientific paradigms and historical certitudes are nowadays perhaps too rapidly – and with perhaps too much unthinking post-Nietzschean glee – shown to be insubstantial wish-fulfilments after all ('mere' theory, 'mere' fiction), both concepts have prompted a great deal of innovative thinking in the human sciences. Describing the internal organisation or the rhetorical substructure of an existing theory, or organising hypotheses of one's own into a theory of one's own, is in any case a more exacting business than catching on the wing a specimen of ubiquitous desire – as is the perception and articulation of the narrative or discursive logic of fictions. But even here over-production has gone on at an extravagant rate, and much undoubtedly strenuous labour within the 'structuralist', 'post-structuralist', 'deconstructionist' and 'narratological' conventions has had a low intellectual yield. For years, the realms of 'theory' and 'fiction' have exerted upon each other a strong attractive force, and nowhere more plainly than in the academic study of imaginative literature. Many critics, it seems, are willing to grant seriousness and coherence to a given social or psychological theory only if they are able to show that theory to be pre-eminently applicable to novels, plays or poems. It is only after an ordeal by literature that the theory merits professional accreditation – although, as ordeals go, the process is not a particularly arduous one. There is no need for the critic to feel exhausted or forlorn as he reaches the end of his Lacanised *Wuthering Heights*, his Foucauldian *Jane Eyre* or his Derridified *Villette*. Other perfectly compliant vehicles for his chosen methodology remain: *Agnes Grey*, *The Tenant of Wildfell Hall* . . . and *bien d'autres encor!* Comparably urgent appropriative energy has been directed by the theorists themselves towards literary texts, especially in France. And although few of them would claim that a theoretical statement has also to be a 'text' or to contain an implied poetics in order to establish its authority, their theories have certainly gained prestige in some quarters – and ridicule in others – from their self-dramatising search for 'literary' effect. From whichever side of the increasingly dilapidated partition between 'theory' and 'fiction' such efforts of annexation begin, the result is to create a wide terrain of near-synonymy between the two terms. 'Theory' and 'fiction' are, after all, alternative names for the verbal productions of those who indulge in 'as if' thinking about the world,[4] and further would-be synonyms may easily be enlisted for short or long spells of duty: myth, model, analogy, metaphor, paradigm, schema, construction. Where *can* one begin in this world of semantic overlap and redundancy?

Before I answer this question and so bring the present fragment of complaining autobiography to its close, I shall describe one way in which I am helped and simultaneously not helped by my three authors themselves. Each of them has an extraordinarily keen perception of the human mind as the fabricator and refurbisher of wishful constructions, and each of them willingly occupies for long stretches of his writing the middle realm in which theories and fictions are only fitfully distinguishable. The problem is not that no criterion exists by which to distinguish them. Indeed for Freud and Proust the criterion is plain and beyond dispute: a theory conduces to truth, a fiction to more fiction. But in the daily world of speculative exertion that each author inhabits this criterion is prevented from producing a series of reliable practical tests by a salient quality that the materials being speculated and theorised upon possess. These materials are fictions. Proust's narrator enquires of Albertine's pronouncements, one by one: 'what sort of construction is this – lie, half-lie, alibi, well-intentioned whimsy, camouflaged truth?' Freud and Lacan ask of their patients: 'what are you really telling me when you tell me all this, when you clothe the fiction of your dreams and phantasies in the secondary fiction of your consulting-room narratives?' For all three writers the panoramic spectacle of fiction in human affairs creates both an extreme scepticism about their own constructs – 'why are my own pronouncements any less mendacious than Albertine's? why are my interpretations any less delusional than my patients' stories?' – and an extreme appetite for styles of awareness and philosophical vantage points that would allow the notion of veracity to be rescued and rehabilitated. At the end of *The Interpretation of Dreams* Freud used the term *theoretical fiction* ('theoretische Fiktion')[5] (v, 603; *GW*, III, 609) to describe a state of affairs that a given theory seemed to require or predict but for which no supporting evidence could be found. Among epistemological categories the 'theoretical fiction' was a sorry amphibian with a low chance of survival, but its sturdy-looking neighbours – theories proper – were themselves constantly threatened by predatory invaders entering science from the worlds of fairytale and romance.

Lacan's answer to the problem of being both 'for' and 'against' fiction, both inside and outside its province, both enslaved and liberated by it, sounds at first more radical than anything in Proust or Freud. Speaking of 'The Purloined Letter' and of his reasons for attaching a precise psychoanalytic importance to Poe's tale, he writes: 'la vérité y révèle son ordonnance de fiction' (17).[6] He does not suggest, here or elsewhere in *Écrits*, simply that the path to truth lies by way of fiction, nor even that a willing self-immersion in fiction is a necessary initiatory rite for students of the unconscious mental life. What Poe's tale says to Lacan, and Lacan to us, is that whoever is immersed in fiction yet in pursuit of truth – desiring it – has already reached his destination. Seek and you have already found. Truth about the human mind and about human speech is fiction accepted and espoused at its unstemmable unconscious source. Proust and Freud do not protest in this way and are both too fastidious as problem-solvers to offer peremptory solve-all formulae of this kind. Yet each of them attends tirelessly to fictions held to be fictions, to the fabricatedness and mediatedness of speech and to the wishful mental underworld that speech reveals. Each of them, that is to say, while having a powerful urge towards Truth, is prepared to suspend that urge for indefinite periods during which the mere verbalised wishes of the self and others are lingeringly sketched and compared – as if the truth-seeker who dwelt knowingly among fictions were indeed already at his journey's end.

All this knowingness is helpful to the commentator on Proust, Freud and Lacan as portraitists of the mental life in that his terms of reference have already been expertly prepared and inflected before his enquiry begins, but unhelpful in that he can easily feel that his writers have left him with nothing to prophesy about their works but that which their works have already plainly declared. In writing the essays that follow and in making a book of them, I have of course tried to resist the pre-emptive power of the writers I discuss – sometimes by reading them against the grain of the reading methods that they themselves recommend and sometimes by reading them jointly rather than singly. I have also tried to suggest why it is that the combined role of theorist and fictionalist as played by Proust, Freud and Lacan may be thought to be a peculiarly exciting and disconcerting one, and why the *intermundium* between theory and fiction still offers a crucial area of study to scientist and 'human scientist' alike. (I do not, however, suggest that the three writers form an exclusive cross-cultural club

– how could I, when Plato, Montaigne, Goethe, Kierkegaard, Musil and Sartre among many others – and to speak only of the European tradition – play comparable combined roles quite as instructively?) Two aspects of my approach to these goals are perhaps worth declaring here, if only to warn my reader of what not to look for in the following pages. I have often chosen (i) to present the relationships between the three writers tangentially and (ii) to discuss the theoretical positions of each writer in their relatively inchoate, indecisive or self-defeating versions. (And from the copious works of each writer I have selected a restricted range of topics and examples and make no claim to have been exhaustive even in my discussion of these.[7])

The special virtues that I ascribe to tangentiality in matters of critical comparison will become plain if I quote briefly from a number of writers whose work I admire and who have, mostly briefly, brought psychoanalytic theory into contact with *A la recherche du temps perdu*. Harold Bloom ends his essay 'Freud and the Sublime' on a global comparison of Freud and Proust:

> Freud has more in common with Proust and Montaigne than with biological scientists, because his interpretations of life and death are mediated always by texts, first by the literary texts of others, and then by his own earlier texts, until at last the Sublime mediation of otherness begins to be performed by his text-in-process. In the *Essays* of Montaigne or Proust's vast novel, this ongoing mediation is clearer than it is in Freud's almost perpetual self-revision, because Freud wrote no definitive, single text; but the canon of Freud's writings shows an increasingly uneasy sense that he had become his own precursor, and that he had begun to defend himself against himself by deliberately audacious arrivals at final positions. (117–18)

In Richard Wollheim's *The Thread of Life*, rapid cross-references between Freud and Proust help to organise much of the argument. Here is Wollheim's comparative style in its most laconic form:

> . . . such is the nature of these mental states [those which show the surviving influences of past events] that they can have the effect of modifying or refashioning the dispositions that they manifest as well as the more standard effect of reinforcing them. They can impinge not only on the strength of the dispositions, or the way in which they bind the energies of the person, but also on their content or intentionality. And they can bring about these changes through their mere occurrence if the circumstances are propitious – Proust's 'involuntary' memories, Freud's 'abreaction' are examples – or through their deliberate exploitation in conditions cunningly organized – the confessional or the transference. The feedback from mental state to mental disposition is an essential element in the way in which we try to contol the lives that we lead. (99–100)

My third and fourth excerpts are both more directly concerned with the epistemological theme in the works of the two writers, and both present the female protagonist of Proust's novel as an emblematically inconstant and anomalous object of knowledge. John Wisdom writes in *Philosophy and Psycho-Analysis*:

> The psycho-analyst seeks to bring into the light those models from the past which for good and evil so powerfully influence our lives in the present, so powerfully distort reality and so powerfully illuminate it. For, of course, these models don't only distort. By no means. No doubt the lover sees what we see isn't there. But doesn't he also see what we can't see? Unquestionably Miss E. Brown is not Aphrodite nor Diana. But then may be she isn't the Miss Brown we think we know. Hate may blind, but hate, even neurotic hate, also reveals. The subtle evidence assembled to prove suspicions of Albertine may not prove precisely those suspicions but they don't prove nothing.
>
> The phantasies and models, illuminating but distorting, which metaphysical philosophers and psycho-analysts try to bring to light are unconscious. (276–7)

Deleuze and Guattari write in *Mille Plateaux*:

> Chacun passe par tant de corps en chacun. Albertine est lentement extraite d'un groupe de jeunes filles, qui a son nombre, son organisation, son code, sa hiérarchie; et non seulement tout un inconscient baigne ce groupe et cette masse restreinte, mais Albertine a ses propres multiplicités que le narrateur, l'ayant isolée, découvre sur son corps et dans ses mensonges – jusqu'à ce que la fin de l'amour la rende à l'indiscernable. (49)

Each of these moments seems to me unusually fertile. Each is in fact two moments in one. Beyond the postulated common features of Proust and Freud there lie, postulated or implied, clear *differentiae*: if the comparison is to tell, the two writers cannot be allowed simply to merge. But beyond these *differentiae* a further, semi-official order of comparison is to be discerned. Freud's 'deliberately audacious arrivals at final positions', designed by Bloom to distinguish the periodicity of Freud's theoretical career and the multiplicity of his writings from the fluent through-composition of Proust's single great novel, may in fact alert us to a continuous characteristic of that novel: by way of the sententious moral statements that punctuate the narrative throughout, Proust's narrator audaciously arrives at 'final' positions and defends himself against the *déjà-dit* of his own text. Similarly, Wollheim invites us to compare what he seemingly merely lists. Proust and Freud each provide one example of that species of mental event wherein a personal past acts with unusual vigour upon a personal present. But how alike are the two examples? To what extent would it make sense to talk of Proust's involuntary memories as having an 'abreactive' power – a power to release the mind from potentially damaging concentrations of affect? To what extent, for that matter, may Proust's cunningly organised narrative be thought of as akin to the techniques listed by Wollheim for deliberately eliciting and exploiting these energetic incursions of past into present – the confessional, the transference?

Wisdom's first paragraph has a fine double backlash at the start of the second: hyper-suspicious neurotic speculation, from being the sort of thing that psychoanalysts observe with detachment in their case-material, becomes – possibly – the sort of thing that they themselves (and metaphysicians) professionally perform; the narrator's distortions of Albertine, from being somewhat sickly and discreditable despite their power of illumination, acquire a new philosophical dignity. Whereas Wisdom stages here a rapid role-reversal between theory and fiction as traditionally understood and evaluated by philosophers, Deleuze and Guattari affect not to know why the effort to distinguish the two notions has ever been thought to matter: for them it is self-evident that the interplay between levels, codes, hierarchies and multiplicities will be as readily observable in fictions of a certain complexity as in theories of mind. The burden of their polemic in the section from which I have quoted is that Albertine as representative of a constant play between differentiation and dedifferentiation in the quest for knowledge, between the discernible and the indiscernible, is representative too of an unconscious so enlarged and so copious as to make the Freudian unconscious seem a miserably stunted affair. But the student of Freud may still find that this epistemic Albertine offers a powerful new way of focusing precisely upon the multiplicities, the involutions and the dialectical reversals, by Deleuze and Guattari only grudgingly acknowledged, that mark the passage of the Freudian unconscious through Freud's own texts.

It is not of course particularly surprising that provocative comparisons should be extendable or reversible in the ways that I have outlined. And my sense that such comparisons are as fertile as they are because their authors have settled for only glancing contact between their terms may have an element of superstition in it. For although long-distance comparers of Proust and Freud have often become flat-footed on the road, exhilarating extended comparisons are still imaginable, as are dull brief ones. But my preference for tangentiality serves a modest purpose, I like to imagine, in discussion of writers who were themselves such versatile exponents of the near-miss and the near-hit – comparers and differentiators, binarists and anti-binarists, systematists and counter-systematists – in their fictional and theoretical recreations of the mental life.

The second of the preferences that I mentioned a moment ago – for the inchoate over the finished – is an even simpler matter to describe. As a reader of Freud, Proust and Lacan, I have found special delight and perplexity in watching theories being made and unmade and in following the rivalry both between alternative theories and between the alternative orders of evidence mobilised in their support. I have come to admire both the inexhaustible model-building inventiveness and *disponibilité* that each of the writers displays and their shared sense that skill in the having of theories, and in the separating of better theory from worse, is an exigent and dangerous matter. Virtuosity has its price, I shall be suggesting in their wake.

'What are theorists desiring when they theorise upon desire?' 'What happens to desire when it pursues models of desire-in-pursuit?' 'In what ways do passions and hypotheses order and disorder one another?' 'What happens to a "scientific" text when it becomes the zone of interference between facts and wishes?' These are my questions in the essays that follow. But such questions already sound too grand for this book: they are of a kind that a work of *theory* might properly address, whereas what follows is a work merely of theory-tinged literary criticism. This book has a 'theory' about its theorists only in the way that a child has a theory about the origin of babies, or a traveller about the lateness of his train, or a very ordinary detective (not C. Auguste Dupin, not Hercule Poirot) about the corpse in the library.

I

Freud's dreams of knowledge

Formel unsres Glücks: ein Ja, ein Nein, eine gerade Linie, ein ZIEL . . .

Nietzsche: *Der Antichrist*

Formula of our happiness: a Yes, a No, a straight line, a *goal* . . .

The Antichrist

Torniamo all'antico e sarà un progresso

Verdi to Francesco Florimo in 1871

Let us return to the past; it will be a step forward

FREUD had many harsh words for those who came to psychoanalysis in search of a world-view to supplant the 'scientific outlook' or to attenuate its rigours. Psychoanalysis has made emotion, illusion and superstition into proper objects of scientific enquiry, he announced in his *New Introductory Lectures* (1933), but science itself has not been compromised in the process; its methods have been made available for the study of 'emotional demands' and 'wishful impulses', but there is no reason to expect those methods to become in any way emotional or wishful in their turn:

> . . .. it would be illegitimate and highly inexpedient to allow these demands to be transferred to the sphere of knowledge . . . It is simply a fact that the truth cannot be tolerant, that it admits of no compromises or limitations, that research regards every sphere of human activity as belonging to it and that it must be relentlessly critical if any other power tries to take over any part of it. (XXII, 160)

Freud's vision of science, and of that intolerant and uncompromising Truth which is its obligatory goal, was a vision in which facts – states of affairs, that which is the case, the nature of the world – would eventually stand revealed; in which knowledge pure and clear would be drawn forth from observation; in which observation would require no more than preliminary, local support from hypotheses and theories; in which hypotheses and theories, their supporting work done, would retire silently from the investigative scene, leaving behind them complete and durable explanations. 'La théorie, c'est bon, mais ça n'empêche pas d'exister', Charcot is reported to have said in Freud's hearing at La Salpêtrière.[1] And this formula ('which left an indelible mark upon my mind', XX, 13) encapsulates an entire dimension of Freud's own thinking: things exist before our theorising begins and the wise scientist will seek to return as rapidly as possible, and whatever the exacting speculative detours he may be compelled to make on the way, to things-as-they-are. Biology and 'pure' psychology, so often presented as competitors in Freud's accounts of his own vocation, are, though different in their objects of study, alike in the kind of knowledge that they strive for – a knowledge born of, and vindicated in, empirical observation and research. When it comes to the false demands that feeling may impose upon the scientific enquirer, biological truth and psychological truth are equally unforgiving. Psychoanalysis itself has not only revealed the mind and its productions as they are but is permanently available as a vehicle for their further study: 'psycho-analysis is a method of research, an impartial instrument, like the infinitesimal calculus' (XXI, 36)...

Yet how remote this vision is from the world of practical intellectual endeavour that we enter when we read Freud's scientific works. For these reveal a fertile and insatiable hypothesiser. Freud, in common with many scientists, declared himself loyal to the principles of inductive thought in his public pronouncements on the responsibilities of his discipline, yet seems seldom to have consulted those principles in pursuing his scientific activities. There his approach was conspicuously hypothetico-deductive in character. Hypotheses do have an occasional shadowy role in Freud's philosophy of science. He was ready to allow that the mind can never simply empty itself of its prior constructions and become pure percipience: ideas will always exert their invisible pressures upon the observing eye. But 'the foundation of science, upon which everything rests ... is observation alone' ('On Narcissism: an Introduction' (1914), XIV, 77), and the ideas which are brought into play as the observer sets to work are granted little methodological dignity. Freud speaks of them as 'nebulous, scarcely imaginable basic concepts' (XIV, 77) and insists that even when such concepts have been delimited, and enshrined in testable definitions, they must still remain pliable: the 'advance of knowledge ... does not tolerate any rigidity even in definitions' ('Instincts and their Vicissitudes' (1915), XIV, 117). Nowhere does he hint that hypotheses of a precise and organised kind may determine the entire cast of an experimental or clinical programme, and nowhere does he fully characterise his own zeal as a hypothesis-maker.

Certain of Freud's hypotheses, as is well known, were so much cherished as imaginative constructions that they proved difficult to abandon when verifiable deductions ceased to flow from them. The early 'seduction theory' of neurosis, for example, which Freud first formulated in 1895, was publicly repudiated by him only in 1906, many years after his last attempt to produce clinical evidence in its defence. His hypotheses, and the theories which embraced them, were of course numerous as well as tenacious. And the story of their emergence now seems to contain many more gaps and accidents than Freud's own smoothly evolutionary accounts of his intellectual development could countenance. Freud, let us remember, was the author of three separate and incompatible 'macro-models' of the psychical apparatus;[2] two separate versions of narcissism;[3] two separate dualistic theories of the instincts (*Triebe*), each containing a number of lesser, supporting hypotheses ('The theory of the instincts is so to say our mythology. Instincts are mythical entities magnificent in their indefiniteness', XXII, 95).[4] In addition, his theoretical inclination took him into regions ostensibly far removed from psychology and psychotherapy, and produced – in *Totem and Taboo* (1912–13), for example, or in *Moses and Monotheism* (1939) – free-standing speculative edifices of an ambitious and defiantly untestable kind.[5] Freud's works in this vein are indeed so ambitious in the explanatory range that they claim for themselves that *The Golden Bough*, to which both are indebted, is quite out-Frazered by them.[6] They have 'the origin and development of human culture' as their theme, and weave from their secondary and tertiary sources an imaginative fabric seductive enough to make the seeking out of facts in fieldwork or in clinical observation seem miserable and intrusive pedantry. The whole of *Moses and Monotheism*, we are told, is subject to a 'factor of doubt': 'I have, as it were, placed that factor outside the brackets and I may be allowed to save myself the trouble of repeating it in connection with each item *inside* them' (XXIII, 31). Freud's frequent gestures of this kind are (and are meant to be) disarming: 'If even I have doubts about it all, your own doubts, reader, need not detain you.' By his 'brackets' and 'factors' he alludes to the realm of mathematical necessity even as he takes us further into that of erudite speculation. It is characteristic of Freud, and of the tension that I shall be discussing in what follows, that he should cast himself as algebraist at the very moment of embarking on a work for which he was elsewhere to suggest the sub-title 'a historical novel' (J, III, 206; *Letters*, 418).

Hypotheses were, then, both frowned upon and assiduously cultivated by Freud. He was a patient experimentalist haunted by the idea that knowledge of the real world might be had, far from the laboratory bench or the consulting room, by the disinterested exercise of thought. He was an expert observer powerfully drawn towards grandiose unobservables. Freud's writings derive something of their extraordinary intellectual density from their capacity to superimpose and interconnect these alternative views of knowledge. They are works of strict psychological science bathed in epistemological dreams and phantasies. The anti-theoretical and philo-theoretical tendencies that I have sketched so far are both available for inspection on the invitingly intelligible surface that

Freud imparted to his 'public' essays: to be clear about his own motives as a scientist – even and perhaps especially when those motives were mixed or contradictory – was a matter of civic responsibility for Freud when he spoke in any of his self-appointed lay roles, whether as philosopher of science, moralist, mythographer or historian of culture. My intention here is to review these tendencies in their less official and less responsible guises. For much of our information about Freud's views of knowledge – and of the power that knowledge might confer, the desires it might serve and the delights and torments to which it might summon the mind – is to be had from the jumps, repetitions and hesitations in his writing; from its incidents, accidents and switches in direction; from its footnotes, asides, analogies, exempla and autobiographical reminiscences; from scruples often or vigorously protested; from that intricate machinery of self-doubt under cover of which unexamined certainties may infiltrate an argument. Desire and wish-fulfilment, adamantly rejected by Freud in his public accounts of scientific procedure, adamantly return and display themselves in his writing. Discussing the utility of his own current hypotheses in *Beyond the Pleasure Principle* (1920), Freud remarked: 'There is no reason, as it seems to me, why the emotional factor of conviction should enter into this question at all' (XVIII, 59). In the wake of psychoanalysis, according to its founder, 'nothing is altered in the attitude of science as a whole . . . no new sources of knowledge or methods of research have come into being' (*New Introductory Lectures* (1933), XXII, 159). But Freud's cumulative record of his discoveries and theoretical innovations so completely re-immerses the scientific enterprise in the desires and convictions of its practitioners that the very notion of a single, immutable scientific 'attitude' or 'outlook' comes to seem a fanciful alibi. Who has done more than Freud, in the present century, to imagine the consequences for science of its admitting rather than repressing the elementary desiring impulses on which the quest for knowledge is founded?

In exploring the wishful substratum of Freud's scientific writings, I shall be particularly concerned with the admiring side-glances that he took at professions other than his own and with the lessons about his science that are to be had from watching him on holiday from scientific activity. I shall discuss in turn Freud's self-images as archaeologist and as *conquistador* – the two favourite means whereby this redoubtable theoretician of a timeless unconscious sought to endow his discoveries with the resonance and prestige of history.

II

Archaeology was for Freud the supreme combination of art and science and exerted a special fascination upon him throughout his career.[7] And that career, we need hardly remind ourselves, spanned a golden age of archaeological discovery: Schliemann was unearthing his many-layered Troy at Hissarlik during Freud's school and university years;[8] Evans was exploring and then excavating Knossos during the period of Freud's self-analysis and of his collaborative friendships with Breuer and Fliess; Freud was writing *The Ego and the Id* in the year Carnarvon and Carter discovered the tomb of Tutankhamen,[9] and *The Future of an Illusion* and *Civilization and its Discontents* during Woolley's excavations of Sumerian Ur. Freud was an avid reader of archaeological memoirs and a spendthrift collector of antiquities. In a letter of 1931 to Stefan Zweig, he strove to correct Zweig's recently published portrait of him in the following terms: 'despite my much vaunted frugality I have sacrificed a great deal for my collection of Greek, Roman and Egyptian antiquities, have actually read more archaeology than psychology, and . . . before the war and once after its end I felt compelled to spend every year at least several days or weeks in Rome, and so on' (*Letters*, 402).

But archaeology was much more than Freud's *violon d'Ingres* and provided him both as a clinician and as a writer with a versatile set of conceptual models. This celebrated moment from his essay on 'Female Sexuality' (1931) is characteristic of one use to which archaeological material may be put: 'Our insight into this early, pre-Oedipus, phase in girls comes to us as a surprise, like the discovery, in another field, of the Minoan-Mycenean civilization behind the civilization of Greece' (XXI, 226). Psychoanalysis, like archaeology, is the quest for, and the systematic study of, anterior states: for Freud *that which came before*, whether in the life of a civilisation or in the life of the mind, has a peculiar and unparalleled capacity to organise our perception of *that which is*. 'Le thème de l'antérieur,' Paul Ricœur has said of the Freudian theoretical corpus, 'est sa propre hantise'.[10] Freud's early paper on 'The Aetiology of Hysteria' (1896), which was written as the full riches of the Minoan-Mycenaean world were first being revealed, contains a developed and heightened analogy of the same kind. The archaeologist – who, Freud is already telling us, so much resembles the student of primitive mental life – may, on arriving at a site, simply ask the local inhabitants for their folklore accounts of such remains as are visible. Or

> he may act differently. He may have brought picks, shovels and spades with him, and he may set the inhabitants to work with these implements. Together with them he may start upon the ruins, clear away the rubbish, and, beginning from the visible remains, uncover what is buried. If his work is crowned with success, the discoveries are self-explanatory: the ruined walls are part of the ramparts of a palace or a treasure-house; the fragments of columns can be filled out into a temple; the numerous inscriptions, which, by good luck, may be bilingual, reveal an alphabet and a language, and, when they have been deciphered and translated, yield undreamed-of information about the events of the remote past, to commemorate which the monuments were built. *Saxa loquuntur!* ['Stones talk!'] (III, 192)

This is hyperbolic archaeology: excavation reveals not workshop or stable but palace, treasure-house and temple, just as inscriptions, once deciphered, are seen to record notable events rather than, say, the contents of a granary or a warehouse. It seems that the local people, who labour in a servile, late-colonial present, have had nothing but magnificence in their tribal past. Freud's analogy speaks of the kingly and hieratic scale on which his own scientific ambitions were already conceived – and sets the stage for a sequence of later theatrical gestures, including the departure of an intrepid male explorer into the *terra incognita* of female sexuality.

Archaeology and psychoanalysis are, then, both concerned with burial and excavation, with the making present of a previously lost past. In the life of the mind, the primitive sexual desire or traumatic event is inhumed by repression and may be exhumed within the analytic dialogue. The point is made at its plainest in Freud's commentary (1907) on Wilhelm Jensen's Pompeian tale *Gradiva*:

> There is, in fact, no better analogy for repression, by which something in the mind is at once made inaccessible and preserved, than burial of the sort to which Pompeii fell a victim and from which it could emerge once more through the work of spades. (IX, 40)

The speaking stones uncovered by the archaeologist's spade provided Freud with a promise of completeness and adequacy in his own scientific explanations. Indeed the collection of antiquities that figured so prominently in his consulting rooms – and that continues to play its part in the mythology of the psychoanalytic movement – seemed to offer palpable corroboration for his theories and was available as a pedagogical aid in his dialogue with patients:

I then made some short observations [to the Rat Man] upon *the psychological differences between the conscious and the unconscious*, and upon the fact that everything conscious was subject to a process of wearing-away, while what was unconscious was relatively unchangeable; and I illustrated my remarks by pointing to the antiques standing about in my room. They were, in fact, I said, only objects found in a tomb, and their burial had been their preservation: the destruction of Pompeii was only beginning now that it had been dug up. (X, 176)[11]

In these and other passages Freud understates by far the complexity of the archaeologist's inferential task and the factors that may obscure the original form and function of the artefacts he discovers. 'If his work is crowned with success, the discoveries are self-explanatory', Freud had said in 'The Aetiology of Hysteria'. Yes, but if not he will be obliged to resort to conjecture, to place constructions upon his material, to piece together merely possible anterior worlds. The archaeological object *par excellence*, for Freud in this mood, is a complete, three-dimensional, tangible, tractable thing, an 'antiquity', an explanation of itself, an answer to its own question. In purging archaeology of any significant conceptual or theoretical component, Freud is of course performing a parallel operation upon its analogue: would not the best proof of psychoanalysis be for it to become a collection of simple whole things, preserved from time and destruction, a self-explaining world, a semantic and epistemological plenum . . . like Pompeii?

In other moods, Freud refashions his analogy to accommodate the sorry need for guesswork that besets both professions. 'In face of the incompleteness of my analytic results', he writes in the preface to his case-history of 'Dora' (1905),

I had no choice but to follow the example of those discoverers whose good fortune it is to bring to the light of day after their long burial the priceless though mutilated relics of antiquity. I have restored what is missing, taking the best models known to me from other analyses; but, like a conscientious archaeologist, I have not omitted to mention in each case where the authentic parts end and my constructions begin. (VII, 12)

Metaphorical transactions between the two professions thus remain smooth even when their characteristic difficulties are being discussed. In both, gaps often occur in the material and it is self-evidently the practitioner's business to fill these in; his mind, as it conjectures, is drawn irresistibly backwards to the lost wholeness of the object before him; whether his chosen object is material or psychical, he is a 'conscientious' artist in restoration. Whereas elsewhere in Freud's writing psychoanalysis is a lacunary mode of interpretation – one which collects gaps, interrogates and systematises them – it here presses towards plenitude with impatient speed. Lacunae are not to be allowed their lack.

Freud's final and most elaborate version of the analogy is to be found in his essay 'Constructions in Analysis' (1937). It is here that the delights available to the restorer are most firmly offset by ungrateful duties and risks of error:

> . . . just as the archaeologist builds up the walls of the building from the foundations that have remained standing, determines the number and position of the columns from depressions in the floor and reconstructs the mural decorations and paintings from the remains found in the débris, so does the analyst proceed when he draws his inferences from the fragments of memories, from the associations and from the behaviour of the subject of the analysis. Both of them have an undisputed right to reconstruct by means of supplementing and combining the surviving remains. Both of them, moreover, are subject to many of the same difficulties and sources of error. One of the most ticklish problems that confronts the archaeologist is notoriously the determination of the relative age of his finds; and if an object makes its appearance in some particular level, it often remains to be decided whether it belongs to that level or whether it was carried down to that level owing to some subsequent disturbance. It is easy to imagine the corresponding doubts that arise in the case of analytic constructions.
>
> (XXIII, 259)

Exactly at this point, when the common destiny of archaeologist and psychoanalyst has been so enthusiastically established, and with such an array of corroborative detail, Freud at last introduces a discrepancy between them. But this, as we shall see, is a matter not of prompting the psychoanalyst to consider alternative explanatory methods, but of watching him beat the archaeologist at his own game. Introducing a further favourite theme, Freud allows the mental scientist access to an archaic order that the archaeologist as archaeologist cannot know.

We might expect competition to arise between disciplines that share so many methods and goals, and we might expect the junior discipline in particular, still lacking secure public ratification and support, to be jealous in protecting its privileges. Signs of competitiveness with archaeology are apparent elsewhere in Freud. Discussing the prehistory of Greek civilisation in *Moses and Monotheism* (1939), he writes: 'With our present psychological insight we could, long before Schliemann and Evans, have raised the question of where it was that the Greeks obtained all the legendary material which was worked over by Homer and the great Attic dramatists in their masterpieces.' And the answer he goes on to provide is decidedly archaeological rather than psychological in its emphasis: 'this people had probably experienced in their prehistory a period of external brilliance and cultural efflorescence which had perished in a historical catastrophe and of which an obscure tradition survived in these legends' (XXIII, 70). If only Schliemann and Evans had possessed Freud's 'present psychological insight', they too could have reached a new knowledge of the past by thought rather than by excavatory toil . . . But in 'Constructions in Analysis' the factor that finally sets mental science apart from archaeology has to do not with the techniques used by the two disciplines, nor yet with the insight of their practitioners, but with the durability of the archaic material on which each operates. Whereas the archaeologist's material may be incomplete, or broken beyond repair, the psychoanalyst's is indestructible. This theme, which had had cautious beginnings (the lesson of Freud's antiquities as taught to the 'Rat Man' was merely that 'what was unconscious was relatively unchangeable', X, 176), was to develop into a guiding principle of clinical observation:

> Since we overcame the error of supposing that the forgetting we are familiar with signified a destruction of the memory-trace – that is, its annihilation – we have been inclined to take the opposite view, that in mental life nothing which has once been formed can perish – that everything is somehow preserved and that in suitable circumstances (when, for instance, regression goes back far enough) it can once more be brought to light.
>
> (*Civilization and its Discontents* (1930), XXI, 69)

In 'Constructions in Analysis', a statement of the same principle – that psychical objects cannot perish and are exhumable intact – is preceded by an extensive list of the misfortunes that may befall the fragile objects of archaeology. Complete preservation of the past, rare in the one field, is common in the other:

> Here [with the psychical object] we are regularly met by a situation which with the archaeological object occurs only in such rare circumstances as those of Pompeii or of the tomb of Tut'ankhamun. All of the essentials are preserved; even things that seem completely forgotten are present somehow and somewhere, and have merely been buried and made inaccessible to the subject. Indeed, it may, as we know, be doubted whether any psychical structure can really be the victim of total destruction. (XXIII, 260)

The psychoanalyst's victory in the contest with archaeology is thus a spectacular one: he not only regularly discovers in his daily practice relics that can vie in their completeness and coherence with those of Pompeii, but recognises these relics as belonging to a superior order of durability. Within the all-too-destructible human organism, within the endlessly mobile world of desire and phantasy that it houses, something permanent is to be found: a fixed psychical structure which, in its fixity, *explains*.

Freud's archaeological models and metaphors are occasionally supplemented by material drawn from the neighbouring sciences of geology and palaeontology. In his *Introductory Lectures* (1916–17), he looked forward to an eventual encompassing taxonomy of the neuroses:

> Consider the difference between the study of minerals and of rocks in mineralogy. The minerals are described as individuals, no doubt on the basis of the fact that they often occur as crystals, sharply separated from their environment. Rocks consist of aggregations of minerals, which, we may be sure, have not come together by chance but as a result of what determined their origin. In the theory of the neuroses we still know too little of the course of their development to produce anything resembling petrology. But we are certainly doing the right thing if we start by isolating from the mass the individual clinical entities which we recognize and which are comparable to the minerals. (XVI, 390)

The taxonomist of mental states and dispositions has to be a time-traveller across epochs if his classification is to find secure anchorage in 'what determined their origin'. And the voyages of Freud's time-machine may sometimes be improbably swift and straight: 'With neurotics it is as though we were in a prehistoric landscape – for instance, in the Jurassic. The great saurians are still running about; the horsetails grow as high as palms(?)' (XXIII, 299). Archaeology, geology and palaeontology, which all make use of stratigraphy in the ordering of their material, all offer psychoanalysis the same enticing picture of time made perfectly legible in layered deposits of matter. 'That which is earlier is deeper,' all three proclaim. 'That which is deeper is closer to the origins', Freud also heard them say, 'and it is only in the origins that scientific explanations can find their guarantee.' The analyst's search for the hard, indestructible, 'original' psychical material from which, if only it is responsibly manipulated, trustworthy science and positive therapeutic results will issue is not of course without its problems, and as early as the Freud–Breuer *Studies on Hysteria* (1895) Freud acknowledged these: 'To begin with, the work becomes more obscure and difficult, as a rule, the deeper we penetrate into the stratified psychical structure' (II, 298). The 'site' may be confused or ruinous; the strata may need to be re-ordered before investigation proper can begin; the psychical material may be organised in a 'complicated and multi-dimensional' way (II, 291). Yet despite the dangers of uncertainty and error that any penetration of the depths involves, it is in the deepest depths and nowhere else that the firmest promise of simplicity and explanatory completeness is offered. The traumatic event 'explains' the neurotic symptom just as the prior existence of Minoan-Mycenaean civilisation 'explains' the glorious richness of Greek art. But the question that might readily be asked of the Minoan achievement thus envisaged – 'what still earlier civilisation in turn explains it?' – is inappropriate to the original structures of mind and personality. These structures are bedrock – earlier than which, deeper than which, more comprehensively explanatory than which, there is nothing.

It is again in *Moses and Monotheism* that this predilection for 'deep' and 'buried' meaning reaches its most explicitly phantasmal form. Freud's main radical conjectures in this work are that Moses was an Egyptian and that, having introduced the Israelites to a primitive Egyptian variety of monotheism, he was killed at their hands. The divergence between this view and the account of Moses's career to be found in Exodus and Numbers is easily explained:

> The poetically embellished narrative which we attribute to the Yahwist, and to his later rival the Elohist, were like mausoleums beneath which, withdrawn from the knowledge of later generations, the true account of those early things – of the nature of the Mosaic religion and of the violent end of the great man – was, as it were, to find its eternal rest. And if we have guessed what happened correctly, there is nothing left about it that is puzzling . . . (XXIII, 62)

The true history of Moses was entombed by the first historians of the Mosaic faith because it was too scandalous to form part of the public record; their text is a political contrivance to which the imposing weight and solidity of an official burial monument have been artfully given. But beneath the 'mausoleum' that the surviving narrative comprises, an alternative and truer truth still resides: this truth, while having no text of its own, can be reconstructed by way of the lapses and incoherences that the available text displays. Freud's imagery works hard to suggest that the real origin and the real fate of Moses are – no less than antiquities or mental causes – 'objects found in a tomb', and that their burial has been their preservation. Yet at the same time this buried reality, this truer truth, this *fons et origo* of our knowledge, is avowedly the product of simple conjecture: 'if we have guessed what happened correctly, there is nothing left about it that is puzzling'. But as no texts are available to confirm or refute Freud's hypothetical biography of Moses it is able to enjoy an unearned inviolability. Whereas earlier, in the *Introductory Lectures*, Moses had appeared in the company of Nimrod as a figure of notoriously dubious historicity (xv, 19), he has now taken a classic Freudian return route to the realm of fact – that route which leads to a lucid cognitive present by way of an ancient and obscure past. In the phantasy of *Moses and Monotheism*, the buried palaeo-Moses has acquired the familiar characteristics of Freud's archaeological objects proper: he is deeper than the rival personage offered by Biblical narrative, earlier, closer to the origins and, in consequence, superior in his capacity to explain the later development of Judaic and European civilisation.[12]

Freud's archaeology is, therefore, a dream of unitary and unidirectional knowledge. The objects to be known may be intact or fragmentary, but in either state they offer the same sort of stimulus and the same sort of reward. If they are still intact they need only to be discovered for their meaning to be revealed, while in the less fortunate case, although informed guesswork and skilled reconstruction will be necessary, the direction in which meaning may best be pursued is still plain – back towards the lost wholeness of each fragmentary thing. The objects of mental science are thus rescued in advance from the perils of multiple causation. They are not situated within a simultaneous field of interactive determining forces and in their production there has been no competitive play between the psychical and the physical or between the personal and the social. Within this archaeological perspective, the psyche has domestic politics but no foreign relations, internal scenes but no public stage. For all that the neurotic symptom may represent an uneasy compromise between conflicting desires, the structure of that symptom is completely explainable by reference to episodes within the early emotional history of the subject, during which desires came singly and were satisfied or not. Such pathogenic episodes, however conjectural, fiction-filled or patched together they may be, are Freud's first causes,[13] just as neurological lesions were Charcot's, and he is as suspicious as Charcot had been of explanatory methods that might complicate the passage of any such cause through the indefinite sequence of its effects. Theory was complication. The task of theoretical model-building in mental science thus conceived was to release the mind by the shortest available path from the obligation to have theories. By way of the detours that its successive models and 'constructions' represent, the mind returns to things as they originally were. And from that point to things-as-they-are the road is straight. The straight causal road opened up by archaeology provides not so much a logical foundation for Freudian historical and hermeneutic procedure as an escape from that procedure at its moments of crisis or overspill. For Freud, in his discussions of case-material, is a multilinear historian of the psychical life, and in his dream-interpretations the manipulator of ramifying and imbricated causal schemes.[14] Archaeology was more than a mere escape from all this analytic intrication: it was the dream of an alternative logic to the threatening and insidious logic of dreams.

Freud often presents his fascination with antiquities as an amiable fad. Discussing 'misreadings' in *The Psychopathology of Everyday Life*, he reports: 'There is one misreading which I find irritating and laughable and to which I am prone whenever I walk through the streets of a strange town on my holidays. On these occasions I read every shop sign that resembles the word in any way as "Antiquities". This betrays the questing spirit of the collector' (IV, 110). And he saw wish-fulfilment of the same kind in his own dream-material. There, the thought of death – 'this most unwished-for of all thoughts' – may be transmuted into an archaeological satisfaction. Discussing a dream in which two men were seen lying on benches in a wooden house, Freud commented:

> I had already been in a grave once, but it was an excavated Etruscan grave near Orvieto, a narrow chamber with two stone benches along its walls, on which the skeletons of two grown-up men were lying. The inside of the wooden house in the dream looked exactly like it, except that the stone was replaced by wood. The dream seems to have been saying: 'If you must rest in a grave, let it be the Etruscan one.' (*The Interpretation of Dreams* (1900), V, 454–5)

Many years later, in Freud's account of religion as wish-fulfilment in *The Future of an Illusion* (1927), the same example was to be used again: 'the dreamer sees himself in an ancient Etruscan grave which he has climbed down into, happy to find his archaeological interests satisfied' (XXI, 17). There is something not faddish but passionate and obsessional about these holiday incidents, especially when seen as part of the archaeological dream-work that permeates Freud's science. The collector whose Midas glance turns the world before him to antiquities finds for himself an appropriate fate: he becomes a voluntary grave-dweller, an archaeological object, an antiquity in his turn. And this fate is a happy one indeed if such objects, having 'rested in a grave', are eventually to be brought back to daylight as the very emblems of Truth.

III

Archaeology was, therefore, a world of hard, glaring facts before which hypotheses and theories could be expected to melt away. Yet Freud's appetite for theory was voracious, and his sense of intellectual potency was reliant upon his capacity not simply to have many theories – *mille e tre* – but to make certain of them indefinitely expansible.[15] His investigation of psychopathology having first been attempted upon himself, he told Romain Rolland, he 'went on to apply it to other people and finally, by a bold extension, to the human race as a whole' (XXII, 239). I now turn to the complementary order of Freudian self-images that I mentioned earlier: those which depict the overreaching mobility of the scientific imagination. From the power of the archaeologist, the emblem of which is the single, stable, 'speaking' object, I shall move to the power of the conqueror, whose emblems are legion and to be found in the chronicle of his deeds, in the length of his itineraries, in the variety of the lands he traverses and of the populations he subdues.

An exemplary transition from the first to the second of these metaphorical modes is to be found in the elaborate Roman episode that occurs in the opening pages of *Civilization and its Discontents*. There are two ways of entering Rome, Freud had said in *The Interpretation of Dreams* – as Winckelmann the archaeologist or as Hannibal the commander-in-chief (IV, 196).[16] In this passage from the later work the two ways, deliberative and executive, tender and tough, are shown to be mutually confirming. Freud first summarises what 'historians tell us' about the physical development of the city and mentions the role that archaeology may have in placing the stages of that development in their correct temporal sequence. He then begins to imagine what Rome would be like if it were not a physical entity but a psychical one, 'in which nothing that has once come into existence will have passed away':

This would mean that in Rome the palaces of the Caesars and the Septizonium of Septimius Severus would still be rising to their old height on the Palatine and that the castle of S. Angelo would still be carrying on its battlements the beautiful statues which graced it until the siege by the Goths, and so on. But more than this. In the place occupied by the Palazzo Caffarelli would once more stand – without the Palazzo having to be removed – the temple of Jupiter Capitolinus; and this not only in its latest shape, as the Romans of the Empire saw it, but also in its earliest one, when it still showed Etruscan forms and was ornamented with terracotta antefixes. Where the Coliseum now stands we could at the same time admire Nero's vanished Golden House. On the Piazza of the Pantheon we should find not only the Pantheon of to-day, as it was bequeathed to us by Hadrian, but, on the same site, the original edifice erected by Agrippa; indeed, the same piece of ground would be supporting the church of Santa Maria sopra Minerva and the ancient temple over which it was built. And the observer would perhaps only have to change the direction of his glance or his position in order to call up the one view or the other. (XXI, 70)

Having spun this phantasy at length, Freud proceeds at greater length to heap negations upon it. The phantasy must be stopped because 'it leads to things that are unimaginable and even absurd'; its only useful purpose is to show how limited pictorial representations of the mind are; a *city*, where 'demolitions and replacement of buildings occur in the course of the most peaceful development', is in any case unsuited for such comparisons; although the development of the human or animal body may be thought to offer a better pictorial analogy, even this has major flaws. Freud's final disclaimer is characteristic of an essay in which self-doubt is presented as a precondition for responsible moral utterance and in which *praeteritio* and *dubitatio* are favoured rhetorical figures: perhaps the very imperfection of these analogies means that the underlying principle which they are designed to reinforce – that psychical material is indestructible – is itself subtly wrong or over-ambitious. 'Perhaps we ought to content ourselves', Freud writes, 'with asserting that what is past in mental life *may* be preserved and is not *necessarily* destroyed' (XXI, 71). But what is it about the phantasy that requires a denial so copious? And why extend the denial so far beyond its original object that an otherwise firm principle of psychoanalytic explanation is threatened?

In Freud's Rome power increases exponentially. The previous masters of the place – whether Caesars or Popes, Gods or Goths – have left such striking mementoes of themselves on the face of the magically restored city that the observer becomes powerful in the contemplation of their power. A similar magic has transformed his senses too: seeking to know Rome, he has only 'to change the direction of his glance or his position' for phase upon phase of Roman history, palace upon palace, to rise before him.[17] This is the scientific quest beatified. The objects of study are no longer refractory or partial or intermittently available for inspection; as the eye moves, so the mind knows; none of these objects can ever be ruined and none need ever be discarded as unworthy of attention. This heady phantasy of omnipotence and omniscience may well have taken Freud uncomfortably close to things 'unimaginable and even absurd'. For here was science, in the very pursuit of strictness, swooning away into mysticism, or into that 'oceanic feeling' which the remainder of his chapter gently mocks and patronises.[18] Yet how much of this vision do Freud's denials deny? In the elaboration of his own text, he places himself in exactly the position occupied by his imaginary observer of Rome. The mind is in turn pictured zoologically, archaeologically and anatomically, and each analogy is superseded yet preserved. That a given model of the psychical apparatus (*psychischer* or *seelischer Apparat*)[19] is found to be inappropriate or inexact does not mean that it should be left unspoken. On the contrary, each model remains desirable when its deficiencies have been named. The cognitive satisfactions that each failed comparison seemed to promise are repudiated yet still savoured within the itinerary of the text. 'Failure' of this kind is success by another name. Freud's phantasy of omnipotence is being adhered to even as it faces his barrage of denials, and not simply because the text preserves its speculative edifices from ruin. For all the analogies drawn from other sciences are reversible. Psychoanalysis does not merely receive structural models from elsewhere and pay homage to their explanatory power: it is a fully equipped supplier both of explanations and of analogical aids to its neighbours. Its concentration of powers makes it the veritable Rome of science and provides a new forum and a new arena for scientific debate.[20]

Freud writes at length and without apology about himself as power-seeking Hero. At the time of the first publication of *The Interpretation of Dreams*, he offered this piece of self-exalting self-ridicule to a correspondent: 'I am not really a man of science, not an observer, not an experimenter and not a thinker. I am nothing but by temperament a Conquistador – an Adventurer, if you want to translate the word – with the curiosity, the boldness and the tenacity that belongs to that type of being' (J, I, 382). In his scientific writings he not only discusses this continuing boyhood phantasy in great detail but bases a higher-level claim to the consideration and respect that are the hero's due upon his fearlessness in dismantling this part of his personal mythology. Although Freud's commentators regularly speak of themselves as having 'discovered' his combative and self-aggrandising tendencies, these features are perfectly visible on the surface of his works. (But then even commentators are seekers after buried meaning and aspirants to heroic status.) The temperamental affinity that he claimed with such illustrious predecessors as Hannibal, Alexander, Cromwell and Napoleon[21] not only outlasted his boyhood but was amply remotivated by his professional struggles to gain acceptance for his teaching.

In his article 'On the History of the Psycho-Analytic Movement' (1914), for example, Freud's followers are reported as having compared him with Columbus (XIV, 43) and, without accepting or rejecting this comparison in his text, he borrows from the Parisian coat of arms a defiant seafarer's epigraph: *fluctuat nec mergitur* ('it is tossed about but does not sink') (XIV, 7).[22] Elsewhere, in the *Introductory Lectures* (1916–17), he illustrates his own dictum that 'success does not always go along with merit' by pointing out that America was not named after Columbus (XVI, 257). Authorship and authority need the protection of appropriate names: the achievement of Columbus, imperfectly commemorated, has in effect been stolen from him; the deeds of Alexander are in danger of being forgotten because, as Alexander himself complained (Freud reminds us), he had no Homer to record them (VI, 108 and XXIII, 71); and, unless precautions are taken, the discoveries of a scientist may easily be betrayed, or annexed, or trivialised. Freud–Columbus's main purpose in writing a history of psychoanalysis in 1914 was to draw clear boundary lines between his own ideas and those of his lapsed followers Adler and Jung; the lecture in which Columbus reappears guards the frontier between Freud and Janet.[23]

Freud's most spectacular attempt to disengage himself from his competitors by aligning himself with men of legendary prowess is to be found in his response to Otto Rank's *The Myth of the Birth of the Hero* (1909). Rank wrote this work at Freud's suggestion and illustrated the underlying structure of the myth with an imposing cast of characters: Moses, Oedipus, Perseus, Gilgamesh, Romulus, Hercules, Jesus and Siegfried, among others. Freud, summarising the book in *Moses and Monotheism* (1939), gives an account of the 'average legend' that emerges from Rank's researches and indicates the one enabling quality that intending heroes must possess: 'A hero is someone who has had the courage to rebel against his father and has in the end victoriously overcome him' (XXIII, 12). It is courage of this kind, but raised to a special intensity, that entitles Freud to join Rank's inventory. He is not only a victorious son but in the pursuit of his victory has become the supreme theoretician of the parricidal impulse. Freud's paper on 'Family Romances' (IX, 237–41), which gives a brief theoretical account of the mechanisms of projection whereby such self-elevations to heroic rank become possible, originally appeared as an insertion in Rank's monograph: Freud had found a Homer to sing his deeds, but ironised *intra muros* against heroism even as he accepted Rank's tribute.[24]

Freud's fullest and most moving account of his own career as one of perpetual travel and conquest is to be found in the letter, quoted above, which was written as a seventieth-birthday gift for Romain Rolland: 'A Disturbance of Memory on the Acropolis' (XXII, 239–48). In Freud's narrative, travel and theory, conquest and cognition, reconnaissance and recognition, are counterpointed to form a complete portrait of scientific desire. The essay, written in 1936, had been half-promised ten years earlier in *The Future of an Illusion* (XXI, 25). It describes events that had taken place in 1904 during a short holiday in Greece taken by Freud and his brother Alexander. This holiday, like Schliemann's excavation of Hissarlik, brought with it the fulfilment of a childhood wish.[25] At Trieste the travellers had been advised by a business acquaintance of Alexander's against going to Corfu, their original destination, and had decided to visit Athens instead. In the hours between their taking this decision and their being able to book passages on the Athens boat, the brothers wandered about the town in a 'discontented and irresolute frame of mind'. In view of their keen wish to see Athens, this depression seemed mysterious. When they finally stood on the Acropolis, Freud had the surprising thought, the disturbance of memory, that gave him a second mystery to explain: 'So all this really *does* exist, just as we learnt at school!' (XXII, 241).

The 'derealization' to which Athens had momentarily been subjected is finally explained in the following terms:

> It is not true that in my schooldays I ever doubted the real existence of Athens. I only doubted whether I should ever see Athens. It seemed to me beyond the realms of possibility that I should travel so far – that I should 'go such a long way'. This was linked up with the limitations and poverty of our conditions of life in my youth. My longing to travel was no doubt also the expression of a wish to escape

from that pressure . . . I had long seen clearly that a great part of the pleasure of travel lies in the fulfilment of these early wishes – that it is rooted, that is, in dissatisfaction with home and family. When first one catches sight of the sea, crosses the ocean and experiences as realities cities and lands which for so long had been distant, unattainable things of desire – one feels oneself like a hero who has performed deeds of improbable greatness. I might that day on the Acropolis have said to my brother: '. . . We really *have* gone a long way!' So too, if I may compare such a small event with a greater one, Napoleon, during his coronation as Emperor in Notre Dame, turned to one of his brothers – it must no doubt have been the eldest one, Joseph – and remarked: 'What would *Monsieur notre Père* have said to this, if he could have been here to-day?' (246–7)

And the depression at Trieste had had the same fundamental cause:

It must be that a sense of guilt was attached to the satisfaction in having gone such a long way: there was something about it that was wrong, that from earliest times had been forbidden. It was something to do with a child's criticism of his father, with the undervaluation which took the place of the overvaluation of earlier childhood. It seems as though the essence of success was to have got further than one's father, and as though to excel one's father was still something forbidden. (247)[26]

There had been two mysteries; there was one solution. Although Freud cannot have expected that solution to surprise any reader acquainted with his earlier works, it is placed at the culminating point of an intricate narrative design. And his tale of detection has its full measure of misleading trails and unverifiable conjectures. The incidents in Trieste and in Athens seem each to provide clues for the understanding of the other, but the connection between them is at first elusive. When this connection, which lies in the experience of *incredulity*, begins to emerge, Freud announces 'now we know where we are' but proceeds to a detailed recapitulation of an earlier paper (XIV, 316–31) on those who have been 'wrecked by success', who 'fall ill . . . because an overwhelmingly powerful wish of theirs has been fulfilled'. The brothers' depression in Trieste is presented as a minor instance of this disorder. But the theory expounded in the earlier paper and now laboriously rehearsed cannot explain the anomalous and gratuitous-seeming event completely. A complete explanation already exists but the moment of its unveiling is being resisted and deferred. Discussion of the Athenian incident contains its own complicating excursions. If the incongruous thought on the Acropolis in fact expressed Freud's 'joyful astonishment' at finding himself there, why, he asks himself, should this meaning have been subjected to such a 'distorted and distorting disguise'? The search for an answer to this further problem involves lengthy consideration of such psychical phenomena as 'derealisation', 'depersonalisation', '*fausse reconnaissance*' and '*déjà vu*', although Freud's own theory of repression would have allowed him a number of legitimate short cuts to the solution that he eventually proposes. The latent cause lying beneath the ostensible cause lying beneath the event itself must not be reached prematurely: that latent cause, which is the heroic contest of son with father, is to be arrived at by a process of slow analytic delectation. The victorious son permits himself, in the act of scientific explanation no less than in that of literary composition, to perform again in thought 'deeds of improbable greatness'.

Freud has, then, created a homology between the structure of his argument and the fulfilment of two related childhood wishes: to see Athens and to vanquish his father. The intellectual delays occasioned by the testing of hypotheses and the marshalling of supplementary evidence are delays too in the satisfaction of a libidinal goal, and the essay is organised in such a way that the two kinds of climax are reached at once. Even the casual play of Freud's phantasy around his principal characters and scenes contributes to the self-apotheosis of the final paragraphs: the safely wise Rolland is replaced by Napoleon;[27] Trieste, that centre of mere business and trade ('our father had been in business') is replaced by the supreme sanctum of European civilisation.

A framework of stoical restraint is placed around this portrait of intellectual hubris and militancy. Freud's opening address to Rolland – 'I am ten years older than you and my powers of production are at an end. All that I can find to offer you is the gift of an impoverished creature who has "seen better days"' – is echoed in his leave-taking: 'now you will no longer wonder that the recollection of this incident on the Acropolis should have troubled me so often since I myself have grown old and stand in need of forbearance and can travel no more'. Yet there are energies of the speculative mind that infirmity and old age cannot quell. The essay relaunches the quest for scientific explanation even as each cherished *explicandum* yields: first, as we have seen, by teasing out the central mystery of the tale and then, once the full solution is in sight, by pointing to the tantalising residue of mystery that psychical events of this kind still possess. In the traveller immobilised by age the appetite for travel persists, and for the hero, even in his moments of exultant conquest, there are deeds of prowess still to perform. During his final journey from Austria to Britain, in flight from the Nazis, Freud dreamed that he had landed at Pevensey – in the footsteps of the Conqueror, as he explained to his son (J, III, 244).

What had happened on the Acropolis? According to the selective account of events given to Rolland,[28] a momentary mistake had been made. Placing himself upon a site that had been more thoroughly sanctified and suffused with myth than any other by the nineteenth-century historians of Greece, Freud had discovered nothing about the Acropolis other than that it was there. In Renan's *Souvenirs d'enfance et de jeunesse*, on the other hand – to take the most obvious contrary instance – an entire Athenian cult had reached its apogee: 'Il y a un lieu où la perfection existe; il n'y en a pas deux: c'est celui-là. Je n'avais jamais rien imaginé de pareil. C'était l'idéal cristallisé en marbre pentélique qui se montrait à moi.'[29] Renan's account of the Acropolis contains a portable distillation of supposed Greek virtues: 'Ce qu'il y a de surprenant, en effet, c'est que le beau n'est ici que l'honnêteté absolue, la raison, le respect même envers la divinité.'[30] To be sure his 'prière sur l'Acropole' had turned into a sorrowful anathema: in the end perfection of this kind was too intense to be tolerable and drove him back to the 'romantic' anxieties and depravities that he associated with the Breton landscapes of his childhood. But where for Renan the Acropolis, whether praised or blamed, had been a place of moral and intellectual plenitude, for Freud it was the place where an infinitesimal mental vacuity had occurred. At another moment Freud could have cast a properly archaeological eye upon the scene, although it had of course already been too much studied and despoiled to offer the same excitements as Hissarlik or Knossos. But in refusing archaeology on this occasion, and contemplating a purely mental chain of causes and effects, he discovered an improbable alternative route to the glory that was Greece. His pause at the Parthenon was as mythopoeic and self-exalting as Renan's had been. For the disturbance of memory that he describes to Rolland is a derivative of the inextinguishable heroic impulse that scientist and conqueror share. As Freud stood on the Acropolis looking at monumental remains that did not themselves, at that moment, detain the mind, he was poised before the indestructible psychical fact that had caused the Athenian monuments to be raised, just as it had propelled Napoleon in his conquests and the scientist of the unconscious in his. Here again was an explanatory bedrock, but one which now offered the scientific mind no other destiny than that of interminable speculative motion.[31]

IV

Although the phantasies that I have been outlining under the headings 'archaeologist' and 'conqueror' provide Freud with the raw material for two divergent intellectual autobiographies, these phantasies do often interpenetrate and either of them may be used to refine or redramatise the other. Of the numerous temples to Diana built on a single site in the stratified city of Ephesus, for example, one is especially noteworthy: the fourth, destroyed by Herostratus 'during the night in which Alexander the Great was born' (XII, 342, XXII, 102). He who studies strata studies, and acquires, power. I shall end my survey of this material with what strikes me as the most complex hybrid instance to be found in Freud's writings. It again involves Alexander and appears as an extended footnote in the second chapter of *The Interpretation of Dreams*. At this point the main text is discussing the decoding procedures used by the ancients in the study of dreams:

[1] [*Footnote added* 1909:] Dr. Alfred Robitsek has pointed out to me that the oriental 'dream-books' (of which ours are wretched imitations) base the greater number of their interpretations of dream-elements upon similarity of sounds and resemblance between words. The fact that these connections inevitably disappear in translation accounts for the unintelligibility of the renderings in our own popular dream-books. The extraordinarily important part played by punning and verbal quibbles in the ancient civilizations of the East may be studied in the writings of Hugo Winckler [the famous archaeologist]. – [*Added* 1911:] The nicest instance of a dream-interpretation which has reached us from ancient times is based on a play upon words. It is told by Artemidorus [Book IV, Chap. 24; Krauss's translation, 1881, 255]: 'I think too that Aristander gave a most happy interpretation to Alexander of Macedon when he had surrounded Tyre [*Τύρος*] and was besieging it but was feeling uneasy and disturbed because of the length of time the siege was taking. Alexander dreamt he saw a satyr [*σάτυρος*] dancing on his shield. Aristander happened to be in the neighbourhood of Tyre, in attendance on the king during his Syrian campaign. By dividing the word for satyr into *σά* and *τύρος* he encouraged the king to press home the siege so that he became master of the city.' (*σὰ Τύρος*=Tyre is thine.) – Indeed, dreams are so closely related to linguistic expression that Ferenczi [1910] has truly remarked that every tongue has its own dream-language. It is impossible as a rule to translate a dream into a foreign language and this is equally true, I fancy, of a book such as the present one. [*Added* 1930:] Nevertheless, Dr. A. A. Brill of New York, and others after him, have succeeded in translating *The Interpretation of Dreams*. (IV, 99)

James Strachey's Standard Edition text, which I reproduce here, gives us information not to be had from the plain German text of the *Gesammelte Werke* (II/III, 103–4): the footnote was begun nine years after the first appearance of Freud's work and completed after further intervals of two and nineteen years. The stratigraphy revealed by Strachey's interpolated dates would suggest that an enduring matter of personal concern is present in the text at this point. One way of guessing at this matter would be to say that Freud is preoccupied here with his own claims to originality – the ancients, who clearly knew much more than Freud's immediate predecessors about the structure and significance of dreams, cannot be allowed to have pre-empted his own major insight – and that he is using Alexander as a heroic alias, just as he used Columbus in the comparable demarcation disputes that I mentioned earlier.[32] Artemidorus himself was a special case among the early dream-interpreters whose techniques are described in the opening chapters of *The Interpretation of Dreams*, for the technique employed in his *Oneirocritica* had come exceptionally close to Freud's own. (A further long footnote, added in 1914, seeks to differentiate them.)[33] But Artemidorus here provides Freud with a term of comparison far grander than the *Oneirocritica* for his interpretative enterprise: Alexander's capture of Tyre. Among the exploits of Alexander, the capture of Tyre seems particularly to have fascinated Freud: he refers to it again in a later supplementary footnote to *The Interpretation of Dreams* (V, 614) and recounts the whole story twice in his *Introductory Lectures* (XV, 85–6 and 236). Indeed he had already placed the entire lecture-series under the sign of heroism by offering his lay audience the question 'how do we know that Alexander the Great existed?' as a way of understanding the sorts of question that the nascent science of psychoanalysis was obliged to handle (XV, 18–19).

But the hero's success at Tyre was not a simple feat of arms or of strategic imagination. Alexander had provided a fragment of dream-material and was later to provide the required military strength. Between his dreaming and his doing, however, a technically skilled student of dreams had intervened. Without Aristander's interpretation, Alexander's dream would have led nowhere; once interpreted, it was a trigger for purposeful and decisive action.[34] The seductiveness of Artemidorus's story as cited by Freud lies in its capacity to marry two of his favourite self-images. Here the decoder of dreams provides a single, crucial explanation. That explanation, born of a complex knowledge of language in dreams, is not in itself complex: once the equivalence *σάτυρος = σὰ Τύρος* has been found the relevant play of language is over. Aristander's explanation is complete, stable and without those loose ends that elsewhere in *The Interpretation of Dreams* may provoke a series of hermeneutic postscripts. Cognitively, he has reached the same happy terminus as Freud's archaeologist at the conclusion of his dig. But that explanation, far from producing a quiet glow of scholarly satisfaction, facilitates the progress towards Egypt of a conqueror without equal, a supreme master of focused and unidirectional aggression.[35] Here in miniature, in the mutual dependence of Aristander and Alexander, is that dialectic of scholar and warrior which gives Freud's autobiographical accounts of his science their characteristic tension. It is fitting that the final layers of this footnote should describe a stubborn obstacle to the progress of Freud's own scientific campaign. For want of a decoder and re-encoder, *Die Traumdeutung* had been halted at the frontiers of Germanic culture; A. A. Brill, and others after him, have now removed the obstacle, allowing the work and its author to travel further along the path of conquest.[36]

V

The unofficial, wishful material that penetrates into Freud's science by way of his metaphors, analogies and fragmentary autobiographical narratives creates an instructive topological space in which to consider the principles and conventions underlying that science. Instructive but erratic. For the images of conqueror and archaeologist that I have polarised in order to highlight the contrasts between Freud's liking for expansive theorising and his liking for seeming theory-freeness – and between the hypothetico-deductive and inductive strains in his scientific work – have a number of main expressive capacities in common. Archaeologist and conqueror are both topographers, surveyors of terrain; both wield incisive metal implements; both return home with trophies and expect clamorous public recognition for their deeds; both are enthusiasts for *hardness* – whether of durable stone relics or of intransigent martial will. Both phantasies involve exclusively 'masculine' ambition and conduct in accordance with the definitions of masculinity Freud provides in the *Three Essays on the Theory of Sexuality* (VII, 219–21) and elsewhere. Indeed one might see the conquistadorial as well as the archaeological imagery as a repeated attempt to impart a surface of phallic self-assertion to what could otherwise have seemed, to a former cerebral anatomist, the 'feminine' softness and deliquescence of mere theorising. Both phantasies seek to accredit a new science by reference to the historical past, and to remove the objects of that science from the sphere of social and political actuality.[37] Besides, it is by no means always plain, as my suggestion has been, that the hero must perform many notable deeds or produce many notable theories in order to win his glory: one sublime exploit – slaying the Minotaur, unearthing the Oedipus complex – may be sufficient to place him among the immortals. (This, in outline, is the Freud story that Ernest Jones told.)

But these anti-theoretical and philo-theoretical phantasies are still separate enough, despite the zone of interference between them, to suggest that no single 'scientific attitude' could provide a satisfactory outlet for the disparate desires that they reveal. If we turn from Freud as the biographer of those desires to Freud as the biographer of his own theories of desire, we find that a similar indecision about the status of theory itself is continually apparent. Theory is wished for and distrusted; having theories – more of them, better ones – is now the goal of science, now a lapse from scientific rectitude. We are able to trace these fluctuations even in Freud's most abstract writings because, far from merely stating his hypotheses and describing the tests to which they have been submitted, it is his custom to tell the story of their emergence. In 'Instincts and Their Vicissitudes' (1915), for example, he writes in partial answer to his own question 'what instincts should we suppose there are, and how many?':

> I have proposed that two groups of such primal instincts should be distinguished: the *ego*, or *self-preservative*, instincts and the *sexual* instincts. But this supposition has not the status of a necessary postulate, as has, for instance, our assumption about the biological purpose of the mental apparatus; it is merely a working hypothesis, to be retained only so long as it proves useful, and it will make little difference to the results of our work of description and classification if it is replaced by another. The occasion for this hypothesis arose in the course of the evolution of psycho-analysis, which was first employed upon the psycho-neuroses, or, more precisely, upon the group described as 'transference neuroses' (hysteria and obsessional neurosis); these showed that at the root of all such affections there is to be found a conflict between the claims of sexuality and those of the ego. It is always possible that an exhaustive study of the other neurotic affections . . . may oblige us to alter this formula and to make a different

classification of the primal instincts. But for the present we do not know of any such formula . . . I am altogether doubtful whether any decisive pointers for the differentiation and classification of the instincts can be arrived at on the basis of working over the psychological material. This working-over seems rather itself to call for the application to the material of definite assumptions concerning instinctual life, and it would be a desirable thing if those assumptions could be taken from some other branch of knowledge and carried over to psychology. The contribution which biology has to make here certainly does not run counter to the distinction between sexual and ego-instincts. (XIV, 124–5)

The vertigo described here, and its suggested cure, both recur throughout Freud's career. What happens when the mental scientist departs from biology and from the 'definite assumptions' and 'necessary postulates' that biology seems to provide? He is cast adrift in the fluid world of the psychological model-builder. For working over the accidental materials of clinical observation involves the production of expendable hypotheses about the underlying structure of the instinctual life, and without firm anchorage in some existing corpus of knowledge the flow of such hypotheses could continue indefinitely. Biology, which Freud had repudiated in the 1890s in order to pursue the calling of 'pure' psychology, remained permanently available to him as that 'other branch of knowledge' which would finally bring psychological speculation to completeness and rest. The classification of instincts that Freud makes in this passage was indeed to be supplanted – in and beyond *Beyond the Pleasure Principle* (1920). But, in fulfilment of his own prediction, biology was to retain its role as external guarantor even when the primal instincts first classified as 'self-preservative' and 'sexual' were reclassified as those of 'life' and 'death'. In the closing paragraph of 'Analysis Terminable and Interminable' (1937), for example, biology is reintroduced with a familiar terminal and closural force. The female's supposed wish for a penis teases the speculative psychologist out of thought; it gives him 'the impression that . . . we have penetrated through all the psychological strata and have reached bedrock, and that thus our activities are at an end. This is probably true, since, for the psychical field, the biological field does in fact play the part of the underlying bedrock [*des unterliegenden gewachsenen Felsens*]' (*GW*, XVI, 99; XXIII, 252).

Much useful analytic and theoretical work, Freud repeatedly reminds us, can be done in terms of purely psychical stratigraphy, and 'bedrock', for most of his chosen scientific purposes, need be envisaged as no more than the deepest and most enduring psychical stratum. Psychoanalysis itself had provided psychology with 'its substructure and perhaps even its entire foundation' (*The Question of Lay Analysis* (1926), XX, 252). But, when psychological constructions begin to proliferate uncontrollably, the desire for 'depth' and stable explanation undergoes its last displacement: rather than have no stopping place, no bedrock of his own devising, the author of a new science of mind imagines his discipline re-assimilated to the very science of organisms from which it had originally, by slow degrees, emancipated itself. At this extreme point in Freud's reflection on his own science, all psychology was mere theory while biology was the lost kingdom of truth and certitude.[38]

Within biology it was neurophysiology in particular that seemed to offer the firmest bulwark against euphoric theoretical speculation. The nervous system called the theorist back from his contingent fabrications to a world that was necessary, determinate and secure. But although psychoanalysis was to rejoin biology at some unforeseeable future time – and have its findings checked by reference to mappable neural structures and measurable neural energies – it could until then expect little practical support from biology in such crucial areas of its scientific work as the theory of the instincts: biological knowledge offered not a procedure for verifying or falsifying new theories but a rough test of their verisimilitude. In this extended interim period before arrival at bedrock, psychoanalytic theory had to develop its own criteria of coherence and its own internal checks and controls. And for Freud this meant designating and strenuously preserving schisms and dualisms within his field of enquiry.

The clearest example of this is to be found in Freud's custodianship of 'libido' itself. Throughout the long and eventful history of this concept within his instinct theories, Freud insists upon the limits of its range. In *Group Psychology and the Analysis of the Ego* (1921) he gives this informal pre-biological definition: 'Libido is an expression taken from the theory of the emotions. We call by that name the energy, regarded as a quantitative magnitude (though not at present actually measurable), of those instincts which have to do with all that may be comprised under the word "love"' (XVIII, 90). But this definition is a restrictive rather than a permissive one. In each of the major classifications that I mentioned earlier, libido occupies one side only of a dualistic system: it corresponds in the first to the sexual as opposed to the self-preservative instinct and in the second to the 'life' as opposed to the 'death' instinct. 'I give the name of *libido*', Freud wrote, summarising the first phase of his thinking on the matter in *An Autobiographical Study* (1925), 'to the energy of the sexual instincts and to that form of energy alone' (XX, 35); while in *Beyond the Pleasure Principle*, at the moment of transition from the earlier to the later theoretical phase, he had placed still greater emphasis upon the need to preserve the dualistic character of psychoanalysis in the face both of those critics who felt able to dismiss it as 'pansexualism' and of Jung, for whom 'libido' had come to mean 'instinctual force in general' (XVIII, 52–3). Such monisms misrepresented a main feature of his thought, but not libellously. For the monistic style was a constant hazard to which that thought could fall prey. In *Beyond the Pleasure Principle*, Freud describes how he had come to recognise that the self-preservative instincts themselves were of a libidinal character and had thus seen his original dualism beginning to decay. The 'death instinct' was a conceptual innovation for which a number of virtues could be claimed. But the first of these was that it circumscribed a wantonly expansive concept and thereby rescued Freud from an intellectual vice. The death instinct was what libido was not; it was libido's new interlocutor. No mental agency was entitled to the absurd grandeur of existing alone and uncontested.

Freud's dialectical theories of human desire are dialectically written and refer copiously to the conflicting wishes and predilections of himself as theorist. And his restless pursuit of a coherent instinct theory is nowhere more plainly an attempt (among other things) to make sense of his own wishes than in his accounts of libido as self-divided. For libido is not simply attended and contested by other instinctual forces: it has its own domestic conflicts. On the one hand, 'the sexual instinctual impulses . . . are extraordinarily *plastic*' (*Introductory Lectures*, XVI, 345),[39] and this plasticity (*Plastizität*) – the resourceful mobility that they display in their search for satisfaction – may in certain clinical cases impede treatment and produce short-lived therapeutic results ('Analysis Terminable and Interminable', XXIII, 241). Libido also displays, on the other hand, a characteristic variously described by Freud as 'adhesiveness' (*Haftfähigkeit*), 'viscosity' (*Klebrigkeit*) or 'pertinacity' (*Zähigkeit*). The sexuality of the Wolf Man illustrated this perfectly: 'Any position of the libido which he had once taken up was obstinately defended by him from fear of what he would lose by giving it up' ('From the History of an Infantile Neurosis' (1918), XVII, 115). Both qualities of libido – its 'plasticity' and its 'adhesiveness' – were a source of theoretical and therapeutic difficulty for Freud. The images of flowing liquid that he often used in his descriptions of libido scarcely disguise and indeed often pinpoint the inscrutability of this essential concept. Here was a 'flow' of energy which, whether it was slowed down or accelerated, dammed up or diverted, seemed still to obey its own elusive laws. And it was in the attempt to regulate this apparently self-regulating flow of desire that the task and the tragic incompleteness of psychoanalysis lay. The difference between the fixated and the mobile libidinal types met with in analytic practice was comparable, Freud wrote in 'Analysis Terminable and Interminable', 'to the one felt by a sculptor according to whether he works in hard stone or soft clay' (XXIII, 241). In cases of extreme mobility, one had the impression not even of having worked in clay, but of having 'written on water'. As a sculptor of theories Freud was subject to the same anxiety as he here attributes to the clinician. For strive as the psychoanalytic model-builder might to make the 'hard stone' of science or the 'speaking stone' of archaeology into a repository for his desire, he could always, in the act of building, find his stone turning to clay or re-encounter that desire as a flow upon which his writing left no trace. Am I Winckelmann or Hannibal?[40] Schliemann or Alexander? a monument or an itinerary?

'Instincts and their transformations are at the limit of what is discernible by psycho-analysis', Freud wrote at the end of *Leonardo da Vinci and a Memory of his Childhood* (1910) (XI, 136). But exactly this horizon, beyond which lay biology and the other sciences, attracted his gaze inexhaustibly. It was there that the intelligibility of psychoanalysis and its claims to scientific status faced their most stringent test, and there too that the *Wißtrieb*, the 'instinct for knowledge' – which was itself a derivative of the infant's wish to understand his or her sexuality – became a legitimate object of scientific enquiry.[41] Apart from the Leonardo essay, which shows the *Wißtrieb* in headlong pursuit of itself,[42] Freud's major contributions to this enquiry are to be found in his descriptions of the intellectual life as lived, thwartedly, by obsessional neurotics. The transformational stages by which intellection proper emerges from self-gratifying sexual research are relived in reverse by these patients: the 'thought-process itself becomes sexualized, for the sexual pleasure which is normally attached to the content of thought becomes shifted to the act of thinking itself' ('Notes upon a Case of Obsessional Neurosis' (1909), x, 245). But such is the percipient generosity of Freud's descriptions that the very features which seem to place neurotic intellectual performances in a category apart – repetition, regression and compulsive brooding – also give them emblematic stature: 'the interminable character of the child's researches is . . . repeated in the fact that this brooding never ends and that the intellectual feeling, so much desired, of having found a solution recedes more and more into the distance' (xi, 80). The obsessional neurotic thinks vacantly, and without achieving purchase upon the material and mental worlds that lie outside him. But as he broods, repeats and regresses he reveals *in vitro* the inescapable conditions of thought by which all seekers for knowledge are bound – the conditions that are to be seen again, *in vivo*, in Freud's writing.

For Freud mental science, the history of which was a tissue of competing fictions, could never be expected to outgrow the need for fiction and it was a point of agnostic honour not to pretend otherwise: 'In psychology we can only describe things by the help of analogies. There is nothing peculiar in this; it is the case elsewhere as well. But we have constantly to keep changing these analogies, for none of them lasts us long enough' (xx, 195).[43] His *Moses* was a 'historical novel' (J, iii, 206); his theory of instincts, and perhaps even his theories at large, a 'mythology' (xxii, 95 and 211); the psychoanalyst's 'constructions' were similar in function to the delusions of his patients (xxiii, 268). The desire-laden phantasies that I have been discussing are the fertile psychical soil from which Freud's working fictions and conceptual models sprang. What sort of inferential procedure brings them forth, however? We might imagine an orderly process, occurring in the mind of a representative scientist, in the course of which, by successive acts of filtration and refinement, phantasies yielded models, models theories and theories, if suitably tested, Truth; by patient coaxing Dionysus would become Apollo. But Freud does not observe any such sequence. His epistemological phantasies are insistent and reiterative. They interrupt and deflect the construction of theories. They compromise the 'scientific outlook' and offer divergent paths for the pursuit of truth. The extraordinary intellectual authority that Freud's work still possesses comes in part, of course, from his willingness to divulge and discuss the unruly dreams of knowledge among which his formal contributions to knowledge were born. But that authority comes too from his inadvertences, from the multifarious secret life that science leads within his texts.

As a theorist Freud was, in his own terms, both an adhesive and a mobile libidinal type. The conflict between these tendencies, first intimately acted out within his scientific works, is now played – sometimes as tragedy, sometimes as *grand guignol* – on the public stage of the psychoanalytic profession. In Freud's writing a legitimate despair makes itself felt: what if theories of mind were indefinitely mutable, and what if such credibility as any one of them might command were based upon the simple reiteration of the theorist's verbal formulae? What sort of claim to be science could theories make if they were creatures merely of a self-corroborating text? And the palliative to this despair – the exit from 'theory' and 'text' alike – was forcibly imagined by Freud as antiquity, bedrock, the first cause. But professions handle such matters less delicately. When psychoanalysis declares itself bedrock, and in the process loses the dialectical edge and the internal contention that characterised its founder's finest work, it faces a severe intellectual danger – and one to which religion had already, in Freud's view, notably succumbed. Freud's most vigorous objection to religion was not that it provided an adult-seeming sanctuary for infantile modes of thought, but that it positively damaged and debilitated the mind (XI, 79 and XXI, 47). It did this by its superstitious adherence to antiquity and to the first cause that it located there. Such adherence – such adhesion – limited the range of permissible questions about nature and placed narrow constraints upon speculative mental activity. Freud's critique of religion was based upon inside knowledge of the satisfactions that religion could afford. He had craved them for himself, and in the name of science. But refusing those satisfactions, refusing bedrock, was a continuing responsibility for the discipline Freud created. As he wrote to Marie Bonaparte, with a characteristic blend of humility and self-heroising: 'Mediocre spirits demand of science a kind of certainty which it cannot give, a sort of religious satisfaction. Only the real, rare, true scientific minds can endure doubt, which is attached to all our knowledge. I always envy the physicists and mathematicians who can stand on firm ground. I hover, so to speak, in the air' (J, II, 466).

2

Proust, jealousy, knowledge

Das Wissen ist ein Verhalten, eine Leidenschaft. Im Grunde ein unerlaubtes Verhalten; denn wie die Trunksucht, die Geschlechtssucht und die Gewaltsucht, so bildet auch der Zwang, wissen zu müssen, einen Charakter aus, der nicht im Gleichgewicht ist. Es ist gar nicht richtig, daß der Forscher der Wahrheit nachstellt, sie stellt ihm nach. Er erleidet sie.

Musil: *Der Mann ohne Eigenschaften*

Knowledge is an attitude, a passion. Actually an illicit attitude. For the compulsion to *know* is just like dipsomania, erotomania, and power mania, in producing a character that is out of balance. It is not at all true that the scientist goes out after truth. It is out after him. It is something he suffers from.

The Man without Qualities

'PROUST has listed a great many reasons why it is impossible to be happy, but, in the course of being happy, one finds it difficult to remember them.'[1] Few readers of *A la recherche du temps perdu* will disagree with this remark of William Empson's and few, I imagine, would wish to remember the book more faithfully if a lessening of their happiness were the price. Happy or not, we forget whole stretches of Proust's long and intricately argued text. Of course we do. How else, without a willingness and a capacity to forget, could we read it at all? How else, once we have penetrated some distance into the book, could we prevent the accumulated mass of Proust's analysis from overwhelming each new sentence with echoes and associations? But, beyond the ordinary forgetfulness to which the practical-minded and pleasure-seeking reader of Proust is subject, there exists another, thoroughly disturbing, amnesic tendency.

This is the tendency to repress from one's consciousness as reader or critic the knowledge that certain sections of Proust's book exist at all, or, their existence granted, that those sections have their own characteristic complexity. I am thinking principally of *Sodome et Gomorrhe*, *La Prisonnière* and *La Fugitive* – those sections in which the narrator discusses at length such 'negative' emotional states as jealousy, distrust or envy and such 'negative' activities of the human intelligence as lying, dissimulation or self-deception. These inner volumes are so little discussed – while the volumes that flank them are analysed and extolled by generation upon generation of commentators – not because they are thought to have no place in Proust's overall scheme but because their place in that scheme is held to be obvious and uncontentious. (This 'obvious' place has the advantage of allowing the profoundly unsettling view of human sexuality enshrined in these volumes to be held at a tranquillising distance.) What Proust discovers and urges upon us in *Le Temps retrouvé* – so the argument familiarly runs – is that certain activities of mind are better than others: remembering involuntarily is better than remembering deliberately, intuition better than rational argument, synthesis better than analysis. Other supposed Proustian preferences are available as supporting evidence: metaphors are superior to abstractions, art to science, being outside time to being inside it. A novel that, in its ending, converges weightily upon these values and virtues, and in so doing solves all its problems and consolidates its structure, may also of course have space generously allotted within it to those disreputable negative states and activities of mind. Indeed the negative cannot properly be discredited without being imaginatively enacted in the text. What Proust is doing in *La Prisonnière* – so the argument continues – is showing us just how bad the bad things are: take *La Prisonnière* and its neighbouring volumes away and the opulently affirmative ending of the book will have no dialectical counterweight; its recommended virtues will not have been tested; it will risk seeming shallow. Besides, the whole book is the story of a successful spiritual quest: the narrator's passage through the fallen world of lying, cheating, social pretence and anxious physical desire is one of those ordeals of spirit to which aspirants after wisdom and virtue are traditionally expected to submit themselves.

This view of the structure of Proust's novel seems to me at best misleading and, in its crudest versions, absurd. It is, of course, understandable that readers who are disturbed by the complexity of the novel should wish to persuade themselves that it is 'really' quite simple and ordinary. But if the simplicity one elicits can be preserved only by ascribing a single, dull-witted purpose to a thousand complex pages of text it is surely time to begin looking at the evidence again. The view I have outlined is one that, while receiving little support from the finest critics of Proust, remains popular and is still promoted as 'official' by numerous manuals and introductory guides. This view may contain, or be accompanied by, many confusions, and I shall mention briefly the most notable of these. It may assume that a novel accommodating elaborately articulated ethical and aesthetic values should itself be judged in accordance with those values; that *Le Temps retrouvé* is mysteriously truer than the rest of the book; that Proust and his narrator, having been distinct throughout the major part of the novel, become the same person by the end. It knows little of the ways in which the parts of a narrative discourse relativise and ironically displace one another. In short, *A la recherche du temps perdu* is less an exhaustive work of fiction in this view than a fictional kernel surrounded by a commentary; this commentary requires of us the same sort of credence as a work of aesthetics or moral philosophy. What is often overlooked is that all the narrator's theoretical pronouncements – including the celebrated 'Une œuvre où il y a des théories est comme un objet sur lequel on laisse la marque du prix' (882)[2] – are caught up in the fictional texture, infused with desire and intention, and subject to the same ironic action-at-a-distance from the remainder of the book as any other of its parts. The question 'what do the narrator's theories in *Le Temps retrouvé* tell us about the structure of Proust's book?' is not, in any case, a particularly illuminating one. We are more likely to be helped towards an exact appraisal of that structure by some such cautious series of questions as 'what main artistic and moral judgements does the narrator make in the course of the novel?', 'by what routes does he reach them?', 'what relationships of affinity or contrast are to be observed between those judgments and between those routes?' Answering these questions warily may prevent us from thrusting a false simplicity upon the book and remind us that Proust brought to the making of his fictions a superbly versatile intelligence.

My discussion of the eclipsed volumes will centre upon *La Prisonnière*. And I shall begin by quoting from the middle of it a sentence that will give the general critical problem that I have sketched an immediate practical form:

> Le mensonge, le mensonge parfait, sur les gens que nous connaissons, les relations que nous avons eues avec eux, notre mobile dans telle action formulé par nous d'une façon toute différente, le mensonge sur ce que nous sommes, sur ce que nous aimons, sur ce que nous éprouvons à l'égard de l'être qui nous aime et qui croit nous avoir façonnés semblables à lui parce qu'il nous embrasse toute la journée, ce mensonge-là est une des seules choses au monde qui puisse nous ouvrir des perspectives sur du nouveau, sur de l'inconnu, puisse ouvrir en nous des sens endormis pour la contemplation d'univers que nous n'aurions jamais connus.[3]
> (216)

What an outrageous discrepancy there is between this encomium to the practice of lying and the values for which Proust's book is best remembered. Lying considered as one of the fine arts and as a source of exquisite sensation; the cool liar as a privileged person; the world made large and various again by the human power of deceit . . . These notions are handsomely confuted elsewhere in the book. But here, for the moment, as we read, we are being invited to embark upon a singular adventure of the moral imagination. We may shrink from it, or parenthesise it, or write it off as a passing indiscretion. But nothing in Proust's book invites us to respond in this way. We need a view of the book and its narrator that can encompass his many statements of this sort not by tidying them away into a special sub-category – that of the casual Proustian jest – but by allowing them to be scandalous, calculatedly inconsistent with things the narrator says elsewhere and full contributors to the argumentative texture of the whole.

Proust has marshalled a brilliant parade of liars.[4] But early on it becomes clear that one motive for lying and being attentive to lies – sexual jealousy – exerts a special fascination upon him. Those characters who suffer from such jealousy are presented as having, in addition to their woe, a special privilege. Their woe is vast and well known. The jealous lover is lied to, and tells lies in his turn; he may spend hours and days on worthless ruses and futile feats of espionage. At one phase, while everything else about his relationship becomes an object of doubt, his desire dumbly and immovably persists; at another phase, desire is lost to boredom and worry. His jealousy may be complicated by envy: he may envy the sexual satisfactions that he imagines his partner to be enjoying in the company of others; he may envy, as he machinates, the superior machinating power that is mobilised against him. But over and against these emotional and moral penalties the jealous lover hears, and heeds, an imperious call to *know*. His privilege is to be summoned to the limits of what is thinkable, and to risk everything for a glimpse of what lies beyond. Overshadowing the promise of sexual satisfaction another, improbable, order of pleasure is seen: that of a mind suddenly confronted by, and able to grasp, 'une étroite section lumineuse pratiquée à même l'inconnu' (I, 283).[5]

Here, from *Du côté de chez Swann*, is the passage in which this long-distance migrant among themes makes its first full appearance. It occurs during the episode where Swann, waiting outside an apartment that he takes to be Odette's, makes up his mind to knock on the illuminated shutters:

Et peut-être, ce qu'il ressentait en ce moment de presque agréable, c'était autre chose aussi que l'apaisement d'un doute et d'une douleur: un plaisir de l'intelligence. Si, depuis qu'il était amoureux, les choses avaient repris pour lui un peu de l'intérêt délicieux qu'il leur trouvait autrefois, mais seulement là où elles étaient éclairées par le souvenir d'Odette, maintenant, c'était une autre faculté de sa studieuse jeunesse que sa jalousie ranimait, la passion de la vérité, mais d'une vérité, elle aussi, interposée entre lui et sa maîtresse, ne recevant sa lumière que d'elle, vérité tout individuelle qui avait pour objet unique, d'un prix infini et presque d'une beauté désintéressée, les actions d'Odette, ses relations, ses projets, son passé . . . cette curiosité qu'il sentait s'éveiller en lui à l'égard des moindres occupations d'une femme, c'était celle qu'il avait eue autrefois pour l'Histoire. Et tout ce dont il aurait eu honte jusqu'ici, espionner devant une fenêtre, qui sait? demain peut-être, faire parler habilement les indifférents, soudoyer les domestiques, écouter aux portes, ne lui semblait plus, aussi bien que le déchiffrement des textes, la comparaison des témoignages et l'interprétation des monuments, que des méthodes d'investigation scientifique d'une véritable valeur intellectuelle et appropriées à la recherche de la vérité.[6] (I, 273–4)

At last Swann has discovered a coherent intellectual purpose, and a problem worthy of his energy and ingenuity. In his own eyes he has become a historian, an archaeologist, a decipherer of texts, a scientist. All in a sudden exhilarating access of self-awareness he has been promoted, within the intellectual community, from day-labourer to polymathic hero. And all because he urgently wishes to know whether his mistress is alone and, in order to find out, has resorted to prying.

This comedy of misapplied intellect is intensified and darkened in the narrator's account of his own relationship with Albertine: in *La Prisonnière* the idea that the lover may become an honorary scientist or scholar by virtue of his jealous calculations and hypotheses is present as an insistent refrain. The asking of questions about Albertine – has she had lesbian relationships in the past? is she having, or contriving to have, such relationships now? how can truth be distinguished from falsehood in Albertine's reports on her actions and feelings?[7] – is presented as one of the narrator's inescapable emotional needs. His mind comes to specialise ever more devotedly in the production and transformation of anxiety, and in the telling of tactical lies designed to surprise Albertine into self-disclosure.

By holding Albertine captive and scrutinising her every word and movement he confines himself to an unpromisingly narrow and understocked observational world. But within that world he observes and speculates expertly, and relives in the solitude of his own body the general human quest for knowledge.[8] He refers, sometimes briefly and sometimes at length, to the technical languages and characteristic intellectual operations of workers within a wide range of scientific and scholarly disciplines; he envisages himself in turn as chemist, philologist, pathologist, cryptanalyst, logician, biologist, physiologist, ornithologist, ichthyologist, astronomer, grammarian, philosophical analyst both deductive and inductive, historian, psychologist of perception, physicist, botanist, mathematician and meteorologist. He discusses certain of Albertine's pronouncements with the seriousness and the hope of a biblical exegete, or with the psychoanalyst's cunning ear for lapses and omissions.

There is nothing casually suggestive about this array of comparisons. Many of the narrator's ambitions, in this section of the work, are strictly scientific ones: he wants to get behind appearances to the real structure of things; he wants to organise his data in such a way that everything observed is explained, and that nothing extraneous and unobserved, no 'occult qualities', are required in order to make his explanations complete; he judges theories by their power of prediction; he sees theory and observation as interdependent; in the construction of general law he admires simplicity and elegance, while readily discarding laws that subsequent experience shows to be false. Moreover he adheres, in true Newtonian fashion, to a principle of parsimony in his search for the causes of human behaviour; nature for Proust's narrator, as for Newton, 'affects not the pomp of superfluous causes': causes are required in sufficient number to explain the appearances – and no more.[9] He knows too how difficult these ambitions are to sustain, and what powerful mechanisms of tendentious perception are at work in human minds to compromise the integrity of experimental results: 'Le témoignage des sens est lui aussi une opération de l'esprit où la conviction crée l'évidence' (190).[10] His despair at the seeming futility of his task is the scientist's despair *par excellence*: 'L'inconnu de la vie des êtres est comme celui de la nature, que chaque découverte scientifique ne fait que reculer mais n'annule pas' (391).[11]

Proust's understanding of the goals of scientific enquiry, and his references to the individual languages and nomenclatures of science, sometimes produce writing of astonishing metaphorical density. Consider, for example, the following passage in which the narrator describes how he came to realise that Albertine's repeated expressions of uninterest in a proposed visit to Mme Verdurin's were dissimulations of an intense desire to go:

> J'avais suivi dans mon existence une marche inverse de celle des peuples qui ne se servent de l'écriture phonétique qu'après n'avoir considéré les caractères que comme une suite de symboles; moi qui, pendant tant d'années, n'avais cherché la vie et la pensée réelles des gens que dans l'énoncé direct qu'ils m'en fournissaient volontairement, par leur faute j'en étais arrivé à ne plus attacher, au contraire, d'importance qu'aux témoignages qui ne sont pas une expression rationnelle et analytique de la vérité; les paroles elles-mêmes ne me renseignaient qu'à la condition d'être interprétées à la façon d'un afflux de sang à la figure d'une personne qui se trouble, à la façon encore d'un silence subit. Tel adverbe . . . jailli dans une conflagration par le rapprochement involontaire, parfois périlleux, de deux idées que l'interlocuteur n'exprimait pas et duquel, par telles méthodes d'analyse ou d'électrolyse appropriées, je pouvais les extraire, m'en disait plus qu'un discours. Albertine laissait parfois traîner dans ses propos tel ou tel de ces précieux amalgames que je me hâtais de 'traiter', pour les transformer en idées claires.[12] (88 9)

Here we have a rapid procession of scholars, invited to contribute in a variety of ways to the discussion: the historian of languages, tracing the development from hieroglyphic to alphabetic script; the philosopher, seeking after rational coherence in his analysis; the animal ethologist, making connections between environmental stimulus and physiological response; the psychoanalyst, interpreting certain accidental features of speech as indicators of repressed wishes;[13] the stylistician, recording those inflections of normal usage that constitute the individuality of a given discourse;[14] the chemist, seeking to break down an amalgam into its component substances. In all these cases, except that of the philosophical analyst, the same sort of contrast is being enacted: a contrast between apparent and real, manifest and latent, sense and seeming nonsense. A complicated network of analogies is thus established between the successive phases of the text. And, although the passage contains no general statement about the pursuit of knowledge, a powerful general point emerges from this play of heterogeneous languages and investigative methods. The path towards meaning, or insight, or system is a circuitous one: it is only by paying attention to such low and unworthy things as blushes, silences, involuntary acts and semantic vacancies or redundancies that truth may be approached, just as it is only by applying an electrical current or a chemical agent, the properties of which are not in themselves of interest, that an amalgam may be analysed.

In this way the entire discussion takes on an epistemological resonance quite different from anything that we could expect from a plain psychological account of jealousy and lying. There is an element of burlesque in such writing: how characteristic of the fretful and egotistically complaining lover that he should wish to rewrite his private uncertainties as the drama of Mind at work upon the secrets of Nature; how ridiculous a subtle intelligence can become when it dedicates itself to trifling goals. But for Proust the presence of burlesque and ironic reservation in no way excludes seriousness: his animated portrait of a single intensely perceptive and reflective mind requires its farcical upheavals and its absurdities quite as much as its moments of heroism or of tragic grandeur.

The narrator's predicament gains its epistemological dimension not simply from these local invasions of the text by scientific or scholarly language, but from numerous sustained descriptions of the speculative mind at work. I shall mention two particularly striking ways in which general questions of intellectual method assume a larger organising role in *La Prisonnière*. The first concerns the production and testing of hypotheses. In the narrator's eyes Albertine's behaviour is never self-explanatory: her motives, desires and intentions have to be construed on the basis of the meagre evidence which that behaviour, and her unreliable words, provide. But his recurrent problem is not that such explanatory constructions are difficult to produce, but that two mutually exclusive constructions, each of them well supported by observation, may be produced by the mind at once or in quick succession. The narrator, seeking to work out whether Albertine has had a sexual relationship with Andrée, manages to interpret one of her sudden changes of plan as resulting either from urgent desire for Andrée or from feelings of friendship towards Andrée and himself (388–93). Or again, he cannot work out whether Albertine is planning to leave him: according to one hypothesis, which is borne out by certain of her glances, or fits of impatience, or eccentric sentences, she indeed intends to bring the relationship to an end; according to the other hypothesis Albertine, who says that she intends to stay, has developed an improbable, eleventh-hour capacity to tell the truth and intends to stay (334–9). Both explanations find support in her actions and in his general understanding of her character. Both cannot be right. 'Laquelle des deux hypothèses était la vraie?' (360).[15]

In these and many similar instances of this 'two-hypothesis' problem each explanation is worked through to its point of maximum coherence and the two are then evaluated comparatively. But long before the comparison is begun Proust isolates and dramatises the moment of transition between the two hypotheses: the narrator pushes his fine first edifice to one side, saying 'that was one way of solving it all; now let's solve it again'. This is the moment at which the speculative intelligence breaks out, moves on, takes risks. With proud ingenuity he builds an alternative model of reality and in so doing persuades himself briefly that his power of speculation is indefinitely self-replenishing. But the new model enters into competition with the old. The two hypotheses, each of them complete but the pair of them incompatible, lock together to produce a new form of mental captivity: 'Il y a ainsi certains états moraux, et notamment l'inquiétude, qui, ne nous présentant que deux alternatives, ont quelque chose d'aussi atrocement limité qu'une simple souffrance physique' (401).[16] His ingenuity now has the enforced task not of constructing something new but of reformulating and re-scrutinising a closed pattern of ideas.

The narrator falls victim to his own parsimony in the tracking down of causes. Whenever Albertine speaks she is either lying or telling the truth. But he provides this unexceptionable main theorem with a set of imperfect corollaries: she desires another person either all-consumingly or not at all; she has formed a project and will pursue it relentlessly or not at all; she cherishes their life together unfailingly or not at all. He is now intellectually incapable of granting in Albertine's case what he so readily grants in his own (and in hers on other occasions):[17] that feelings may be muddled, that intentions may be precarious or half-formed or contradictory and that an action may be prompted by several motives at once. The competition between each pair of hypotheses cannot be resolved until more causes are found, or until the existing causes are allowed to become less precise, less regular and less uniform. Against the need for simple and elegant solutions in the analysis of human conduct, the multidimensional complexity of the individual person has to be restored.

I mentioned two general questions of intellectual method a moment ago. The second of them has to do with finding less painful occupations for the jealous mind and straighter paths towards knowledge. On several occasions the narrator reminds himself that the only certain way of leaping clear of the circularities and double-binds into which his brilliance as a hypothesis-maker leads him would be to make no hypotheses at all. And at these points he invents for himself a complete phantasy world of experimental observation. The trouble is always that the beloved has mental processes of her own; to make matters worse she has a past and, still worse, she thinks, desires and performs actions when she is not in his company:

> Que de gens, que de lieux (même qui ne la concernaient pas directement, de vagues lieux de plaisir où elle avait pu en goûter, les lieux où il y a beaucoup de monde, où l'on est frôlé) Albertine – comme une personne qui, faisant passer sa suite, toute une société, au contrôle devant elle, la fait entrer au théâtre – du seuil de mon imagination ou de mon souvenir, où je ne me souciais pas d'eux, avait introduits dans mon cœur! Maintenant, la connaissance que j'avais d'eux était interne, immédiate, spasmodique, douloureuse. L'amour, c'est l'espace et le temps rendus sensibles au cœur.[18] (385)

If only he could travel freely in the time and space of her hidden deeds. In this recurrent phantasy[19] he would be omnipresent in

Albertine's life; he would possess completely reliable senses and a completely efficient system for the storage and retrieval of information about her; he would watch her every action as it happened, and understand her every motive there and then. Surveillance of this kind would produce the state of 'total intelligence' that undercover agents no doubt dream about in their moments of rest and recuperation. Spasmodic knowledge would be replaced by continuous knowledge. The narrator's impeccable observational results would require of him no more than a small final inductive jump for the abiding truths of Albertine's character to emerge. Those results would relieve him of the anxious need to speculate and construe, and would entitle him to repeat in his turn Newton's celebrated boast *hypotheses non fingo* ('I invent no hypotheses').

What we have, then, in this competition between two modes of jealous enquiry is the rough sketch of a debate between the inductive and hypothetico-deductive methods. Methods that philosophers of science have striven to formulate clearly, and that have been defended in their arguments with formidable mathematical and logical weapons, are rediscovered by Proust's narrator as the spontaneous impulses of a mind under conditions of torment. And this gives the book an additional interrogative dimension. If Proust had done no more than allude to scientists and scholars, or plunder their vocabularies, *La Prisonnière* would have been far less provocative than it is. The emotional condition of the jealous lover would have been seen as an unfortunate threat to the smooth functioning of his cognitive faculties; and in his attempts to counter that threat he would have emerged as a rather paltry and caricatural kind of scientist. The scientist himself, and the integrity of his enterprise, would not have been brought under scrutiny. But as things are in Proust's book – with questions of intellectual method organising long stretches of the narrator's introspection and the cognitive faculties themselves becoming primary material for analysis – the dialogue that goes on between scientist and tormented lover fully engages both parties. Proust compels us to all manner of disconcerting speculations about the emotional substrata that the scientific enquirer and the jealous enquirer might share. This speculation may easily bring us round to the question 'in what kinds of emotional calamity does scientific enquiry begin?' or simply – 'what kind of jealousy is science?'

Until now the hidden factor in my discussion – hidden except for a few comments on lexical matters – has been the texture of Proust's writing in *La Prisonnière*. But this texture is itself caught up in the epistemological drama and serves in countless ways to localise and energise the abstract issues that I have been outlining. The following passage is characteristic of one register; I shall comment on it in some detail:

Comment n'avais-je pas depuis longtemps remarqué que les yeux d'Albertine appartenaient à la famille de ceux qui (même chez un être médiocre) semblent faits de plusieurs morceaux à cause de tous les lieux où l'être veut se trouver – et cacher qu'il veut se trouver – ce jour-là? Des yeux, par mensonge toujours immobiles et passifs, mais dynamiques, mesurables par les mètres ou kilomètres à franchir pour se trouver au rendez-vous voulu, implacablement voulu, des yeux qui sourient moins encore au plaisir qui les tente qu'ils ne s'auréolent de la tristesse et du découragement qu'il y aura peut-être une difficulté pour aller au rendez-vous. Entre vos mains mêmes, ces êtres-là sont des êtres de fuite. Pour comprendre les émotions qu'ils donnent et que d'autres êtres même plus beaux, ne donnent pas, il faut calculer qu'ils sont non pas immobiles, mais en mouvement, et ajouter à leur personne un signe corrrespondant à ce qu'en physique est le signe qui signifie vitesse.

Si vous dérangez leur journée, ils vous avouent le plaisir qu'ils vous avaient caché: 'Je voulais tant aller goûter à cinq heures avec telle personne que j'aime!' Hé bien, si, six mois après, vous arrivez à connaître la personne en question, vous apprendrez que jamais la jeune fille dont vous aviez dérangé les projets, qui, prise au piège, pour que vous la laissiez libre vous avait avoué le goûter qu'elle faisait ainsi avec une personne aimée tous les jours à l'heure où vous ne la voyiez pas, vous apprendrez que cette personne ne l'a jamais reçue, qu'elles n'ont jamais goûté ensemble, la jeune fille disant être très prise, par vous précisément. Ainsi la personne avec qui elle avait confessé qu'elle allait goûter, avec qui elle vous avait supplié de la laisser aller goûter, cette personne, raison avouée par nécessité, ce n'était pas elle, c'était une autre, c'était encore autre chose! Autre chose, quoi? Une autre, qui?

Hélas, les yeux fragmentés, portant au loin et tristes, permettraient peut-être de mesurer les distances, mais n'indiquent pas les directions. Le champ infini des possibles s'étend, et si, par hasard, le réel se présentait devant nous, il serait tellement en dehors des possibles que, dans un brusque étourdissement, allant taper contre ce mur surgi, nous tomberions à la renverse. Le mouvement et la fuite constatés ne sont même pas indispensables, il suffit que nous les induisions.[20]

(91–2)

The passages that I quoted earlier will have made certain features of this one seem familiar. The language of cognition, for example, is often drawn upon: *comprendre*, *calculer*, *mesurer*, *constater*, *induire*. The passage contains in addition several references to physics, including a particularly striking one at the end of the first paragraph: the symbol for velocity may be added to the person of these 'êtres de fuite' because their person is already conceived of not as an irreducible psycho-physical entity but as a complex symbolic system. Understanding such a person is a matter neither of intuiting their inner states nor of empathising with them: it is a matter of deciphering their codes. But what I shall be suggesting in the next few paragraphs is that the passage would remain vigorously alive to problems of knowledge even if these references were missing, and that the writing itself has become a main way of keeping those problems new.

Writing like this may be disappointing to those who think of the elaborately metaphorical 'grand manner' of the earlier volumes as Proust's finest and most important stylistic achievement. And indeed Proust does do a number of ostentatious things here that any self-respecting 'fine' writer would usually be expected to avoid. The movement of his prose is poorly controlled by argument or sustained metaphor. The passage reads as a string of discrete pronouncements; a few perfunctory efforts to establish causal connections have been made, but the prose still jerks its way along; ideas are not developed but reiterated in a slightly modified form. And, perhaps worst of all, certain single words or the members of certain groups of cognates are insolently and coarsely repeated: *personne* appears seven times, *être(s)* (the noun) five times, *goûter* (noun and verb) five times, *avouer* or its near-synonym *confesser* four times – and so forth. To take afternoon tea may well be a sign of good breeding, but to mention the fact five times in a short paragraph is surely not.

But do these jolts and repetitions really represent a lessening of Proust's artistry? We might be alerted to the possibility that something willed and coherent is going on by the fact that the 'faults' that I have listed are all of the same order: they all involve either a dearth or an excess of connectedness between the successive phases of the text. While the connections between one syntactic unit and the next are reduced, those between certain main lexical items are greatly strengthened. This means that within the sequence of propositions, which forms a pattern of its own, other patterns, insistent but unsynchronised, are to be heard. Let us consider the case of the five occurrences of *être(s)* in the first paragraph and the six occurrences of *personne* in the second. The two words refer to distinct classes of people: the first to the beloved herself, whose eyes become mobile in response to the promptings of erotic adventure; the second to the friends named in the many alibis that such adventure necessitates. But the two words also have a common function: they both represent the shifting and ungraspable goal of a mind seeking to know. Albertine, like those who populate her self-protective fictions, is fugitive and multiform. What is being repeated throughout the *être* refrain, and the *personne* refrain that continues and re-genders it, is the fact that this persistent obstacle to knowledge exists. If 'reality' were suddenly to be revealed, the narrator tells us, this process would have a stop. But his mind is now caught within a welter of mere possibilities, within a world irremediably other: 'c'était une autre, c'était encore autre chose! Autre chose, quoi? Une autre, qui?' As the plain fact of otherness is itself grasped, this fourfold repetition of *autre* continues the refrain. Otherness in the narrator's experience finds its way as a desperate sameness into his words.

Thus several rhythms are running at once in this writing. The prose both proceeds and repeats; it both suggests and insists. By means like those that I have described, Proust has created in *La Prisonnière* a dynamics of knowing, a portrait of the mind in process. Not only have the mind's indeterminacies and indecisions been given a palpable form, but its risks feel like risks: its ideas now sing, now stammer. Prose of this kind – precisely because it takes chances – can of course sometimes seem extravagant and confused, but it is an achievement of style comparable in originality to the 'grand manner' I mentioned a moment ago. And it is writing like this which, as we read, returns epistemological enquiry to our nerves and pulses.[21]

What I've been trying to do so far is suggest how complex Proust's handling of jealousy is in *A la recherche du temps perdu* and analyse some of the recurrent intellectual mechanisms that he describes and reconstructs. Jealousy in this view is the quest for knowledge in a terrifying pure form: a quest for knowledge untrammelled and unsupported by things actually known. It is a continuous journey towards a receding goal, an itinerary with no stopping-places and no landmarks; it is an appetite for knowledge, but knows nothing: 'La jalousie, qui a un bandeau sur les yeux, n'est pas seulement impuissante à rien découvrir dans les ténèbres qui l'enveloppent, elle est encore un de ces supplices où la tâche est à recommencer sans cesse, comme celle des Danaïdes, comme celle d'Ixion' (151).[22] The narrator keeps his word, and bears out his theory of jealousy in the detail of what he says: by the end of *La Prisonnière* the crucial questions about Albertine – has she had lesbian relationships in the past? is she having, or contriving to have, such relationships now? how can truth be distinguished from falsehood in her reports on her actions and feelings? – are still unanswered. Whereas 'the truth' about Odette is eventually revealed to Swann and confirmed by fresh evidence from all directions, Albertine's sexuality remains an enigma. Even after four hundred pages of energetic and fastidious truth-seeking, the narrator can still write: 'ma raison, d'ailleurs, ne demandait qu'à me prouver que je m'étais trompé sur les mauvais projets d'Albertine, comme je m'étais peut-être trompé sur ses instincts vicieux' (367).[23] He speaks of his delight in his capacities as a 'modeller of nebulae', as one whose self-appointed task it is to elicit intelligible structure from the diffuse and inconstant raw materials provided by experience (372). Albertine is one such nebula; each of his models accommodates some only of her features; features excluded from one model prompt the building of the next. But the process is unstoppable. Albertine cannot be known, unless this interminable passage from structure to structure is itself knowledge and our other notions of what it is to know are the products of a lingering infantile wish for comfort or mastery.

I began this discussion of 'negative' states and activities of mind in Proust by quoting an extended passage in praise of lying and by suggesting that statements of that sort had to be taken seriously. I hope that it has by now become clear how serious and how guileful these statements are and how multifarious their contributions to the book. Lying itself, to take just one example of those negative activities, has been seen to be important in two main ways: as a stimulating obstacle in the search for truth, and as the presence within the everyday world of the glorious human impulse to make fictions. But it would be ridiculous for me to over-promote the role of the jealous intellect in the book, especially as I have already expressed my impatience with an equal and opposite over-promotion – that of the intuitive faculty and its satellites – and my regret that Proust's conceptual range has so often been diminished in the process. I am seeking to ensure simply that certain neglected voices should be heard as clearly as possible within the contrapuntal texture of Proustian argument. The time has come for us to remind ourselves of what that argument is like and of the ways in which the discussion of jealousy is itself framed, complicated and contested by other elements of the book. I shall look first at *La Prisonnière* as a whole, and then at the place of jealousy within the complete novel.

The narrator's relationship with Albertine occupies, of course, the major part of *La Prisonnière*; his main detailed account of this relationship is given in a series of large, spaced blocks, and Albertine is present at least as a mental reference-point in all the intervening sections. The other scenes and subjects upon which the narrative dwells include: the death of Bergotte; the death of Swann, which had been mentioned without comment in *Sodome et Gomorrhe* (II, 870); the relationship between Charlus and Morel; the first performance of Vinteuil's unpublished septet; the Verdurins' conspiracy against Charlus and their successful attempt to deprive him of Morel. These sections are arranged in such a way that they form a pattern of sharp contrasts – silent introspection against noisy public talk, the sequestered world of passion against the world of social ostentation, the politics of the salon against the politics of sexual intimacy – and, at the same time, echo and reflect one another in countless details. Charlus, to take a familiar example, appears as an inventive player within the social comedy and as an epitome of self-opinionated verbosity; his performances take place far beyond the narrator's introspective orbit. But Charlus afflicted by jealousy, arrested by one sinister phrase in a letter, is cast into a state of disarray that closely resembles the narrator's own: '[le baron] se sentait torturé par une inquiétude de l'intelligence autant que du cœur, devant ce double mystère, où il y avait à la fois de l'agrandissement de sa jalousie et de l'insuffisance soudaine d'une définition' (215).[24] As so often happens in this book, two distinct temperaments and two distinct predicaments have suddenly revealed an improbable kinship.

Just as jealousy is observed by the narrator elsewhere than in himself, so the scientific language which pervades his analysis of jealousy is available for many other uses. On the way to the Verdurins', for example, the narrator meets Brichot and is struck by his new spectacles:

> Elles étaient en merveilleux état. Mais derrière elles j'aperçus, minuscule, pâle, convulsif, expirant, un regard lointain placé sous ce puissant appareil, comme, dans les laboratoires trop richement subventionnés pour les besognes qu'on y fait, on place une insignifiante bestiole agonisante sous les appareils les plus perfectionnés.[25] (198)

What complex malice is here. Proust's attack on the excesses of the scientific establishment – the excess of apparatus over experimental imagination and of financial outlay over intellectual yield – is of a trenchancy to make even the staunchest defenders of 'big science' feel uncomfortable. But this same attack gives telling concrete shape to one of the narrator's own errors of proportion: he too brings powerful instruments to bear upon trivial subjects. He stands accused by his image not simply because the fault in question is, in a general way, one of his own, but because he is committing exactly this error of proportion now. Brichot's failing sight and thick spectacles have called forth a display of metaphorical apparatus (in the previous sentence the spectacles were 'puissantes et compliquées comme des instruments astronomiques')[26] cruelly at odds with its human occasion. The image broadly implies and pointedly implicates; and its several mobile, intersecting planes cannot be arrested upon a single main sense. The narrator's sympathy for Brichot surges, shrinks and is drawn elsewhere all within a single sentence; his delicate moral attention moves alertly on and his moment of irreversible moral decision is yet again deferred. In the next sentence he offers Brichot a supporting arm. His cruelty just before and his kindness now each attract something of the other's colouring.

This ability to manipulate images, to segment them and, by devices of syntax, to keep their many components in play simultaneously is of course one of Proust's essential literary gifts. And, although the gift is used sparingly in *La Prisonnière*, certain of his images work hard within the text and together confront the narrator's analysis with a strong alternative order of meaning. The dying Bergotte has withdrawn from society: 'Il allait ainsi se refroidissant progressivement, petite planète qui offrait une image anticipée de la grande quand, peu à peu, la chaleur se retirera de la terre, puis la vie' (184).[27] Bergotte has died: 'On l'enterra, mais toute la nuit funèbre, aux vitrines éclairées, ses livres, disposés trois par trois, veillaient comme des anges aux ailes éployées et semblaient, pour celui qui n'était plus, le symbole de sa résurrection' (188).[28] Whereas each of these tender and expansive images is a complete event and has a sentence to itself, other images do their reconciling work from within the texture of the long analytic sentence and release us momentarily from its asperities:

> Dissipe-t-elle, au contraire, d'un mot adroit, de tendres caresses, les soupçons qui le torturaient bien qu'il s'y prétendît indifférent, sans doute l'amant n'éprouve pas cet accroissement désespéré de l'amour où le hausse la jalousie, mais cessant brusquement de souffrir, heureux, attendri, détendu comme on l'est après un orage quand la pluie est tombée et qu'à peine sent-on encore sous les grands marronniers s'égoutter à longs intervalles les gouttes suspendues que déjà le soleil reparu colore, il ne sait comment exprimer sa reconnaissance à celle qui l'a guéri.[29] (192)

Feeling of this kind is both respite from pain and a new discovery of love – a particularising love that allows us to see not just the rain droplets on the chestnut trees but the play of light within each droplet. And it is also an achievement of intelligence in its own right: a searching, punctilious intelligence has discovered, late but unmistakably, when to let go.

These few moments of tenderness or reciprocity or joy give another mode of feeling, strongly present elsewhere in the book, its precarious foothold amid the analyses of *La Prisonnière*. And in one extended episode – the first performance of Vinteuil's septet (248–65) – that other mode of feeling is explored at length. At length but not in isolation. For this is the episode in which the entire project of the book is encapsulated; the septet, unlike the earlier violin sonata with which it is compared, has harshly dissonant passages within it. It speaks of joy, but a joy in diversity. The narrator's keen elation is produced by a musical work in which differences of key, tempo and motif are precisely articulate to the point of stridency, and contains the promise of a literary work on the same plan. This promise is kept by the narrator in his description of the mingled artistic, social and sexual events which take place in the Verdurins' salon during the performance. He attends closely to the music, is deeply moved by it and notices within it a multitude of inventive details. But he notices too Mme Verdurin whose famed hypersensitivity to music reduces her, as usual, to simulated agony; the cellist, who plays his instrument as if he were stripping a cabbage; Morel, whose brow is suddenly adorned with a tantalising lock of hair; Mme Verdurin's dog, who is snoring; Charlus, who, between movements, seeks to confirm an assignation he has made with a footman. Albertine comes to mind: the narrator wonders about her relationship with the composer's daughter. Mlle Vinteuil's lesbian friend comes to mind and is situated at the point of convergence of two causal chains: as a member of a lesbian circle in which Albertine is thought to participate she is one cause among many of the narrator's jealous misery; as decipherer and editor of Vinteuil's manuscript, she is one cause among many of his present exhilaration in art. Whatever his projected literary work is to be like it cannot be allowed to make token accommodating gestures towards the heterogeneous materials of experience. It will be a celebration of heterogeneity, as the septet and this passage are; it will have room within it for cabbage-stripping cellists and snoring dogs as well as for triumphs of artistic invention; it will allow jealousy and joy their indissociable alliances; it will be articulate, inclusive and unsubduably diverse.

When the narrator's supreme moment of artistic and moral decision is at last reached in *Le Temps retrouvé*, many readers are perplexed to find that so much creative energy should be held to depend, for its eventual release, upon a small commonplace accident of memory. William Empson, with whose words I began, has caught this perplexity well:

> . . . you remember how Proust, at the end of that great novel, having convinced the reader with the full sophistication of his genius that he is going to produce an apocalypse, brings out with pathetic faith, as a fact of absolute value, that sometimes when you are living in one place you are reminded of living in another place, and this, since you are now apparently living in two places, means that you are outside time, in the only state of beatitude he can imagine. In any one place (atmosphere, mental climate) life is intolerable; in any two it is an ecstasy. Is it the number two, one is forced to speculate, which is of this encouraging character? Is to live in $n+1$ places necessarily more valuable than to live in n?[30]

Two things are missing from this wicked retelling of the narrator's culminating discovery: first that those famous tiny sensations – the unevenness of paving stones, the chink of a spoon against a plate, the roughness of a napkin – precipitate the narrator not simply into his past, but into a state of complete physical and intellectual well-being: 'une joie pareille à une certitude, et suffisante, sans autres preuves, à me rendre la mort indifférente' (867);[31] and secondly that this state has been prepared for within the book not simply by the periodic promises and early warnings that the narrator gives us, but by the entire intellectual grain of the narrative. For this latecoming joy, which resembles certainty and has the status of a proof, is the receding goal of the jealous quest finally brought to a stop; it is no vacant swooning of the mind, but knowledge itself. Baudelaire had spoken of 'une extase *faite de volupté et de connaissance*'.[32] Roland Barthes, reminding us that the very notion of pleasure has come to seem politically and intellectually suspect, wondered in *Le plaisir du texte*: 'et pourtant: si la connaissance elle-même était *délicieuse*?'[33] The delicious, sensuously immediate, knowledge that Proust's narrator finally discovers, and from which he draws his major creative lesson, has been prefigured in many earlier moments of delight. These moments are lengthily recapitulated and repatterned in *Le Temps retrouvé*. But the peculiarly urgent sense that these moments together make, and the symmetry that they introduce into Proust's voluminous fiction, should not cause us to overlook the many subtle ways in which the 'negative' episodes in the novel are themselves prefigurings of the final knowing-in-delight that he describes. Jealousy is an alertness of eye and ear and intellect; it is an experience of manifold potentiality; it is a stimulus to the making of fictions; it is a comprehensive way of inhabiting space and time. When these things are produced by pain and absence they may be called jealousy. But the same things, rediscovered in joy, and by joy transformed, may as fittingly be called *knowledge*.[34]

The advantage of seeing the discussion of jealousy and the discussion of involuntary memory as mutually implying, as each of them introducing heterogeneity into the other, is that superb sections of the book that might otherwise be ignored, or condescended to as the record of a spiritual pilgrim's temporary trials, are thereby allowed to remain rich and absorbing. Once Proust's fictional enactment of the problems of knowledge in these inner volumes has been fully examined and pondered, his attitudes to the scientific or analytic intelligence may perhaps finally be credited with their full discriminateness and complexity. The narrator does, of course, criticise this intelligence on numerous occasions: operating alone, it was superficial and incomplete.[35] In an early state of the novel, the character now known as Vinteuil was called Vington and he was not a musician but a naturalist. What did Proust do in eliminating his scientist? He maintained a uniformity of pattern: he made sure that all those characters who had exemplary insight and creative power, and who were to influence the narrator decisively in the working out of his own vocation, were *artists*.[36] But he was not attempting to remove science from the book. As we have seen, Proust's critique of science is an extraordinarily subtle and colluding one. His awareness of the ambitions, excitements and disappointments of the scientific vocation penetrates even into the fine texture of his writing. Vinteuil's supreme achievement was to be not a formula, or a theorem, or an equation, or a taxonomic system – but a septet. Yet Swann, listening to Vinteuil's sonata in the first volume of the novel, knows better, even in his artistic delight, than to demote the scientific imagination: 'O audace aussi géniale peut-être, se disait-il, que celle d'un Lavoisier, d'un Ampère, l'audace d'un Vinteuil expérimentant, découvrant les lois secrètes d'une force inconnue' (I, 351).[37] Time and again in *A la recherche du temps perdu*, Proust has delved down into those areas of the human mind where the scientific and the artistic imagination have their common origin. And by making the jealous lover, as he heeds his call to know, the main intermediary between the worlds of art and science, Proust has reminded us in the simplest possible way that all works of the mind – Lavoisier's as well as his own – are works of passion too.

The reminder is a simple one, but the working out of its consequences within Proust's novel is not. That novel is indeed one of the most elaborate and circumstantial portrayals of the theorising mind that European culture possesses. In it, all theories are made within the force-field of human desire and in their turn provide that desire with unsuspected opportunities and restrictions. For every new access of awareness that the impassioned theorist achieves, a new amnesia is exacted.

3
Freud and Proust

Es ist die Höflichkeit Prousts, dem Leser die Beschämung zu ersparen, sich für gescheiter zu halten als den Autor.

An der Psychoanalyse ist nichts wahr als ihre Übertreibungen.

Adorno: *Minima Moralia*

It is Proust's courtesy to spare the reader the embarrassment of believing himself cleverer than the author.

In psycho-analysis nothing is true except the exaggerations.

I

THE WRITINGS of Proust and Freud invite comparison at so many points that the avoidance of comparison by those critics who have been willing to link their names must be accounted a thing of wonder. For Proust and Freud culture informs and is informed by sexuality, and both write urgently and at length about the manifold forms of sexual desire that meet and compete in the moral, artistic and intellectual spheres. For both of them language is the hugely unstable medium in which desire is socialised and in which constant failures of that socialisation occur: language is at once a retreat from, and a surreptitious return route to, the libidinal substratum. Add to this a willingness on the part of each to disclose the desiring impulses and gambits that underlie his own productions and the two writers begin to seem irresistibly, perhaps even cloyingly, comparable.

But until now most joint discussion of Proust and Freud has been content to pursue lesser quarries. First, it has addressed the questions: how much, if anything, of Freud's work did Proust know? if he had read nothing or little, what sort of hearsay acquaintance with Freud's ideas could he be expected to have derived from his casual reading, from salon conversation, from his many medical acquaintances? Secondly, it has taken a few bare and sometimes incompletely understood concepts from primers of psychoanalysis, named or nicknamed them 'Freudian theory', and applied them to Proust's imaginary narrator in the context of his imaginary family. What both these approaches have for the most part overlooked is that Proust and Freud have many psychological, sociological and linguistic interests in common, that their works, whatever knowledge the one author may have had of the other, are reciprocally illuminating to a remarkable degree, and that the two sets of texts mesh together and interact, and at the same time contest and diffract each other, in numerous ways.[1]

In order to give some idea of the scale of the terrain to be explored I shall simply list ten sample areas of common interest (there are many others), of which I have chosen two for discussion here:

(i) infantile sexuality and the Oedipus complex
(ii) sadism, masochism and their various hybridisations

(iii) pathological jealousy
(iv) bisexuality and homosexuality
(v) dream analysis and the rules of interpretation
(vi) the theory of the unconscious
(vii) the 'accidental' emergence of the unconscious in errors, slips, symptoms, mannerisms and jokes
(viii) the theory of consciousness
(ix) the role of free association in the investigation of mental process
(x) theories of writing

A joint exploration of the two writers will of course proceed differently in different areas. In certain cases Proust's narrator's fluctuating theoretical pronouncements can be measured against one or other of Freud's theories. For example, one of the narrator's accounts of conscious thought in *La Fugitive* – 'la pensée ayant un pouvoir de renouvellement ou plutôt une impuissance de conservation' (III, 644) – is directly comparable to Freud's account of consciousness, in *Beyond the Pleasure Principle* and elsewhere, as a system through which stimuli pass without leaving any permanent trace (XVIII, 25) or as a magically self-erasing writing-pad (XIX, 227–32).[2] In certain other cases, Freud provides versatile exploratory tools for the analysis of Proust's text: Freud's discussion in *The Interpretation of Dreams* of condensation and displacement as primary modes of mental functioning (IV, 279–309), for example, illuminates Proust's convoluted and mobile metaphorical textures. In still other cases broader kinds of comparison are available: between Proust and Freud as artists in interpretation, or as sufferers from that hypertrophy of the interpretative function of mind that Deleuze and Guattari have called *interpretosis*.[3] Most instructively of all, perhaps, Proust may be called upon to provide a complex phenomenology for mental processes – those associated with bisexuality, jealousy and sado-masochism, for instance – upon which Freud performed certain of his most adventurous pieces of theoretical modelling.

This high degree of comparability and commutability between the Freudian and Proustian corpuses should not lead us to understate the wide gaps between them. Apart from the generic discontinuity, which is far from trivial, between the novel and the scientific treatise, the most notable of these gaps involves the kind of psychology, or rather of psychologising, that Proust's narrator himself chiefly does. Let us remember a tone and an analytic diction used throughout *A la recherche du temps perdu* in the narrator's discussion of mental process. The passage below is part of the extended Venetian episode which occurs towards the end of *La Fugitive* (and from which most of my later quotations will also be taken). Like much of that episode, it is concerned with the death of Albertine and with the disruption, provoked by that death, of the narrator's own sense of coherence and continuity as a person:

> on ne s'afflige pas plus d'être devenu un autre, les années ayant passé et dans l'ordre de la succession des temps, qu'on ne s'afflige, à une même époque, d'être tour à tour les êtres contradictoires, le méchant, le sensible, le délicat, le mufle, le désintéressé, l'ambitieux qu'on est tour à tour chaque journée. Et la raison pour laquelle on ne s'en afflige pas est la même, c'est que le moi éclipsé – momentanément dans le dernier cas et quand il s'agit du caractère, pour toujours dans le premier cas et quand il s'agit des passions – n'est pas là pour déplorer, l'autre l'autre qui est à ce moment-là, ou désormais, tout vous; le mufle sourit de sa muflerie car on est le mufle, et l'oublieux ne s'attriste pas de son manque de mémoire, précisément parce qu'on a oublié.[4] (III,642)

This is a subtle language, abstract yet untechnical, for the introspective analysis of mind in action, and has of course deep roots in the French intellectual tradition: in the work of Montaigne, Descartes, Pascal, La Rochefoucauld and La Bruyère; in the psychologising philosophies of Maine de Biran or Bergson and in the *romans personnels* of Constant, Nerval, Fromentin and others. Into this commodious ready-made language certain kinds of Proustian speculation could insert themselves smoothly: it enabled the narrator to seize upon and discuss such dangerous topics as the multiplicity of the self, forgetfulness, psychical numbness, depersonalisation, and the inconstancy or contradictoriness of desire, yet at the same time to suggest that this teeming world of dispersed and discontinuous personal life was indefinitely, and at will, retrievable to consciousness and subject to the control of the single, imperturbable self that resided there. Later on the same page we read: 'ma pensée était déjà habituée à son nouveau maître – mon nouveau moi';[5] in one gesture the fragmentation of the self is espoused and superseded. At these moments Proust's narrator is an associationist psychologist of an entirely traditional stamp. All experience is the writing of complicated and superimposed messages on the mental *tabula rasa*; given proper knowledge of the modes of association between idea and idea, and given lucidity, patience and dedication in the required measure, what experience has ravelled the mind can of itself, acting freely upon itself, unravel.

Such introspective analytic performances are of course not only unassimilable to psychoanalysis, they are based on theoretical suppositions to which it was and remains hostile. For psychoanalysis *repression* is an unavoidably central fact about the mental life: Freud's theory concerns itself precisely with the limitations under which the retrieval capacities of the conscious mind labour, and with the indirect, devious and unmasterable routes by which the repressed contents of the unconscious may become available to conscious reflection. Psychoanalysis may have been born by agonising parthenogenesis within Freud's introspective mind – this is the view of Ernest Jones, who celebrates at length in his biography the solitary acts of heroism by which Freud discovered within himself the Oedipus complex – but in its theoretical elaboration, and in the practical work that it does as a therapeutic method, psychoanalysis is relentlessly dialogical and dialectical. (A marked introspective capacity in the analysand may assist but may also impede analytic treatment.) The dynamic relationship between the unconscious and the preconscious–conscious systems is such that resistance may be overcome, repression lifted and previously unconscious material made available to reflection only by way of the mediations and displacements of the analytic dialogue. Over and against the introspective model, in which the mind is transparent from level to level and permeable part by part, Freud offers us models of the mind in which part is radically extrinsic to part and in which barriers and opacities may occasionally be attenuated but never definitively removed.

Clearly, if the encounter between *A la recherche du temps perdu* and psychoanalytic theory is to be close and informative, we shall be obliged to look beyond the smooth psychological speculations of Proust's narrator, to distrust his masterful voice and to ask whether an alternative psychology – more unstable, more dialectical and more discontinuous – may not also be ingrained in Proust's text. The psychological topics of common interest to Proust and Freud that I have chosen from my original list for more detailed discussion are: (i) errors and slips and (ii) bisexuality.

II

Both writers are hyper-acute observers of error; for both the erroneous, the erratic and the errant are powerful sources of meaning; and for both the ready flow of such material within everyday human exchange creates problems of organisation and makes their own claims to error-freeness difficult to sustain with confidence. Precisely the everydayness of the perceptual and verbal events anthologised in *The Psychopathology of Everyday Life*, and the gaiety of Freud's anecdotal manner, have made this his most popular and least menacing work. And many a 'popular' dilution of psychoanalytic thinking has taken its cue from this volume and from its companion study of jokes: errors, slips and jokes have allowed the unconscious to be portrayed as desultory – only momentarily audible and hence, seemingly, a thing of the moment – and likely to make itself felt in the world of purposeful speech and behaviour as no more than an occasional benign purveyor of witticisms or as an ineffectual subversive whose attacks leave their target institutions intact. But although Freud's serried catalogues of lapses, gaffes and embarrassments may seem to give support to this view, the most disconsolate themes of *The Interpretation of Dreams* are also amply present in the *Psychopathology*. In both books unconscious desire, however briefly glimpsed, is in fact obdurate and unstoppable and exerts a continuous pressure upon all human activity. And words, which when spoken may indeed acquire certain of their accidental-seeming inflections in direct response to that pressure, are also a facilitating medium for all unspoken mental productions. This 'compliance of the linguistic material', as Freud called it in the *Psychopathology* (VI, 222), allowed unconscious motives and wishes to find local expression in slips but, more gravely, made the elimination of error, whether from the language of neurosis or from the language in which the theory of psychoanalysis itself was articulated, into an exacting and unfinishable task.[6]

Proust too is a pathologist of speech-habits, and his inexhaustible fund of comic case-material, which extends from the malapropisms of Françoise to the proliferating banalities of Norpois and the clannish affectations of the Guermantes, may suddenly give way to linguistic aberrations that are ominously charged with emotion. 'Failed performances' – if I may hazard an alternative translation for the German term (*Fehlleistung*) that is usually obscurely rendered as 'parapraxis'[7] – of the exact kind that Freud discusses are relatively rare in *A la recherche*. But certain of these provide the narrator with a direct route to the realm of unconscious motivation, absorb several pages of text and are placed at major points of transition within the narrative. In the case of Albertine's 'me faire casser [le pot]' (III, 337),[8] for example, a slip of the tongue reveals in her an unsuspected mode of 'perverse' sexual desire (for anal intercourse) and launches the narrator upon a protracted analysis that characteristically blends puzzlement, indignation and envy (III, 337–41). This desire, once revealed and analysed, allows the narrator to contemplate dispassionately, and thereafter to provoke, Albertine's flight from captivity.

During the Venetian episode this eloquent 'failed performance' of Albertine's is answered by another, a mis-transcription or a mis-reading by which Albertine, now dead, seems to have been resurrected. By telegram the narrator had summoned the fugitive Albertine back to him; by an almost simultaneous telegram he had been told of her death (III, 476); and a telegram now revives her (Proust dramatises his account of self-enclosed subjectivity in *La Fugitive* – its distance from others, its resistance to penetration – by having all these portentous messages travel at the speed of light):

> . . . le portier me remit une dépêche que l'employé du télégraphe était déjà venu trois fois pour m'apporter, car à cause de l'inexactitude du nom du destinataire (que je compris pourtant à travers les déformations des employés italiens être le mien), on demandait un accusé de réception certifiant que le télégramme était bien pour moi. Je l'ouvris dès que je fus dans ma chambre, et jetant un coup d'œil sur un libellé rempli de mots mal transmis, je pus lire néanmoins: 'Mon ami, vous me croyez morte, pardonnez-moi, je suis très vivante, je voudrais vous voir, vous parler mariage, quand revenez-vous? Tendrement. Albertine.'[9] (III, 641)

By this stage in the novel Venice is a place where memory and forgetfulness are inseparably woven together; it offers release from the traumatic residues of passion yet at the same time provides countless associative paths by which that passion may by accident be revived. In this telegram, Albertine's precarious afterlife within the narrator's *oublieuse mémoire*[10] finds its most laconic form: in a wrong name. But what kind of error has been made? The name 'Gilberte' has been confused with its near-miss anagram 'Albertine'. But by whom?

> La dépêche que j'avais reçue dernièrement et que j'avais crue d'Albertine, cette dépêche était de Gilberte. Comme l'originalité assez factice de l'écriture de Gilberte consistait principalement, quand elle écrivait une ligne, à faire figurer dans la ligne supérieure les barres de *t* qui avaient l'air de souligner les mots ou les points sur les *i* qui avaient l'air d'interrompre les phrases de la ligne d'au-dessus, et en revanche à intercaler dans la ligne d'au-dessous les queues et arabesques des mots qui leur étaient superposés, il était tout naturel que l'employé du télégraphe eût lu les boucles d'*s* ou d'*y* de la ligne supérieure comme un 'ine' finissant le mot

de Gilberte. Le point sur l'*i* de Gilberte était monté au-dessus faire point de suspension. Quant à son *G*, il avait l'air d'un *A* gothique. Qu'en dehors de cela deux ou trois mots eussent été mal lus, pris les uns dans les autres (certains, d'ailleurs, m'avaient paru incompréhensibles), cela était suffisant pour expliquer les détails de mon erreur, et n'était même pas nécessaire. Combien de lettres lit dans un mot une personne distraite et surtout prévenue, qui part de l'idée que la lettre est d'une certaine personne? combien de mots dans la phrase? On devine en lisant, on crée; tout part d'une erreur initiale; celles qui suivent (et ce n'est pas seulement dans la lecture des lettres et des télégrammes, pas seulement dans toute lecture), si extraordinaires qu'elles puissent paraître à celui qui n'a pas le même point de départ, sont toutes naturelles. Une bonne partie de ce que nous croyons, et jusque dans les conclusions dernières c'est ainsi, avec un entêtement et une bonne foi égales, vient d'une première méprise sur les prémisses.[11] (III, 656)

The erratic anagrammatising of Gilberte's name has had at least three possible phases: Gilberte's ornate handwriting could have provided cues for misreading (her flourishes have an irresponsible semantic power); the telegraph clerk, responding to one or other of these cues, could have made a mistake (Freud, analysing his own example of error in telegrams, singled out these clerks as artists in 'secondary revision', VI, 129–30); the wishful narrator himself could have read 'correctly' the incorrect name or distorted further an already distorted message or introduced the whole distortion himself. The narrator does not adjudicate between the alternative prehistories of 'his' error, for in the face of his powerful unconscious wish – that Albertine should be alive – each of them is equally credible. In withholding judgment on the merely precipitating causes involved, the narrator is continuing in miniature a procedure already familiar to readers of *La Prisonnière* and *La Fugitive* – that procedure whereby a number of successive or imbricated hypotheses are left permanently unresolved. In the passage that separates the error from its explanation, two clear examples of this occur. The 'real' death of Albertine – the only one that matters to the narrator – is her death as a structure of his own thought; the creation, flowering and extinction of that structure are subject to their own causal laws and these are not reducible, or even coherently relatable, to the laws which govern the life and death of Albertine's body (641–2). But within two pages an interference between the two causal orders is allowed: news of Albertine's apparent return to life accelerates the onset of forgetfulness and indifference (643), despite the narrator's earlier claim that this process had run its full course before the arrival of the telegram. A similar equivocation takes place on the nature of the self: can the self be subject to definitive mutation, severed from its own past states, or, on the contrary, can it be defined only by its improbable power to endure? In one view the self is endlessly in eclipse (642) and thought incapable of conserving anything (644). In another the self anxiously returns in thought to the scene of its losses and, without seeking continuity, endlessly finds it: 'Notre amour de la vie n'est qu'une vieille liaison dont nous ne savons pas nous débarrasser. Sa force est dans sa permanence' (645).[12]

One thing seems to the narrator certain despite these conceptual and emotional indecisions: there had been an initial mistake from which all subsequent mistakes flowed. The misreader of a letter is one who begins from an erroneous idea – 'l'idée que la lettre est d'une certaine personne'. The point is repeated and reinforced: 'tout part d'une erreur initiale'; '[une] bonne partie de ce que nous croyons . . . vient d'une première méprise sur les prémisses'.[13] But these anxious repetitions suggest that there is something singularly unstable about the narrator's claim. A passage that discusses one near-miss anagram (*Gilberte* → *Albertine*) as the revealer of a hidden wish ends with another, emphatic and still more complex: *première* → *méprise* → *prémisses*. In this culminating piece of word-play, notions of temporal or logical priority threaten to dissolve into the centrally placed notion of misapprehension or mistake. And the narrator's most distinctively 'Freudian' account of misreading earlier in the passage has already allowed that error may have no origin or beginning: 'ce n'est pas seulement dans la lecture des lettres et des télégrammes, pas seulement dans toute lecture'.[14] Error may simply be an inescapable condition of mental performances.

This is an episode, then, in which analytic and interpretative mastery is ostensibly being sought, but in which, detail by detail, mastery is being undermined. As explanation vies indecisively with explanation and as the copious narrative self reinvents its characteristics, factual *erreur* turns into textual *errance*; in the discussion of lapses further lapses occur; and the attempted correction of symptomatic misreadings becomes symptomatic in its turn. If we were looking for straightforward conclusions on 'Freud and Proust' at this premature stage, if conclusions were to be allowed at all on such a narrow range of evidence, we could say that both are searchers for the latent beneath the manifest and in particular for that which is insistently and informingly desired beneath all that is casual and contingent in human conduct; both are attentive to the derivatives of the unconscious and regard 'failed performances' as accurate pointers to unconscious motivation; and for both the discovery of this instructive material is a disquieting one, an invitation to disorder. The couplet from the second part of Goethe's *Faust* that appears on the title-page of *The Psychopathology of Everyday Life* could also serve as an epigraph to *La Fugitive*:

> Nun ist die Luft von solchem Spuk so voll,
> Daß niemand wieß, wie er ihn meiden soll.
>
> Now fills the air so many a haunting shape,
> That no one knows how best he may escape.[15]

But comparative conclusions like this are far too simple. For while indicating a certain degree of congruence between the two writers, or prominent moments of conceptual overlap between their works, they omit the complex middle-distance. The major lesson of Freud's theory for observers of Proust's text is that symptomatic slips are likely to be visible elsewhere than in the narrator's theoretical discussion of such slips, and indeed that his fluent discussion and his propensity for theory may themselves become suspect once a fuller range of unconscious motives has been revealed. Freud alerts us to the ways in which Proust's text means on the margins of its oratorical declarations and in the interstices of its famously penetrating analyses. In the passage I have discussed, for example, the alternative order of slips and of motives would have to do with the killing of Albertine rather than with her involuntary resuscitation. For her death – whether real or imaginary, bodily or mental, telegrammatically confuted or anagrammatically confirmed – is relentlessly reiterated as the ingenious analytic texture spreads, and the unconscious that revives her is providing itself with the opportunity to despatch her again. Freud helps us to see how many kinds and levels of interlocution Proust has inserted into his narrator's tireless soliloquy, and to distrust his psychologising even when this is of a seemingly clairvoyant psychoanalytic kind.

III

Freud and Proust were both consummate dialecticians of human sexuality, and the scale and complexity of their enquiries are still astonishing today. Only very rarely in the later twentieth century –

but unmistakably in, say, Foucault's *Histoire de la sexualité* – has analytic subtlety comparable to theirs been devoted to the procedures by which sexual attitudes and identities are fabricated within culture. Both conferred unusual epistemic privileges upon 'aberrant' configurations of sexual desire; both were impassioned relativists in their surveys of sexual behaviour yet had recourse to the strong-minded normative categories of their age in their moments of moral or intellectual exhaustion. And both made the unsettling discovery that in order to present a coherent account of what sexual creatures did the phenomenon of bisexuality had to be entirely rethought: it had to be retrieved from the wild and distant shores to which the cumulative *psychopathia sexualis* of modern Europe had consigned it and given a central role in the new literature of sex.

'Without taking bisexuality into account', Freud wrote in his *Three Essays on the Theory of Sexuality* (1905), 'I think it would scarcely be possible to arrive at an understanding of the sexual manifestations that are actually to be observed in men and women' (VII, 220). The bisexual constitution of human beings at large made the description 'homosexual' unreliable and imprecise and, in conjunction with other factors, prompted Freud to speak of the 'manifold permutations' to which homosexual desire was subject (XVIII, 170). In *The Ego and the Id* (1923) that same constitution was presented as a permanent obstacle to the intelligible description of the child's early development (XIX, 33): the young child cannot be other than uncertain in his or her choice of sexual object and uncertainty preys too upon any theorist who seeks to trace the developmental routes by which this or that variety of adult sexual preference is reached. For Proust's narrator in *La Prisonnière* and *La Fugitive*, bisexuality similarly figures as an epistemological outrage and moment by moment frustrates the search for intelligibility in his personal relationships. Albertine's mobile desires are the object of interminable speculation and analysis – of *albertinage*, as these irremediably anxious textual performances have been called. To answer the question that her sexuality poses would be to reach the blissful outcome of a tormented philosophical quest.

'Male and female created He them.' But in Paris and Vienna by the early years of the present century, the Creator's original distribution of sexual kinds had gone seriously awry. Teasing sexual indeterminacy of a kind that had long been familiar in works of art – in Leonardo's Saint John the Baptist or Caravaggio's angels and urchins, in Shakespeare's comedies or Balzac's *Séraphîta* and *Sarrasine* – was now being raised to the level of theory. An obscure middle zone seemed to be drawing into itself the once clearly counterposed notions 'male' and 'female' and to be hastening an immemorially ancient classificatory tradition to its close. Proust and Freud each responded to this crisis with a vein of historico-biological whimsy that was characteristic of their time. If 'male' and 'female' were no longer available to the observer of human sexuality as an efficient system of classes then the reason for their shortcomings was to be sought not in the recent history of European culture, not in the changing pressures which that culture placed upon the sexual instinct, but in the early history of biological species. The journey back through biological time led not to an Eden of bipolar sexual difference but to a primordial hermaphroditism:

Enfin, l'inversion elle-même, venant de ce que l'inverti se rapproche trop de la femme pour pouvoir avoir des rapports utiles avec elle, se rattache par là à une loi plus haute qui fait que tant de fleurs hermaphrodites restent infécondes, c'est-à-dire à la stérilité de l'autofécondation. Il est vrai que les invertis à la recherche d'un mâle se contentent souvent d'un inverti aussi efféminé qu'eux. Mais il suffit qu'ils n'appartiennent pas au sexe féminin, dont ils ont en eux un embryon dont ils ne peuvent se servir, ce qui arrive à tant de fleurs hermaphrodites et même à certains animaux hermaphrodites, comme l'escargot, qui ne peuvent être fécondés par eux-mêmes, mais peuvent l'être par d'autres hermaphrodites. Par là les invertis, qui se rattachent volontiers à l'antique Orient ou à l'âge d'or de la Grèce, remonteraient plus haut encore, à ces époques d'essai où n'existaient ni les fleurs dioïques ni les animaux unisexués, à cet hermaphroditisme initial dont quelques rudiments d'organes mâles dans l'anatomie de la femme et d'organes femelles dans l'anatomie de l'homme semblent conserver la trace.[16] (II, 629)

In this passage from the incomparably passionate and witty exordium to *Sodome et Gomorrhe*, Proust's narrator has naturalised homosexual desire by moving its main field of action from the cultural to the biological sphere and its golden age from Greek antiquity to the remote first stirrings of terrestrial life: homosexuality, far from being a psychological predisposition of certain individuals within human society, is part of man's archaic biological inheritance. Freud, in his account of bisexuality or 'psychical hermaphroditism' in the *Three Essays*, entertained the same biological analogy in his search for an explanation of what were indisputably mental and social facts:

. . . it appears that a certain degree of anatomical hermaphroditism occurs normally. In every normal male or female individual, traces are found of the apparatus of the opposite sex. These either persist without function as rudimentary organs or become modified and take on other functions.

These long-familiar facts of anatomy lead us to suppose that an originally bisexual physical disposition has, in the course of evolution, become modified into a unisexual one, leaving behind only a few traces of the sex that has become atrophied. (VII, 141)

The analogical explanation that biology seemed about to provide was promptly but with some regret rejected by Freud: 'The truth must therefore be recognized that inversion and somatic hermaphroditism are on the whole independent of each other' (142) – although explanations of this sort continued to fascinate him throughout his career. If the development of minds could not in the end be thought of as imitating that of bodies, and if ontogenesis did not in exact and determinate ways recapitulate phylogenesis, nature could not, strictly, be blamed. But by refusing such replications of structure nature had certainly, in Freud's view, missed an opportunity for beauty and elegance in its organisation of itself.

In *Beyond the Pleasure Principle*, Freud, like Proust's narrator, uses the Greek golden age as a staging post on his way to a possible biological explanation and chooses from that age the text that has always marked, for theorists of sex, its most resplendent moment: Plato's *Symposium*.[17] Science has little to tell us, Freud says, about either of the two sets of forces – the instincts of 'life' and 'death' – that *Beyond the Pleasure Principle* sets against each other. Yet Plato's fabulous hermaphrodites (*Symp.*, 189) may perhaps suggest one way in which science, destitute of illuminating hypotheses about the origin of sexuality, could proceed:

In quite a different region, it is true, we *do* meet with such a hypothesis; but it is of so fantastic a kind – a myth rather than a scientific explanation – that I should not venture to produce it here, were it not that it fulfils precisely the one condition whose fulfilment we desire. For it traces the origin of an instinct to *a need to restore an earlier state of things*.

What I have in mind is, of course, the theory which Plato put into the mouth of Aristophanes in the *Symposium*, and which deals not only with the *origin* of the sexual instinct but also with the most important of its variations in relation to its object. 'The original human nature was not like the present, but different. In the first place, the sexes were originally three in number, not two as they are now; there was man, woman, and the union of the two. . . .' Everything about these primaeval men was double: they had four hands and four feet, two faces, two privy parts, and so on. Eventually Zeus decided to cut these men in two, 'like a sorb-apple which is halved for pickling'. After the division had been made, 'the two parts of man, each desiring his other half, came together, and threw their arms about one another eager to grow into one'.

Shall we follow the hint given us by the poet-philosopher, and venture upon the hypothesis that living substance at the time of its coming to life was torn apart into small particles, which have ever since endeavoured to reunite through the sexual instincts? that these instincts, in which the chemical affinity of inanimate matter persisted, gradually succeeded, as they developed through the kingdom of the protista, in overcoming the difficulties put in the way of that endeavour by an environment charged with dangerous stimuli – stimuli which compelled them to form a protective cortical layer? that these splintered fragments of living substance in this way attained a multicellular condition and finally transferred the instinct for reuniting, in the most highly concentrated form, to the germ-cells? – But here, I think, the moment has come for breaking off. (XVIII, 57–8)

In the years when Freud found it necessary to rebut repeatedly the charge that psychoanalysis was a lubricious 'pan-sexualism', the 'divine Plato' (VII, 134) was the most notable of the character witnesses he called in his own defence (XVIII, 91, XIX, 218, XXII, 209).[18] It was as absurd to accuse psychoanalysis of explaining 'everything' by sex as it would be to make the same charge against Plato's symposiasts in their celebrations of Eros. But the *Symposium* has in this passage a much less diplomatic and public-spirited role. It is called upon to initiate, and confer respectability upon, a characteristic Freudian departure into theoretical reverie. His eventual return to strict and responsible science is announced by an equally characteristic gesture of seeming recantation: 'But here, I think, the moment has come for breaking off.'[19] The pleasures of the speculative intelligence that Freud abandons with this gesture are complex ones. For the intuition about the instinctual life that he introduces by way of Plato – that instincts have their origin in '*a need to restore an earlier state of things*' – is tested by methods that are themselves speculative, if not plainly science-fictional. Freud's search for the origin of the instincts leads him to surmise that the desired origin might be found precisely in the predisposition of animate matter to desire a return to its original state. The theorist's desire for origins is thus written into the book of Nature as the prototype of all desire.[20] His own text returns upon the anterior textual world of Plato just as Plato's returned upon the fabled 'initial hermaphroditism' of the human species, and the 'scientific' hypothesis that the Platonic myth allegedly facilitates in fact does no more than provide for that myth a protective cortical layer of erudite terminology.

In the immediate vicinity of the passages I have quoted from *Sodome et Gomorrhe* and *Beyond the Pleasure Principle*, both authors make as it were ceremonial reference to Darwin[21] as an emblem of irreproachably strict biological science. But both writers in their fantasticated accounts of the yearnings felt by unisexual human creatures for their bisexual pre-existence are closer to the scientific world of Erasmus Darwin's *The Loves of the Plants* than to his grandson's *Origin of Species*. The quest for mental or instinctual 'origins' was at once an austere moral responsibility and a pretext for phantasy and play. For Proust's narrator this quest was the boldest element in an elaborate *deffence et illustration* of the homosexual condition; for Freud it was the psychological scientist's supreme calling. But once anchorage of this kind had been found and praiseworthy intentions declared, the way was opened up to multifarious textual invention. The hermaphrodite who guarded the instinctual origins was also the patron deity of the polymorphous, pleasure-seeking writer at work upon his page.[22]

Elsewhere than in the opening pages of *Sodome et Gomorrhe* there is little evidence to suggest the presence in *A la recherche du temps perdu* of a *theory* of bisexuality. Indeed bisexuality – whether as a term, or as a concept, or even as a phenomenon complex enough to be theorised upon – is almost completely absent from the remainder of Proust's novel.[23] Although the book as a whole is a vast fresco of imperious sexual energy, changes in sexual orientation almost all follow the same pattern: an apparently heterosexual man or woman emerges as homosexual in fact. Such conversions or comings-out accumulate so fast towards the end of the novel that a decidedly comic air of millennial upheaval is created. Most of the narrator's discussion of Albertine's obdurately ambiguous sexuality has to do with the question 'which does she *really* desire, men or women?' Proust prided himself on the creation late in the novel of Morel – who desired both, and with apparently equal intensity – but seems to have had or to have affected doubts about whether any significant number of individuals thus constituted actually existed. 'Ce sont du reste les brutes à qui ce rôle est d'habitude départi', he said in his essay on Baudelaire, while congratulating himself in an aside upon the singularity of Morel's character.[24]

Not possessing the term 'bisexuality', and in a book where homosexuality as distinct from bisexuality provided a major element of teleological structure, Proust nevertheless endowed his narrator with an indefinite capacity for bisexual phantasy and repeatedly allowed a volatile sense of sexual indeterminacy into the fine textures of his writing. Among the many cues for phantasy of this kind that the narrator encounters in everyday experience, works of art – quoted, alluded to or described – have a particularly prominent role. And they offer the novelist handling what was still a shameful theme an opportunity for obliqueness and discretion: in the absence of a full-scale theory of sexual origins, works of art suggest that the modes of desire proscribed by modern Europe have a long, dignified and thoroughly European prehistory.

In my first example, again taken from the episode of the telegram in *La Fugitive*, the work of art involved is a literary one – Racine's *Phèdre*. 'How strange it is that I should be so completely cured of my love for Albertine', the narrator has just suggested:

> Est-ce pour cette fille que je revoyais en ce moment si bouffie et qui avait certainement vieilli comme avaient vieilli les filles qu'elle avait aimées, est-ce pour elle qu'il fallait renoncer à l'éclatante fille qui était mon souvenir d'hier, mon espoir de demain, à qui je ne pourrais plus donner un sou, non plus qu'à aucune autre, si j'épousais Albertine, renoncer à cette "Albertine nouvelle", "non point telle que l'ont vue les Enfers" "mais fidèle, mais fière et même un peu farouche"? C'était elle qui était maintenant ce qu'Albertine avait été autrefois: mon amour pour Albertine n'avait été qu'une forme passagère de ma dévotion à la jeunesse.[25] (III, 644)

As the narrator's dream-like retrospection espouses Phèdre's in her celebrated speech of avowal –

> Je l'aime, non point tel que l'ont vu les enfers,
> Volage adorateur de mille objets divers,
> Qui va du Dieu des morts déshonorer la couche;
> Mais fidèle, mais fier, et même un peu farouche,
> Charmant, jeune, traînant tous les cœurs après soi,
> Tel qu'on dépeint nos Dieux, ou tel que je vous voi.[26] (II. V)

– echoes are sounded back through the intricate Racinian sub-text of the novel. As a child at Combray, the narrator had seen himself as a new Phèdre at the moment of saying farewell to his beloved hawthorns: 'comme une princesse de tragédie à qui pèseraient ces vains ornements, ingrat envers l'importune main qui en formant tous ces nœuds avait pris soin sur mon front d'assembler mes cheveux' (I, 145 quoting *Phèdre*, I.iii).[27] (The narrative voice injects grotesque comedy into the scene by assimilating Phèdre to a self-willed child combed and curled for the photographer and by transforming the Racinian alexandrine into lurching semi-metrical prose.) In *A l'ombre des jeunes filles en fleurs* the narrator, preparing himself to hear La Berma perform (I, 440–3), had schooled himself in an earlier speech of Phèdre's ('On dit qu'un prompt départ vous éloigne de nous . . .') from the scene he quotes in *La Fugitive*.

These and other self-identifications with Racine's heroine are now recapitulated in a symmetrical exchange of sexual roles: the narrator becomes Phèdre to Albertine's Hippolyte. 'I am accustoming myself', Freud wrote to Fliess, 'to regarding every sexual act as a process in which four individuals are involved' (Freud/Fliess, 364; *Origins*, 289).[28] How eloquently Proust has enshrined this fourness in the passage above; and with what economy and wit does he remind us of the book's earlier Oedipal drama: in a turbulent phantasy provoked and abetted by literary art, the narrator becomes an incestuously desiring mother – a mother of the very kind that, as a child, he had most wished to have.

The vicissitudes of sexual desire in Proust's account of Carpaccio, which is my second example, are less quadrilateral and more complex. One effect of the unfortunate publishing history of Proust's novel, both in French and in English, has been to confine Carpaccio to the threshold of the small pantheon of 'Proustian painters'.[29] Asked to name a painter having a kinetic function in the text of *A la recherche*, most readers are still likely to mention Vermeer, or Botticelli, or Giotto, or various of the Impressionists, or Whistler. But not Carpaccio. Carpaccio was in fact inserted into the narrative with great precision and was the subject of one of those minute long-term calculations in which the novel abounds. He appears in the company of Racine in *A l'ombre*: 'Un Carpaccio à Venise, la Berma dans *Phèdre*, chefs-d'œuvre d'art pictural ou dramatique que le prestige qui s'attachait à eux rendait en moi si vivants . . .' (I, 441).[30] Some 2,250 pages later the promise made in these lines is kept: painter and dramatist reappear in close proximity and the narrator demonstrates their continued living presence within him by turning himself first into Phèdre (III, 644) and then into Carpaccio's Saint Ursula (III, 646). I shall quote the main Carpaccio episode in its entirety and then discuss in turn the two works referred to and reinvented by the narrator:

Nous entrions, ma mère et moi, dans le baptistère, foulant tous deux les mosaïques de marbre et de verre du pavage, ayant devant nous les larges arcades dont le temps a légèrement infléchi les surfaces évasées et roses, ce qui donne à l'église, là où il a respecté la fraîcheur de ce coloris, l'air d'être construite dans une matière douce et malléable comme la cire de géantes alvéoles; là au contraire où il a racorni la matière et où les artistes l'ont ajourée et rehaussée d'or, d'être la précieuse reliure, en quelque cuir de Cordoue, du colossal Évangile de Venise. Voyant que j'avais à rester longtemps devant les mosaïques qui représentent le baptême du Christ, ma mère, sentant la fraîcheur glacée qui tombait dans le baptistère, me jetait un châle sur les épaules. Quand j'étais avec Albertine à Balbec, je croyais qu'elle révélait une de ces illusions inconsistantes qui remplissent l'esprit de tant de gens qui ne pensent pas clairement, quand elle me parlait du plaisir – selon moi ne reposant sur rien – qu'elle aurait à voir telle peinture avec moi. Aujourd'hui, je suis au moins sûr que le plaisir existe sinon de voir, du moins d'avoir vu une belle chose avec une certaine personne. Une heure est venue pour moi où, quand je me rappelle le baptistère, devant les flots du Jourdain où saint Jean immerge le Christ, tandis que la gondole nous attendait devant la Piazzetta, il ne m'est pas indifférent que dans cette fraîche pénombre, à côté de moi, il y eût une femme drapée dans son deuil avec la ferveur respectueuse et enthousiaste de la femme âgée qu'on voit à Venise dans la *Sainte Ursule* de Carpaccio, et que cette femme aux joues rouges, aux yeux tristes, dans ses voiles noirs, et que rien ne pourra plus jamais faire sortir pour moi de ce sanctuaire doucement éclairé de Saint-Marc où je suis sûr de la retrouver parce qu'elle y a sa place réservée et immuable comme une mosaïque, ce soit ma mère.

Carpaccio, que je viens de nommer et qui était le peintre auquel, quand je ne travaillais pas à Saint-Marc, nous rendions le plus volontiers visite, faillit un jour ranimer mon amour pour Albertine. Je voyais pour la première fois *Le Patriarche di Grando* [sic] *exorcisant un possédé.* Je regardais l'admirable ciel incarnat et violet sur lequel se détachent ces hautes cheminées incrustées, dont la forme évasée et le rouge épanouissement de tulipes fait penser à tant de Venises de Whistler. Puis mes yeux allaient du vieux Rialto en bois à ce Ponte Vecchio du XVe siècle aux palais de marbre ornés de chapiteaux dorés, revenaient au Canal où les barques sont menées par des adolescents en vestes roses, en toques surmontées d'aigrettes, semblables à s'y méprendre à tel qui évoquait vraiment Carpaccio dans cette éblouissante *Légende de Joseph* de Sert, Strauss et Kessler. Enfin, avant de quitter le tableau mes yeux revinrent à la rive où fourmillent les scènes de la vie vénitienne de l'époque. Je regardais le barbier essuyer son rasoir, le nègre portant son tonneau, les conversations des musulmans, des nobles seigneurs vénitiens en larges brocarts, en damas, en toque de velours cerise, quand tout à coup je sentis au cœur comme une légère morsure. Sur le dos d'un des *Compagnons de la Calza*, reconnaissable aux broderies d'or et de perles qui inscrivent sur leur manche ou leur collet l'emblème de la joyeuse confrérie à laquelle ils étaient affiliés, je venais de reconnaître le manteau qu'Albertine avait pris pour venir avec moi en voiture découverte à Versailles, le soir où j'étais loin de me douter qu'une quinzaine d'heures me séparaient à peine du moment où elle partirait de chez moi. Toujours prête à tout, quand je lui avais demandé de partir, ce triste jour qu'elle devait appeler dans la dernière lettre "deux fois crépusculaire puisque la nuit tombait et que nous allions nous quitter", elle avait jeté sur ses épaules un manteau de Fortuny qu'elle avait emporté avec elle le lendemain et que je n'avais jamais revu depuis dans mes souvenirs. Or c'était dans ce tableau de Carpaccio que le fils génial de Venise l'avait pris, c'est des épaules de ce *compagnon de la Calza* qu'il l'avait détaché pour le jeter sur celles de tant de Parisiennes, qui certes ignoraient, comme je l'avais fait jusqu'ici, que le modèle en existait dans un groupe de seigneurs, au premier plan du *Patriarche di Grado*, dans une salle de l'Académie de Venise. J'avais tout reconnu, et, le manteau oublié m'ayant rendu pour le regarder les yeux et le cœur de celui qui allait ce soir-là partir à Versailles avec Albertine, je fus envahi pendant quelques instants par un sentiment trouble et bientôt dissipé de désir et de mélancolie.[31] (III, 646–7)

Venice, as we have already been reminded by this stage in the novel, is a place where different styles and structures meet and interweave. The acquisitive and assimilative Venetian republic had made heterogeneity into a local rule, and artefacts, ideas and feelings are alike subject to it. The dominant gothic motif in the civic and domestic architecture of the city is 'encore à demi arabe' (625)[32] and, just as orient and occident flow together in the intricate façades of the buildings, so the narrator's possessive sexual passion is directed at once towards his mother, who has accompanied him, and towards the young working women of the town. The townscape is so completely sexualised that his mother, desiring and desired, is described as having left a permanent imprint on his memory of the Venetian gothic style (625), and the network of lesser canals that he explores by gondola as offering an inexhaustible array of erotic itineraries (626–7). Before the re-entry of Carpaccio, that is to say, Venice has already established itself as a privileged site for phantasy and as an ingenious mechanism for the transformation of desire.

The drama of the first paragraph resides in the narrator's improbable rediscovery of maternal power. Having travelled by water to San Marco, he finds the basilica to be not a merely monumental edifice but one that is mobile and fluent, a continuation of the sea. The work of time upon the building has been to replace straight lines by curves and that work is going on now, for the whole place seems to have been 'construite dans une matière douce et malléable comme la cire de géantes alvéoles'.[33] His mother's solicitude in placing a shawl over his shoulders persuades him that a special pleasure exists in seeing, or in having seen, a thing of beauty in the company of this person rather than that. But his commemoration of his mother's tenderness takes a provocative form: in a world where everything else is exuberantly in process, he turns her to stone. While the pavement mosaics themselves become wax, the memory of her becomes 'immuable comme une mosaïque'.[34]

The narrator's mother attends upon his emotion before Venetian art, just as an anonymous old woman attends upon Saint Ursula in two of the eight panels, now in the Accademia, in which Carpaccio depicts her spectacular career (Plates 1 and 2). Ursula, according to Carpaccio's version of the legend,[35] was a Breton princess, who agreed to marry the son of the pagan King of England only on condition that she be allowed to undertake an

1 Carpaccio, *The Arrival of the English Ambassadors* (*St Ursula Cycle*); Venice, Accademia

arduous pilgrimage with a multitudinous following of virgins. It was on this pilgrimage that Ursula was martyred at the hands of the Huns. It is not clear whether Proust had one only of these panels in mind, although the phrase 'ferveur respectueuse et enthousiaste'[36] perhaps suggests the second woman, at prayer, rather than the first, who is depicted in passive contemplation. The question 'which panel did he mean?' is in any case not a particularly sensible one in that the *vecchia* – who was to become a familiar motif in Venetian narrative painting of the *cinquecento*[37] – is one of several elements from the first painting that the second self-consciously recombines.[38] Each of the panels is in the form of an episodic narrative designed to be read from left to right. In the first the arrival of the English ambassadors in an enchanted, Venetianised Brittany, and their homage to the Breton King, are followed by the discussion between father and daughter of the marriage settlement. In the second the slaughter of Ursula and her companions is followed by her funeral ceremony. In both the old woman occupies the bottom right of the painting, is present during the latest narrative stage, and is active within the pictorial design while having no role in the story. In the first work, she is half-turned out of the picture plane and into the space occupied by the spectator; she contradicts the flat rightwards movement of the tale, not simply by turning outwards, but by mirroring the leaning, askew posture of the King in a composition where almost all other figures are seen frontally or in profile. She occupies a point of tension between depth visibly receding into the picture, into the King's private chamber, and depth invisibly projecting from the picture into 'our' world. In the second work her kneeling figure in the funeral scene mirrors Ursula's kneeling figure in the scene of murder. Both praying women are in full profile. Yet despite their mirroring of each other the figure of the old woman still has a contradictory energy: she kneels against the direction of the corpse and the funeral cortège and looks backwards into a now superseded phase of the narrative. Her hands posed diagonally upwards join forces with the episcopal mitres to counteract the diagonally downwards movement of the lethal Hunnish shaft. Both old women are active without doing anything, active by being there; both are placed at the foot of a staircase that neither of them, it is clear, is eligible to ascend. For on the podium to which each staircase leads a sacrament is being prepared or enacted. It is this 'being there', this mute attending upon the suffering, travail or death of another woman, that provides the bridge between Carpaccio's *repoussoir* figure and the figure of the narrator's mother, and this that allows the narrator momentarily to become, in his Venetian rapture, a virgin bride, pious and resolute as she faces martyrdom. But what passion is it that the narrator, having thus become feminine and Ursuline, undergoes? And what entitles him to annex to himself his mother's mourning for her own mother?

2 Carpaccio, *The Martyrdom of Ursula* (*St Ursula Cycle*); Venice, Accademia

In this paragraph, as in earlier ones, the narrator's mother has acquired an extraordinary cadential weight. For the second time in this Venetian episode the word 'mère' has closed a long and elaborate paragraph; for the second time it has both acted as the long-deferred resolution of an intricate syntactic pattern and been associated with Venetian stone.[39] In a world where the stones themselves are labile and capricious, the psychical life of the individual is held to be organised and governed by weighty internal fixtures. Love of this mother and for this mother is the only enduring thing in a mutable world, and is undergone as a passion and a martyrdom.

How close we are in this portrait of petrified human desire to an entire dimension of Freud's thought – not simply to its general drift but to the animated metaphorical substratum of his texts. Freud too was fascinated by the eloquence of worked stone, although Rome rather than Venice was his Italian *lieu d'élection* and archaeology rather than architecture his favourite reservoir of images.[40] Archaeology and psychoanalysis resembled each other in that both were concerned with the excavation and restoration of a previously lost past. But the excavator of mental objects had one central advantage over his archaeological counterpart. For the primitive sexual impulse, the traumatic event, the earliest configurations of libido, belonged to a superior order of durability.[41] Where the material relics of human civilisation were friable and destructible, primitive psychical relics were solid enough to prevail against the innumerable adventitious pressures to which minds are exposed. Proust and Freud, who have a similar gift for dramatic portraiture of mental process, take a similar pleasure in the idea that the mere desires of mere minds should provide firm bedrock in an otherwise dispersive and entropic material world.[42] And both write with particular force about the ways in which libidinal structures first produced in the context of the mother–child relationship persist through adult life. In his last book, *An Outline of Psycho-Analysis*, Freud restated his lifelong maternal theme in perhaps its gravest and simplest form:

> A child's first erotic object is the mother's breast that nourishes it; love has its origin in attachment to the satisfied need for nourishment . . . This first object is later completed into the person of the child's mother, who not only nourishes it but also looks after it and thus arouses in it a number of other physical sensations, pleasurable and unpleasurable. By her care of the child's body she becomes its first seducer. In these two relations lies the root of a mother's importance, unique,

without parallel, established unalterably for a whole lifetime as the first and strongest love-object and as the prototype of all later love-relations – for both sexes. (XXIII, 188)

By way of the milky flow from breast to mouth, a rigid pattern is being created; in the playful caresses that pass between the child and its first seducer an implacable fatality is at work. The infant human mind is already forming for itself the restrictions under which its later pursuit of pleasure and happiness will be conducted: even as the child sucks, sacrifice and martyrdom are its lot.[43]

Where the Carpaccio cadence of Proust's first paragraph establishes the maternal prototype, the paragraph that follows describes an attempt to be free of its determining force. The painting to which the narrator now turns is known by a variety of names in addition to the one that he provides, including *Miracolo della reliquia della Croce* and *The Healing of the Madman* (Plate 3). One can understand readily enough why the author of *A la recherche du temps perdu* should have found this panel singularly absorbing. For here, among numerous shared motifs, are: madness; madness miraculously cured; madness and its cure both placed upon the margins of a populous and variegated social world. Here too are the populace in its variety, and, caught up within that variety, a number of exclusive societies – those of the priesthood, monastic orders, trade guilds and that elegant coterie of young noblemen-about-town known as the *compagnia della Calza*. The miracle-working patriarch himself may well remind us of the curative paternal power so singularly absent from the novel. But despite the wealth of associations between painting and novel, Carpaccio's work is incorporated smoothly into Proust's narrative structure. The relationship between this paragraph and the preceding one, and between this painting and the Ursula cycle that it follows in Proust's narrative is, at its simplest, one of chiasmus: the multifarious Venetian world of the first paragraph comes to rest upon a figure from Carpaccio, and Carpaccio then offers, in the second paragraph, a return route to Venice in its multifariousness; two accounts of mobile desire pivot upon an image of desire fixated. Within the ever-changing topography to which this second painting returns the narrator's attention, a sexual metamorphosis, of man into woman, again occupies a central position. Fortuny, like so many brilliant couturiers, is a plagiarist. He has plundered Carpaccio for his designs, and in removing a cape from fashionable fifteenth-century Venetian men has made it available to fashionable modern Parisian women. Contemplating these sumptuously attired men, the narrator is brought back, in a sudden moment of pained recognition, to Albertine and to those features of her that had been most threatening and most alluring: her seeming duplicity and the indeterminacy of her sexual appetites. This male figure in female-seeming garb in the painting is wearing the cape of one who was 'toujours prête à tout'.[44]

This momentary reawakening of desire for Albertine is announced at the start of the paragraph and explained at some length in the second half. But throughout this remarkable page, an unstoppable transformational machinery is in operation. There are no identities, only trajectories; no original, only derived forms. Carpaccio's work reproduces that of nameless contemporary costume-makers and is itself reproduced in the work of later artists: in Whistler, José-Maria Sert and Fortuny. Carpaccio's paintings become stage designs in the hands of Sert (whom Diaghilev brought together with Richard Strauss as composer and Harry Kessler as choreographer for the *ballets russes* production of the *Legend of Joseph*) and dress designs in the hands of Fortuny – who was a migrant from Spain to Venice to Paris.[45] Thanks to Carpaccio's record of Venice, clothing from across the centuries is reborn as clothing, and paint as paint. Features of San Marco as described in the preceding paragraph are transported to the neighbourhood of the Rialto: material that decorative artists had 'ajourée et rehaussée d'or' in the baptistery is now echoed in the 'cheminées incrustées' of Carpaccio's skyline, just as the 'surfaces évasées et roses' of the arcades are rediscovered in the 'forme évasée et le rouge épanouissement de tulipes' of these same chimneys, the full description of which in *Le Côté de Guermantes* (II, 572) is about to be repeated verbatim (III, 650).[46]

Above all Proust is interested in the many alternative trajectories for the eye that Carpaccio has inserted into his painting. (One has only to see the work in the Accademia in the company of contemporary works also celebrating Venetian scenes and ceremonies – by Gentile Bellini, Mansueti and Bastiani – to become aware of how complex Carpaccio's handling of depth and multiple perspective is.) The narrator traces in some detail one of the routes taken by his eye within the painting: from the chimneys, to the old Rialto, to the palaces on the canal-side, to the water traffic, and back along the teeming canal-bank. The portrait of Venice that emerges as he describes this receding avenue of human types and

3 Carpaccio, *The Healing of the Madman*; Venice, Accademia

trades is of course familiar from generations of earlier writers and artists: Venice as the point of intersection between otherwise remote societies, manners and artistic styles had been celebrated before Carpaccio and by Proust's time had become an essential commonplace of the guide-books and of belletrist travel impressions such as Gautier's *Italia* (1852) and Taine's *Voyage en Italie* (1866).[47] Proust not only re-orchestrates the familiar theme, but distorts the painting in his retelling to improve upon Carpaccio's presentation of this inveterately heterogeneous city. In the painting only one black appears – in the fluent form of the moorish gondolier who occupies the centre foreground. Proust has taken this figure, removed him from the foreground, placed him firmly in the dimension of depth and given him someone else's barrel to carry: 'le nègre portant son tonneau'.[48] Let the rich seam of humankind that plunges into the painting be one of ethnic as well as professional diversity, he seems to be saying: let the eye on its journey into Venetian space move from Europe to Africa to the Levant, and from Christianity to Islam. In Venice such journeys are a chief delight.

This point is repeated a hundred or so pages later in the novel, at the start of *Le Temps retrouvé*, in Proust's last reference to Carpaccio. During the war the presence of allied troops from the outposts of Empire has made Paris resemble Carpaccio's Venice:

> . . . c'était le défilé le plus disparate des uniformes des troupes alliées; et parmi elles, des Africains en jupe-culotte rouge, des Hindous enturbannés de blanc suffisaient pour que de ce Paris où je me promenais je fisse toute une imaginaire cité exotique, dans un Orient à la fois minutieusement exact en ce qui concernait les costumes et la couleur des visages, arbitrairement chimérique en ce qui concernait le décor, comme de la ville où il vivait Carpaccio fit une Jérusalem ou une Constantinople en y assemblant une foule dont la merveilleuse bigarrure n'était pas plus colorée que celle-ci.[49] (III, 763)

The minimal index of cultural diversity is here the same as it had been in Proust's fictional recreation of *The Healing of the Madman*: a cosmopolitan scene must possess at least one person from Africa and several from the East. The black and Muslims are replaced by Africans and Hindus. Whereas in the Carpaccio painting the black wore red on the top half of his body, his counterparts now wear it on the bottom half; white turbans, which had formerly been Islamic emblems, are now emblems of Hinduism. In this final appeal to Carpaccio, then, Proust is re-transforming his earlier revised version of the painting. Carpaccio, under whose patronage the narrator's sexual identities and aims are diversified, is himself transformed by Proust's all-consuming text.[50]

Freud is well known as the tragedian of libidinal fixation. But he also wrote eloquently about that quality of libido – 'plasticity' or 'free mobility' – that made its sublimation and socialisation possible:

> . . . we must bear in mind that the sexual instinctual impulses in particular are extraordinarily *plastic*, if I may so express it. One of them can take the place of another, one of them can take over another's intensity; if the satisfaction of one of them is frustrated by reality, the satisfaction of another can afford complete compensation. They are related to one another like a network of intercommunicating channels filled with a liquid . . . Further, the component instincts of sexuality, as well as the sexual current which is compounded from them, exhibit a large capacity for changing their object, for taking another in its place – and one, therefore, that is more easily attainable.
>
> (*Introductory Lectures* (1916–17), XVI, 345)[51]

Venice – was there ever a more glorious 'network of intercommunicating channels filled with a liquid'? – provides Proust with a model not only of desire in perpetual displacement but of the sublimating and desublimating exchanges that occur between the sexual and the cultural realms. Architecture and painting divert and absorb the narrator's sexual impulses, but precariously. At any moment the gothic trefoil may drive him back upon his Oedipal longing, or a Carpaccio panel reawaken his passion for Albertine. The 'free' mobility of his desire as it plays upon the works of culture constantly stumbles into unfreedom.

In 'Analysis Terminable and Interminable' (1937) Freud drew a brief combined picture of the 'fixated' and 'mobile' libidinal types (XXIII, 241–2). What Proust has done in this passage from *La Fugitive* – and in numerous other sections of the novel – is draw an extended picture of the same kind, but making both types internal to his narrator and enacting each of these desiring styles within the movement of his own text. The narrator, who is capable elsewhere of irate or complacent or defensive statements of sexual preference, achieves by way of works of art, and in the texture of his own discourse, a condition of extreme libidinal mobility. Differences of sexual orientation become, within the texture of Proust's writing, handleable, shimmering *stuff*, a variegated fabric like the costumes of the *compagnia della Calza*. Writing offers a precious escape from a punitive sexual typology.

Yet desire plainly does not run unhindered from one delight to the next, in writing or anywhere else. The interconnected channels of Venice, like those explored by the writer when engaged upon the higher tourism that is textual production, are haunted by emblems of immobilised desire, and the journey that promises displacement and diversification without end may abruptly return the traveller to his point of departure. Proust writes with great scruple and precision about the almost-freedom of desire, and about the helplessness induced by the discovery that the severest limitations placed upon that freedom are internal to the mind, unwilled and indissoluble. At the centre of the Venetian chiasmus, the narrator's mother stands (or sits, or kneels) as an intractable stone guest, calling him back from his erotic adventures and re-infantilising his once-defiant adult emotion. And the mother's power runs across the chiasmus too: her gesture of solicitude ('ma mère . . . me jetait un châle sur les épaules') is repeated by Albertine as a gesture of *sauve-qui-peut* self-interest ('elle avait jeté sur ses épaules un manteau de Fortuny'), and by Fortuny as one of insolent acquisitiveness ('c'est des épaules de ce *compagnon de la Calza* qu'il l'avait détaché pour le jeter sur celles de tant de Parisiennes').[52] Even as the mother's action is travestied and desecrated its prototypical status is reinforced. Quite apart from the internal constraints of forgetfulness and distorted remembrance that organise these paragraphs, the 'merveilleuse bigarrure'[53] of the Carpaccio episode in its entirety and of its brief reprise in *Le Temps retrouvé* is hemmed in by the spectacle of other people's sexuality, which may add little to the variegation of the world and a great deal to the individual's sense of forlornness in his own desires. The 'sentiment trouble . . . de désir et de mélancolie'[54] that a detail of Carpaccio's painting precipitates is to reappear and achieve elegiac intensity in the remaining pages of *La Fugitive*, which are concerned with the narrator's discovery of Saint-Loup's homosexuality.[55] And the reappearance of Carpaccio's Venice acts as a prelude to further sexual researches and to scenes of sado-masochistic excitement and abjection that the narrator observes from a distance, through a peephole. The narrator is formed by others in his capacity to desire, yet perpetually discovers that the desires of others are not, or not yet, his.

IV

The two sample areas in which I have chosen to compare Freud and Proust clearly have much in common. For the student of 'failed performances' who perceives desire errant in discourse is confronting, case by case, segments of the psycho-libidinal motor that propels all performances. That motor may be hypothetically reconstructed from these punctual emergences of the unconscious into the behavioural domain, but may also be modelled by scanning behaviour over time and by sounding its subterranean contours. The momentary *Fehlleistungen* of sexual creatures will have no semantic power and will not be interpretable until they have been exposed to a theory – or inserted into a story – about human sexuality at large. Yet 'sexuality at large' will be a vapid and unwieldy topic of concern for theorist or novelist unless individual events are called upon to exert a continual particularising pressure upon it. Proust and Freud are memorably alike in their capacity to adopt both these approaches – now concurrently, now consecutively – to their overflowing dossiers of observational material, and to sustain relentless dialogue between the freedom and the fixation of desire. For both of them observation confirms unerringly that desire errs. Yet what would their books have been like if they had had no other message? What enchanted verbal confections would we now possess, what extravaganzas of omnivorous appetite and polymorphous passion? The books they in fact wrote are permeated by the knowledge that desire – agile, Protean, acquisitive and experimental as it may be – has in each local instance its inescapable prehistory, its determining pattern of choices already made and its moorings within a sensate organism. Pleasure-seeking *errance* may have been inaugurated long ago by simple *erreur*, and may still bear its traumatic mark. For Proust's narrator, mapping ontogenesis on to phylogenesis as boldly as Freud ever did, the peculiar anxieties of the homosexual disposition may be traced back to an 'erreur initiale de la société' (II, 622),[56] an unfortunate fall from the 'hermaphroditisme initial' (II, 629) of the species.[57] Homosexual desire is founded upon one memory of prelapsarian bliss, heterosexual desire upon another. But both are products of limitation and constraint. Bisexuality remembers the protozoic Eden more completely, and rediscovers its many pleasures more readily, but is preyed upon, as all sexual dispositions are, by that other prehistory – of training and coercion, seduction and counter-seduction – which is the life of the human infant within the family. For both writers the narrative about desire that sets the pre- and postlapsarian states against each other may be duplicated, enlarged or miniaturised at will: it may be told of the species or the individual, of organisms or minds, of legendary monsters or modern nurslings. There was once a paradise in which multiform desires were unfailingly satiated (in the primal oceans, at the mother's breast) and there is now (among unisexual mammals, in the social group) a fallen world of severance, dissatisfaction, envy and pursuit. The two phases of that narrative are connected by an unhappy power of remembrance that visits upon the individual a knowledge of what has been lost.

Most of my discussion has been taken up with fairly obvious similarities between Freud and Proust and I shall end with another. But before ending, I shall speak briefly of a dissimilarity that cannot not be mentioned if a comparative portrait along the lines sketched here is to make sense. Proust and Freud, while remarkably similar in their models of human desire and in their postulation of an unconscious upon which the coherence of those models depends, are dissimilar in their accounts of the main access routes to the unconscious and of the benefits that having access to it may be expected to provide. Where Proust's narrator, in *Le Temps retrouvé*, speaks of joy and ecstasy, Freud speaks of work. Intense moments of contact with the unconscious are, for Proust, a gratuitous grace – spontaneous, uncovenanted, ungoverned by rule; they are the culmination of an unplanned individual journey into the psychical underworld; they are the introspective's best reward, the last leap into apperceptive knowledge of a mind accustomed to solitary exertion. For Freud such moments occur by way of the indirections and mediations of interpersonal dialogue and may be attested by the subject's resistance to their onset, or by the pain they cause; although they too cannot be planned for, the working conditions and conventions in which they are pursued must be rigorously controlled; they may bring further pain, further work and further dialogue in their wake. Even here, points of comparison exist. The narrator, returning to the social world at the end of his introspective trances in *Le Temps retrouvé*, in some respects resembles an analysand emerging from a particularly fruitful analytic session: he is less anguished, less censorious, more versatile in his sympathies and more self-accepting. And Freud would surely not have dissented from Proust's valedictory maxim 'tous les altruismes féconds de la nature se développent selon un mode égoïste' (III, 1036), nor failed to perceive its applications to psychoanalysis. Yet the gulf between Freud and the Proust of *Le Temps retrouvé* is still very wide on the matter of how liberating and enabling discoveries about the mind can best be made. I spoke, at the start, of the tension in *A la recherche du temps perdu* between a narrator who psychologised, who 'did' psychology of a kind that the tradition of the *moralistes* had made familiar, and a narrator who was the instrument of an alternative psychology, resembling psychoanalysis, that the Proustian text itself enacted in its discontinuities, contradictions and reversals. Proust chose at the end of the novel to give one of these narrators a special reward. He provided his psychologising narrator, that is to say, with the apotheosis that his extraordinary introspective gifts most deserved, and so removed him from the anxious interlocutory world in which vast tracts of the preceding narrative had been situated. Freud chose not only to inhabit that world but to create within it a new style of clinical practice and a new scientific profession.

My last resemblance is largely a matter of ambition and scale. The persistence, the limitless emotional investment, the fecundating egotism with which Proust and Freud both pursued their early insights, together with their indefinite capacity to re-organise, re-energise and re-dialecticise their representations of mental process, make them heroes of the speculative mind, upholders of an exacting code of theoretical prowess. Even as they discuss the limitations under which the creative writer labours, their desire-laden writing presses beyond them. Even as they trace the boundaries beyond which their texts have nothing to say, their assimilative and expressive powers are calling those boundaries into dispute. And both of them expend huge energies in the recapitulation, correction and reinforcement of their own ideas – on sexuality as on everything else – as if the supreme test of an existing theory were its capacity to generate alternative versions of itself.

4
Lacan

He does not have a stable existence at all, but he hurries in a perpe [illegible] *g . . .*
Kie[illegible]*ither/Or*

'THE THOROUGH UNDERSTANDING of Aristotle is the highest achievement to which man can attain, with the sole exception of the understanding of the prophets.'[1] Maimonides's words will be offensive, in the docile admiration they seem to display, to many modern ears. For a lingering Romantic conception of genius may still lead us to expect of an original thinker that his ideas will spring in fully formed splendour from within himself, or from nature, or from nowhere. Where lesser minds may find proper employment in reading and elaborating texts from the past, the true innovator is expected to do everything for himself. Guided by an assumption of this kind, we may be embarrassed by thinkers who present themselves proudly as the readers and explainers of existing intellectual monuments, although evidence is plentiful to suggest that thinking done in the light and shadow of an admired predecessor may be thinking of great originality and strength. Plotinus reads Plato; Maimonides reads Aristotle; Averroës reads both; the young Marx reads Hegel. Assessing originality in such cases involves more work than we are perhaps accustomed to: the achievement of each later thinker may be well understood only if we are prepared to return to the works of the earlier and trace in detail the transformations and creative distortions that they have undergone. Yet an investigation of this kind may be exhilarating: it may alert us not only to those ways of being original that our modern pieties overlook but to the large part that *re*thinking and *re*writing play even in the works of those who acknowledge no forbears and present themselves as exceptions to all rules but their own.

Lacan reads Freud. This is the simplest and most important thing about him. But where his fifty-year exploration of Freud's works differs from the celebrated readings that I have already mentioned is in the apparent purity of his motives. Where others have sought either to confront one body of ideas with another (Aristotle meets Islamic philosophy in the works of Averroës and rabbinic Judaism in those of Maimonides) or to elaborate one strain of the original corpus in preference to others (Plotinus dwells upon the metaphysical and would-be mystical Plato), Lacan presents his main task as that of reading Freud well and getting him right.

The 'return to Freud' that he proclaims as his personal mission and slogan follows two distinct paths. The first and more straightforward operation is that of disinterring Freud's ideas from the litter of banalising glosses and explanations that later writers have heaped upon them. And in the strenuous polemical activity that this involves Lacan's main target is the international psychoanalytic movement itself; those for whom Freudian notions have mere commodity value – the sub-academic paperback-writer or the radical-chic conversationalist, for instance – are undeserving even of an incidental jibe. Most later psychoanalysts have done worse than misunderstand Freud: they have lost all sense of the weight, the perplexingness and the innovative power of Freud's ideas as they were first formulated by him. Those ideas have been all too superficially learnt and repeated, and adhered to with such credulity and self-delusion that they form a barrier rather than an inducement to the scientific investigation of mental process. The procedures of initiation into psychoanalysis by which Freud sought to guarantee the continuity of his teaching often produce a disabling side-effect: 'Mais n'ont-elles pas mené à un formalisme décevant qui décourage l'initiative en pénalisant le risque, et qui fait du règne de l'opinion des doctes le principe d'une prudence docile où l'authenticité de la recherche s'émousse avant de se tarir?'[2] (239). In Lacan's writings psychoanalysis is repeatedly made to turn back upon itself and to re-examine its concepts, rituals and institutions from the vantage-point offered by its own discoveries in their original unsystematised state.

The second and more complex operation involves Lacan in a greater risk than that of making enemies among his professional associates. For he sets out to correct certain parts of the Freudian corpus by reference to others. The discovery that Lacan places at the centre of Freud's achievement, and uses as his own essential conceptual tool in this correcting of Freud from within, is that of the unconscious – the unconscious that appears as an independent system, opposed to the 'preconscious–conscious' system,[3] in the second of Freud's major models of the psychical apparatus. (In the first, the posthumously published 'Project for a Scientific Psychology' of 1895 (I, 283–397), the concept makes only the sketchiest of appearances; in the third – the triad comprising id, ego and superego introduced in 1923 (*The Ego and the Id*, XIX, 3–66) – it has a new and complex role: the main characteristics of the unconscious reappear in descriptions of the id, but the ego and the superego are also held to have unconscious portions.) This version of the unconscious dominates Freud's thinking in the great creative phase that extends from *The Interpretation of Dreams* (1900) to the metapsychological papers of 1915. It is at once a topographical and a dynamic concept and, in the papers on 'Repression' and 'The Unconscious' (XIV, 143–58, 161–215), is placed at the centre of Freud's most complex theoretical accounts of mental functioning.

For Lacan, as for many writers, Freud's essential insight was not – clearly not – that the unconscious exists, but that it has structure, that this structure affects in innumerable ways what humans say and do, and that in thus betraying itself it becomes accessible to analysis. The unconscious as presented in *The Interpretation of Dreams*, *The Psychopathology of Everyday Life* (1901) and *Jokes and their Relation to the Unconscious* (1905) is endlessly voluble and self-revealing: in our dreams, forgettings, misrememberings, slips of tongue or pen, jokes, symptoms, verbal and physical mannerisms, it insists on being heard. The psychical energy by which repression takes place, and is maintained, is met and challenged by another energy which seeks, largely by means of dissimulation and subterfuge, to propel the repressed contents of the unconscious into the preconscious–conscious domain. The unending dialectic that this conflict produces exercises a special fascination upon Lacan, and his use of figurative language is never more forcible and involuted than when he depicts the unconscious speaking in the face of repression and censorship. In the following passage, for example, he extends and alters Plato's allegory of the cave:[4]

> La place en question, c'est l'entrée de la caverne au regard de quoi on sait que Platon nous guide vers la sortie, tandis qu'on imagine y voir entrer le psychanalyste. Mais les choses sont moins faciles, parce que c'est une entrée où l'on n'arrive jamais qu'au moment où l'on ferme (cette place ne sera jamais touristique), et que le seul moyen pour qu'elle s'entr'ouvre, c'est d'appeler de l'intérieur.[5] (838)

Whenever we arrive at the cave of the unconscious, it is always closing time; the only way that we have of gaining access is to be inside already. The structure of the unconscious is knowable only by those who are prepared to admit and espouse its inexhaustible capacity for displacement.[6]

Lacan, in his many attempts to re-teach psychoanalysis the provocativeness of its own insights, points to the insistent power of repression as it is exercised both within the analytic process and within the abstract working out of analytic theory. The discovery of the unconscious is itself subject to repression: the unconscious which, according to the very definitions on which psychoanalysis is founded, is the realm of insatiable instinctual energy and knows no stability, or containment, or closure, is immobilised and domesticated by its professional observers. This extraordinary agent of dispersal and scandal becomes an ordinary counter within an ordinary conceptual game.

But the stultification of the unconscious message by post-Freudian analysts has its counterpart within Freud's own works. For Freud's discovery was a terrifying one, and his vision of the mind as self-divided and of the uncontrollably proliferating and self-enmeshing quality of its unconscious portion drove him to seek consolation in the cushioned world of mythical and metaphysical speculation. But although Freud lapsed from his own discovery in ways that his discovery should have allowed him to foresee, his intellectual adventure is exemplary in the very dangers to which he succumbed: Lacan presents him as a new Actaeon turned upon and savaged by his own thoughts for having unveiled the goddess of the unconscious (412, 436).[7] Lacan's self-appointed task is to keep on thinking the intolerable Freudian thought, even at the price of dismemberment, and to allow repressed doctrine to make its disruptive return to psychoanalysis as it is performed and thought. Already we can begin to see how paradoxical Lacan's 'return to Freud' is, and how much disobedience this view of true loyalty might entail.

In Lacan's rethinking of Freud's texts 'from within', the temptations of complete assent and complete dissent are refused with equal consistency. The beginnings of this tension are evident in Lacan's first major publication, *De la psychose paranoïaque dans ses rapports avec la personnalité* (1932). Lacan came to psychoanalysis by way of medicine and psychiatry, and this work, which was his doctoral dissertation, marks a crucial point of transition in his intellectual biography. While observing all the scholarly niceties that the format traditionally requires, he mounts an energetic attack on several dominant modes of psychiatric explanation. The study of paranoia has been impeded by the power that established psychiatry possesses to sanctify feeble or scantily tested hypotheses and turn them into dogma. Those who explain paranoia by reference to its supposed organic basis, or to the inherited disposition or 'constitutional type' of the patient, are resorting to an endlessly re-applicable interpretative trick that allows them to avoid acknowledging the complexity of individual human subjects.

Psychoanalysis offers Lacan a finely tuned mechanism for redirecting attention upon the paranoiac as *person*. Paranoia, no less than the neuroses around which psychoanalytic theory had originally been developed, may be coherently described and analysed by reference to the personality of the sufferer, his sexuality, childhood experiences, emotional development, family relationships, intellectual capacities and wishes for himself. Once this material has been collected and organised, no further point is served by inserting the patient into a pre-existing clinical typology or 'characterology'. Under the inspiration of psychoanalysis, Lacan is able to envisage a science of personality in which the subject retains his past, his intentions and his creative intelligence. But even while drawing this lesson and acclaiming 'l'immense génie du maître de la psychanalyse' (*De la psychose paranoïaque*, 324),[8] Lacan stresses the limits of his debt and draws attention to confusions within Freud's theory. Moreover, and again characteristically, he draws on the work of other thinkers, including Spinoza, William James, Bergson and Russell, in order to keep his own theoretical model permeable by other systems of thought. In the fierce argumentation of *De la psychose paranoïaque* and in its array of fluid and mutually correcting concepts, an astonishing intellectual style has been created.

When Lacan read a paper introducing his notion of the 'mirror phase' to the International Psychoanalytical Congress held at Marienbad in 1936 – and in so doing made his formal entry into the movement – he began to explore a mode of verbal production-in-performance that remained peculiarly his. The bulk of his theoretical work after that date took the form of conference papers and reports delivered to professional bodies; these were improvised from notes, reworked from transcript for publication, and often edited and annotated on subsequent appearances. A copious selection of these papers appeared as *Écrits* in 1966. They bear the marks both of that 'free association' which psychoanalysis enjoins upon the patient as he speaks and of that 'evenly suspended attention' with which the analyst is expected to listen to the patient's words;[9] this means that even Lacan's main ideas and cherished controversial positions are presented to the reader in a consciously ragged and desultory form. The edited transcripts of the weekly seminars that Lacan conducted in Paris over two decades, and that are now in process of publication, take us even further into his speculative workshop.[10] Certain sections of the *Séminaire* serve to clarify the main ideas of *Écrits*, others elaborately rework them, and others still are the record of a surging glossolalia in the face of which critical intelligence falls indignantly or admiringly silent. Lacan's prose aspires perpetually to the condition of speech. And his aims in writing like this are clear: to allow the energies of the unconscious to become palpable in the wayward rhythm of his sentences, to discourage the reader from building premature theoretical constructions upon the text and to compel him to collaborate fully in the inventive work of language.

This characteristic of Lacan's writing makes his contributions to the technical vocabulary of psychoanalysis particularly difficult to summarise. For the terms and concepts with which he has extended and remodelled Freud's are simply not available to us in a stable and circumscribed form. They define each other as they perform analytic work and undergo severe changes of implication as their intellectual context alters. Lacan is a builder of loosely moored conceptual mobiles, faced with which the question 'What does this mean?' is better asked of a given term in the form 'What does it do?' or 'What paths does it travel?' Moreover, all Lacan's concepts, whatever main or subordinate part they play within his psychical models (or 'topologies' as he often calls them), serve too as polemical weapons: no account of them is complete without saying something about the ways in which they are adaptable to the changing needs of argument within his inveterately factional profession.

Consider, for example, the concept of the 'mirror phase' to which I have already referred. This phase occurs in the human individual between the ages of six months and eighteen months. It is a period at which, despite his imperfect control over his own bodily activities, he ('le petit homme') is first able to imagine himself as a coherent and self-governing entity. Such an image is concretely available to him when he sees his own reflection in a mirror:

> L'assomption jubilatoire de son image spéculaire par l'être encore plongé dans l'impuissance motrice et la dépendance du nourrissage qu'est le petit homme à ce stade *infans*, nous paraîtra dès lors manifester en une situation exemplaire la matrice symbolique où le *je* se précipite en une forme primordiale, avant qu'il ne s'objective dans la dialectique de l'identification à l'autre et que le langage ne lui restitue dans l'universel sa fonction de sujet.[11] (94)

This moment of self-identification is crucial, however, not because it represents a stage on the way towards 'adulthood' or 'genital maturity' – such developmental models of the changing human subject come under constant attack from Lacan – but because it represents a permanent tendency of the individual: the tendency that leads him throughout life to seek and foster the imaginary wholeness of an 'ideal ego'. The unity invented at these moments, and the ego that is the product of successive inventions, are both spurious; they are attempts to find ways round certain inescapable factors of lack, absence and incompleteness in human living. Even from my few lines of quotation and summary it will be plain that Lacan's concept of the mirror phase reaches far beyond the confines of child psychology for its fullest validation. Towards the end of the passage a theory of language and a theory of interpersonal perception are taking shape; another order of experience is emerging over and against the order of imaginary identifications which the 'specular' moment inaugurates; and one of Lacan's favourite objections to psychoanalysis as traditionally practised may already be glimpsed: if the ego is no more than an imaginary precipitate, how absurd it is for the proponents of 'ego psychology' to appoint themselves to the task of developing and stabilising that ghostly presence.

In a sense all complex conceptual systems work like this, with each component helping to define and activate the others. But where these systems are customarily divided by their authors into separately tractable sub-units, it is for Lacan a matter of intellectual scruple that no such division should take place. Every concept acts as a nodal point within a network of choices and refusals, and is presented to the reader in a language where the practical business of choosing and refusing remains palpable as a syntactic turmoil. I shall now turn to that central series of insights and conjectures about the structure of the unconscious upon which Lacan's entire theory of psychical process is founded. For his characteristic and much-publicised modes of thinking, talking and writing make their fullest sense, and offer themselves to responsible judgement, only when considered in the context of this theory.

In Freud's central account of the unconscious a series of topographical, dynamic and economic models[12] are fused. His discovery was not of the sort that could be declared and developed in a single, ready-made theoretical language. When, after many years of analytic practice and speculation, he came in his paper 'The Unconscious' (1915) to list the characteristics of the unconscious as a system, he was still using a technical vocabulary to which biology, mechanics, logic and language study had each made a distinctive contribution. The unconscious, he claimed, has at its core a set of instinctual impulses that are able to coexist without mutual influence or contradiction; it knows no negation, no doubt, no degrees of certainty; it is the realm of the primary process, in which psychical energy is freely transmissible between ideas by means of displacement and condensation;[13] it is timeless; it is concerned not with external reality but with the achievement of pleasure and the corresponding avoidance of unpleasure (XIV, 186–9).

A main intuition of Lacan's was that Freud's account of the unconscious and its relations with the preconscious–conscious system could be reorganised around a relatively small number of linguistic concepts, and thereby be made at once more cogent and more elastic. The cue for this innovation was provided by Freud himself, in whose works 'facts of language' are given extraordinary prominence. In analysing the verbal narratives that provided the central fund of evidence for his case-histories and his books on dreams, slips and jokes, he shows much skill and delicacy as a textual critic. The developing functions of human language are a theme particularly dear to him. And the linguistic sciences are often called upon to provide analogies and corroborative evidence in his psychological writings. That Freud himself had not drawn to any appreciable extent upon linguistics proper is, for Lacan, a matter of historical chance (446–7, 799): the foundations of that discipline were being laid by Saussure and others at the same time as Freud's theory was being constructed, and he could not have been expected to have detailed knowledge of, or draw useful inferences from, a neighbouring science *in statu nascendi*.

The lessons that the accident of birth made Freud unable, and Lacan able, to learn are principally those concerning the synchronic analysis of complex signifying systems. Comparative philology, which was still monarch of the linguistic sciences during Freud's formative years, not only had little to teach about such analysis but was sometimes, for the psychologist, a positive encouragement to error. Reviewing in 1910 Karl Abel's conjectural and now largely discredited pamphlet on *The Antithetical Meaning of Primal Words* (1884), for example, Freud drew a parallel between the dreaming mind, which knows no contradiction, and a primitive state of human language postulated by Abel in which certain words had had opposite meanings at once (XI, 155–61). (Old English *bat* ('good') and *badde* ('bad') are assumed to derive from a common ancestor meaning 'good–bad'.) Freud later used Abel's work as his sole support for the view that 'the equivalence of contraries in dreams is a universal archaic trait in human thinking' ('A Short Account of Psycho-Analysis' (1924), XIX, 206). He had, that is to say, based a characteristic wishful phantasy about 'the origin of things' upon a piece of fairytale philology.[14]

Linguistics, on the other hand, inhibits this kind of speculation and suggests a more productive mode of comparison between language and mind. In so far as it studies the minimal differential units that constitute language, and the ways in which those units may be embraced and interrelated within comprehensive systems, it provides a series of testable models for the psychical apparatus. Where philology took Freud into a whimsical no-man's-land, linguistics, as manipulated by Lacan, could return psychoanalysis to the tasks Freud was best at: the working out and the coherent articulation of psychical structure.

'L'inconscient est structuré comme un langage.'[15] This best-known of Lacan's pronouncements makes plain the importance of his debt to linguistics; and, having the form of a mere simile, it serves as a reminder of the problems that the recourse to linguistic concepts raises for psychoanalysis. The first questions that we are likely to ask of Lacan's formula are: how exact and how useful are analogies of this kind? Does the first term take logical priority over the second? Would the same thing, or a different but equally interesting thing, or a lesser thing, be said if the order of the terms were reversed? Lacan's work in this area is a sequence of two-way mappings – of the unconscious upon language and of language upon the unconscious – performed in such sustained defiance of his reader's wish for firm landmarks that these first questions are never definitively answered. Indeed the whole tendency of his thinking on this fundamental issue is to call the logic of such questions into question.

The relationship between language and the unconscious may be looked at broadly in two ways. First, it is clearly possible that intrapsychical tensions and conflicts could have played their part in determining the structure of human language in the first place: the idea that language was created in the partial image of an already existing unconscious offers at the very least an appealing poetic explanation for that sense of a 'natural' interlocking between the two systems which students of the unconscious report. Secondly, language is the sole medium of psychoanalysis: for the patient as he speaks his dreams and his phantasies, and for the analyst as he punctuates the patient's discourse and places constructions upon it, the unconscious is available only in a linguistically mediated form. There is no point in speculating about a possible 'pure', pre-linguistic state of the unconscious, nor in seeking to describe the ways in which the observational instrument of language may imprint its own structures upon the unconscious materials observed. For language is the medium of these secondary investigations too, and having 'tricked' us once with its refractions and diffractions will trick us again.

Lacan has little patience with the first approach, and is inclined to put matters the other way round: language creates the unconscious. And he sees linguistic mediation as extending far beyond the analytic dialogue. He points out that the human subject, as he acquires speech, is inserting himself into a pre-existing symbolic order and thereby submitting his desire to the systemic pressures of that order: in adopting language he allows his 'free' instinctual energies to be operated upon and organised (445). It is the peculiar privilege of man the language-user to remain oblivious, while making things with words, of the extent to which words have made, and continue to make, him.

Lacan's comparison of language and the unconscious as entire systems, and his account of their many possible reciprocities, are supported by detailed work on the elementary structural components of each. He draws in particular upon Saussure's binomial definition of the linguistic sign – signifier and signified in arbitrary association – and on the metaphoric and metonymic poles of verbal organisation proposed by Roman Jakobson.[16] (I shall discuss both these sets of terms in a moment.) These concepts are useful for a number of reasons: because they correspond neatly to certain antithetical pairs of concepts within Freud's thinking; because they are readily combinable and permutable within the pseudo-algebraic representations of mental process that Lacan came increasingly to favour; and because a severe limitation is placed on the larger act of comparison. The limitation is simply this: that there is very little in Freud's presentation of the unconscious that corresponds to the sentence, or to syntactic structure in general.[17] Indeed much of the surprising originality that Freud ascribes to the unconscious stems from its refusal of allegiance to exactly those modes of hierarchical organisation that syntax promotes. The system of a given language as articulated in its grammar could therefore have only a small role in psychoanalytic accounts of mental functioning. Rather than use an ill-adapted set of grammatical categories, Lacan chose to base his models on certain underlying binary structures with a high capacity for recombination.

This application to psychoanalysis of Saussure's teachings received its first full expression in the papers 'Fonction et champ de la parole et du langage en psychanalyse' (237–322) and 'L'instance de la lettre dans l'inconscient ou la raison depuis Freud' (493–528), delivered in 1953 and 1957 respectively.[18] But Lacan does not import a stable linguistic theory into psychoanalysis with a view to bringing a still unruly body of doctrine to order: the encounter between Freud and Saussure will allow each to become re-thinkable in the light of the other.

For Saussure the sign represented a sudden collision and bonding between two distinct realms, each of which was in itself fluid and undifferentiated: thought on the one hand and acoustic images on the other. But once bonding has taken place between a segment of the thought-realm (a signified) and a segment of the sound-realm (a signifier) their relationship is intimate to the point of complete interdependence:

> La langue est encore comparable à une feuille de papier: la pensée est le recto et le son le verso; on ne peut découper le recto sans découper en même temps le verso; de même dans la langue, on ne saurait isoler ni le son de la pensée, ni la pensée du son; on n'y arriverait que par une abstraction dont le résultat serait de faire de la psychologie pure ou de la phonologie pure.[19]

What Lacan questions, even as he borrows the Saussurian terminology, is the state of symmetry and equilibrium between signifier and signified that is described in passages such as this. He uses the formulation $\frac{S}{s}$ (signifier over signified) not only as a minimal summary of Saussure's theory, but as a way of highlighting a stubborn problem within it: the exact status and role of the signified. To this latter end, Lacan treats the algorithm $\frac{S}{s}$, which seems at first glance no more than an operational procedure within a calculus of his own devising, as a concrete poem and a personal emblem. For the bar separating the two symbols is itself more than a symbol: it is the pictorial enactment of a necessary and irremoveable cleavage between them. Similarly, the placing *beneath* of the signified is more than a matter of mathematical convention and convenience. For the signified does indeed, in Lacan's account, 'slip beneath' the signifier and successfully resist our attempts to locate and delimit it. The supremacy of the signifier (capital letter, roman type, upper position) over the signified (small letter, italic type, lower position) is made visible before us. The burden of Lacan's argument is that the quest for the signified in its 'pure' form – the quest, that is to say, for the pristine, word-free structures of thought – is frivolous; language has a constitutive role in human thinking; 'pure psychology' of the kind invoked by Saussure does not exist. The proper object of attention, for the psychoanalyst no less than for the linguist, is the signifying chain itself: the relationships observable within that chain are the surest guide to psychical structure and to the structure of the human subject.

Once the kernel of Saussure's thought has been dramatised in this way, Lacan is able to use it as a means both of organising and of destabilising psychoanalytic theory. At first sight his undertaking looks dangerously restrictive. For the distinction between signifier and signified, in so far as it opposes the manifest to the latent, is adaptable in the extreme and may be assimilated in turn to a variety of distinctions that Freud himself had presented and manipulated separately: those, for example, between the conscious and the unconscious, between dream-images and 'latent dream thoughts', between neurotic symptoms and repressed wishes. But in collapsing these pairs of antithetical categories into an all-purpose two-term code Lacan is not being lazy and is not illicitly schematising Freud's thought. The procedures for structural analysis that he follows as he examines the procession of variously connected signifiers are those that Freud had formulated in his accounts of the dream-work. In this passage from *Jokes and their Relation to the Unconscious*, for example, summarising the notion of displacement, Freud gives a clear portrait of the signifier at play:

> The dream-work . . . exaggerates this method of indirect expression beyond all bounds. Under the pressure of the censorship, any sort of connection is good enough to serve as a substitute by allusion, and displacement is allowed from any element to any other. Replacement of internal associations (similarity, causal connection, etc.) by what are known as external ones (simultaneity in time, contiguity in space, similarity of sound) is quite specially striking and characteristic of the dream-work. (VIII, 172)

On countless occasions in his presentation of case-material, Freud appears as the delighted observer of an unconscious that fulfils its wishes by an ingenious manipulation of extraneous and unwished-for materials. The difference of emphasis between Freud and Lacan is this: Freud, while acknowledging the power of his 'external associations', sees them as making their fullest sense only when measured against the 'internal associations' that they disguise or replace; dream-images require the conjectural 'latent dream thoughts' in order to become legible; the signified, even as it slips from view, invites pursuit. For Lacan this interpretative oscillation between signifier and signified can easily divert attention from the former and into a fluid region of wish-fulfilment phantasy; the relations between signifiers are a neglected resource and provide more than a sufficiency of information for the analyst.

Lacan's stress on the signifier and his winnowing of the structural from the hermeneutic components of Freud's theory entail a further excursion into the linguistic domain. His debt on this second occasion is to Jakobson, in whose two poles of verbal organisation he saw the clue to two underlying and irreducible modes of connection within the signifying chain. For Jakobson the two poles, metaphoric and metonymic, coexist competitively within any symbolic process, and he himself drew attention to a possible overlap between his own categories and those used by Freud in characterising the unconscious. Freud's 'displacement' and 'condensation' were both based on the principle of contiguity, the one being metonymic and the other synecdochic;[20] his 'identification' and 'symbolism' were based on similarity, and are hence metaphoric.[21] Lacan pays no attention to this suggestion of Jakobson's, and puts forward a simpler and more elegant pair of equivalences: condensation (*Verdichtung*) corresponds to metaphor, and displacement (*Verschiebung*) to metonymy (511). These are Freud's crucial categories; his identification and symbolism are easily converted into one or other of them.

But Lacan is not content to leave matters here, with each linguistic term brought into alignment with one mode of unconscious mental functioning. Jakobson's terms no less than Saussure's have a further test to pass: if they are to become what they describe, become signifiers in their own right, then they must show themselves to be multiple, overdetermined,[22] and permanently available for new uses. To this end, which is that of a continual new beginning, an additional pair of crosswise relationships is created (517–18): the psychical mechanism by which neurotic symptoms are produced involves the pairing of two signifiers – unconscious sexual trauma and changes within, or actions by, the body – and is thus metaphorical; whereas unconscious desire, indestructible and insatiable as it is, involves a constant displacement of energy from object to object and is thus metonymic. (An arrest of the metonymic function produces not a symptom but a fetish.)

The result of this double reshuffling of Jakobson's polarity is that the terms 'metaphor' and 'metonymy' not only introduce clear and useful subdivisions within the notion of signifier, but play an enigmatic signifying game of their own. The process is familiar throughout Lacan's work. His theoretical metalanguage becomes, in its constant effort of adaptation to the unconscious, language pure and simple – which means language heterogeneous and complex: 'il n'y a pas de métalangage . . . nul langage ne saurait dire le vrai sur le vrai, puisque la vérité se fonde de ce qu'elle parle, et qu'elle n'a pas d'autre moyen pour ce faire' (867–8).[23]

I suggested earlier that the very form in which the proposition 'l'inconscient est structuré comme un langage' is cast draws attention to its own possible limitations as a theoretical principle. But the ways in which Lacan manages to avoid these limitations should by now be clear. For questions of logical or chronological priority between the unconscious and language begin to dissolve as soon as a 'symbolic order' embracing both is envisaged. Precisely by confining himself to the *fundamentals* of language as described by Saussure and Jakobson, rather than exploring the higher, syntactic modes of organisation, Lacan keeps in contact with the elementary differential components of all symbolic systems. The unconscious, in so far as it becomes visible and audible in speech, symptoms, dreams and involuntary acts of omission or commission, is governed by the same rules as all other systems: the rules that Lacan has expressed in summary form as the 'logic of the Signifier'. So confident is he that he has made contact here with something fundamental and universal, that he draws attention to an element of redundancy in his own phrase 'structured as a language': '"structured" and "as a language" for me mean exactly the same thing';[24] '*Il n'est structure que de langage*' (*Télévision*, 18).[25] It is at points like this that the Lacanian unconscious seems furthest removed from the Freudian predecessor which ostensibly motivates it. Freud not only distinguished between *Wortvorstellungen* ('word-presentations') and *Sachvorstellungen* ('thing-presentations') but designated the unconscious as the specialised field of action for thing-presentations severed from their word-counterparts ('The Unconscious' (1915), XIV, 201–2; *GW*, X, 300).[26] Lacan not only gives priority to *word*-presentations in his definitions of the unconscious, but on occasion presents his own definitions as having dispossessed and supplanted Freud's: 'The unconscious is not Freud's; it is Lacan's'.[27]

The special role – variously called priority, primacy, precedence, pre-eminence, insistence, supremacy – assigned by Lacan to the signifier in the psychical life is accompanied by another major redefinition of terms and another unremitting polemical campaign. I refer to the terms *sujet* ('subject') and *moi* ('ego'). Whereas the ego, first glimpsed at the mirror stage, is the reified product of successive imaginary identifications and is cherished as the stable or would-be stable seat of personal 'identity', the subject is no *thing* at all and can be grasped only as a set of tensions, or mutations, or dialectical upheavals within a continuous, intentional, future-directed process. The ego as a tension-point within Freud's id–ego–superego topography is respected by Lacan as a necessary component of a properly dialectical model of the human subject. But the ego envisaged as an end in itself, as a threatened residence of selfhood needing continually to be refortified against hostile incursions from the id and the superego, is treated with scorn: this stabilised and tranquillised ego plays dumbly into the hands of the 'soul-managers' and the social engineers. Lacan's accounts of the psychical apparatus at work have at their centre the notion not of ego but of subject. The subject does not 'disappear' in Lacan's hands, as a once fashionable phrase had it, but has its manifold trajectories plotted and re-plotted by him.

The basis for the mobility of the subject is supplied by the signifying chain itself. For the signifier not only constitutes and governs the subject – Lacan speaks of 'la suprématie du signifiant dans le sujet' (20) and of 'la prééminence du signifiant sur le sujet' (39) – but positively requires the subject as its mediating term: 'un signifiant, c'est ce qui représente le sujet pour un autre signifiant' (819).[28] Far from being a by-product or an epiphenomenon of the signifier, the subject has a relationship of interdependence with it, and to such an extent that whatever may be claimed for the one must needs be claimed, with appropriate modification or 'skewing', for the other. Both are characterised by their power of indefinite structural displacement, and that power necessarily takes priority over all innate or acquired psychological characteristics:

le déplacement du signifiant détermine les sujets dans leurs actes, dans leur destin, dans leurs refus, dans leurs aveuglements, dans leur succès et dans leur sort, nonobstant leurs dons innés et leur acquis social, sans égard pour le caractère ou le sexe, et . . . bon gré mal gré suivra le train du signifiant comme armes et bagages, tout ce qui est du donné psychologique.[29] (30)

The traditional language of psychology has an inveterate tendency to describe the mind as if it were a stable collection of things, or forces, or faculties, and Lacan's presentation of the subject-in-process may at first seem impossibly flimsy and weightless to those whose expectations of coherence in psychical model-building have been conditioned by that language. What is remarkable is that his view of the subject as 'merely' empty, mobile and without a centre should emerge, in its passage from one analytic task to the next, and through a language in which all expectations of short-term coherence are insistently dismantled, as at once cogent and precise.

Lacan calls the domain of the signifier, in which this perpetual restructuring of the subject takes place, the Symbolic order. And this order is the dominant one in the triad Symbolic–Imaginary–Real that has acquired a creative role in Lacan's thought comparable to that of id–ego–superego in the later thought of Freud. (Although Lacan's three orders and Freud's three agencies are called upon to do the same sorts of analytic work, it would be impossible to establish a strict term-for-term equivalence between them.) Each of Lacan's orders is better thought of as a shifting gravitational centre for his arguments than as a stable concept; at any moment each may be implicated in the redefinition of the others. I have already suggested something of the contrast between the Symbolic and the Imaginary in my remarks on the subject and the ego. Where the one is characterised by difference, disjunction and displacement the other is a seeking for identity or resemblance. The Imaginary grows from the infant's experience of his 'specular ego' but extends far into the adult individual's experience of others and of the external world: wherever a false identification is to be found – within the subject, or between one subject and another, or between subject and thing – there the Imaginary holds sway. Although the two orders are distinct and opposed, the Symbolic encroaches upon the Imaginary, organises it, and gives it direction; the false fixities of the Imaginary are exposed, and coerced into movement, by the signifying chain.

The Real is the most puzzling of the three, and is given much less attention that the others in *Écrits*; Lacan's *Séminaire* contains the fullest and most challenging accounts of it. Two apparently divergent general tendencies may be discerned in Lacan's presentation of this notion. First, the Real is that which is there, already there, and inaccessible to the subject, whether this be a physical object or a sexual trauma; when we appear on the scene as subjects certain games have already been played, certain dice thrown. Things *are*: '*Le réel est ce qui revient toujours à la même place*' (XI, 43).[30] But to become aware of this is not to be compelled to silent acquiescence: 'Ne sentez-vous pas qu'il y a quelque chose de dérisoire et de risible dans le fait que déjà les dés sont jetés?' (II, 256).[31] The way beyond this 'laughable' Real is the uniquely human way offered by the Symbolic order: thanks to that order the dice may be thrown again. Secondly, however, the Real is the primordial chaos upon which language operates: 'C'est le monde des mots qui crée le monde des choses, d'abord confondues dans l'*hic et nunc* du tout en devenir' (276);[32] the Real is given its structure by the human power to name. Neither of these conceptions is particularly original; the language of common sense plays a prominent role in the presentation of each; and their divergence is only apparent. They place a common stress upon the limits of the linguistic power: the Real is that which is radically extrinsic to the procession of signifiers. The Real may be structured – 'created' even – by the subject for himself, but it cannot be named (II, 252). It is the irremediable and intractable 'outside' of language; the indefinitely receding goal towards which the signifying chain tends; the vanishing point of the Symbolic and Imaginary alike. As a result of this view, the Real comes close to meaning 'the ineffable' or 'the impossible' in Lacan's thought. As a term within the triad it has less work to do than the others. But it serves admirably both to reintroduce problems and asymmetries into what could easily have become a facile dualism between the Symbolic and the Imaginary, and to remind Lacan's would-be omnipotent subject that his symbolic and imaginary constructions take place in a world which exceeds him.

Lacan's account of the subject as 'decentred' and dialectical is itself reworked in numerous ways and systematically protected from the danger of promoting or seeming to promote an array of fixed, readily re-applicable concepts. Although there is no fool-proof way for Lacan or anyone else to prevent conscientiously scattered doctrine from becoming centralised doctrine, or the resistance to cant from engendering cant of its own, his precautions have in general worked well. For the near-synonyms that he uses in depicting the discontinuous itineraries of the subject (*refente*, *division*, *Spaltung*, *fading*, and so forth) are kept in motion by a dominant polysemic term: *l'Autre* ('the Other'). More consistently than any other of Lacan's terms, 'the Other' refuses to yield a single sense; in each of its incarnations it is that which introduces 'lack' and 'gap' into the operations of the subject and which, in doing so, incapacitates the subject for selfhood, or inwardness, or apperception, or plenitude, or mutuality; it guarantees the indestructibility of desire by keeping the goals of desire in perpetual flight.

For Lacan as for Freud the primal Other is the father within the Oedipal triangle – who forbids incest, threatens castration, and, by placing an absolute prohibition upon the child's desire for its mother, becomes the inaugurating agent of Law. Lacan is concerned not with the real or imaginary fathers of a given individual but with the symbolic father whose name initiates and propels the signifying chain: 'C'est dans le *nom du père* qu'il nous faut reconnaître le support de la fonction symbolique qui, depuis l'orée des temps historiques, identifie sa personne à la figure de la loi' (278).[33] The original encounter with the legislating *nom-du-père*, and the abiding lack and non-satisfaction to which the subject is thereby condemned, produce the complex pattern of alternating or intermingled aggression and subservience that is to mark the subject indelibly in his dealings with others. (Lacan makes frequent use of Hegel's dialectic of master and slave as an indefinitely reconstruable model for this process.)[34] These dealings, whether in the form of the everyday encounter between people or in that of the dialogue between patient and analyst, are a main concern of Lacan's, and he discusses with extraordinary acuity their determining role in the constitution of the subject.

The subject is made and remade in his encounter with the Other:

> Ce que je cherche dans la parole, c'est la réponse de l'autre. Ce qui me constitue comme sujet, c'est ma question. Pour me faire reconnaître de l'autre, je ne profère ce qui fut qu'en vue de ce qui sera. Pour le trouver, je l'appelle d'un nom qu'il doit assumer ou refuser pour me répondre.[35] (299)

> . . . c'est de l'Autre que le sujet reçoit même le message qu'il émet.[36] (807)

L'Autre est donc le lieu où se constitue le je qui parle avec celui qui entend, ce que l'un dit étant déjà la réponse et l'autre décidant à l'entendre si l'un a ou non parlé.[37] (431)

The relationship between Subject and Other is characterised by desire:

le désir de l'homme trouve son sens dans le désir de l'autre, non pas tant parce que l'autre détient les clefs de l'objet désiré, que parce que son premier objet est d'être reconnu par l'autre.[38] (268)

C'est en effet très simplement . . . comme désir de l'Autre que le désir de l'homme trouve forme.[39] (813)

le désir de l'homme est le désir de l'Autre, où le de donne la détermination dite par les grammairiens subjective, à savoir que c'est en tant qu'Autre qu'il désire (ce qui donne la véritable portée de la passion humaine).[40] (814)

Much deliberate alteration of meaning is visible within and between remarks such as these: the Other is, for example, now one term in the dialectical couple Subject–Other, now the entire locus or condition of 'otherness' (*altérité*, *hétéronomie*) that embraces both terms. And the picture is further complicated when the same term is used to bind the intrapersonal and interpersonal worlds together.

Freud's essential discovery, Lacan tells us, was that man bears otherness within him. The schism between the unconscious and the preconscious–conscious systems brings man face to face with his own 'excentricité radicale de soi à lui-même' (524).[41] When viewed from the vantage point of the preconscious–conscious, the unconscious – the signifying chain through which all desire passes – is another place and another language: 'L'inconscient, c'est le discours de l'Autre' (379).[42] The message that is passed across the gap between the subject and the external Other passes inwardly too, for the supra-individual, social world is installed by language within the individual mind: 'L'inconscient est ce discours de l'Autre où le sujet reçoit, sous la forme inversée qui convient à la promesse, son propre message oublié' (439).[43] In Lacan's later thinking two further 'other' concepts are introduced – the *petit autre* and the *objet a*, which is sometimes referred to simply as the '*a*'. Although both concepts serve to accommodate within Lacan's theoretical model the mobility of desire and the indefinite multiplicity of its objects, they are discontinuous in one major respect. Whereas the *petit autre* has an intermediary role between the ego and the other and therefore belongs to the imaginary realm of specular identifications ('l'autre qui n'est pas un autre du tout, puisqu'il est essentiellement couplé avec le moi', II, 370),[44] the *objet a* is the object of desire permeated and mobilised by lack: it is the *je ne sais quoi* by reference to which desire is revealed in displacement, in incompleteness and 'unspecularisable': 'L'objet *a* n'est aucun être. L'objet *a*, c'est ce que suppose de vide une demande . . .' (XX, 114).[45] In Lacan's numerous overlapping descriptions of it, the *objet a* is the object of desire on its way to becoming the cause and the condition of desire as well.

The reader of Lacan may find himself wondering about the credentials of a term that ranges so promiscuously between arguments: what is this 'Other' that it should be ennobled by a capital letter and so freely convertible? How can the term remain useful as an operational device when it may be variously defined as a father, a place, a point, any dialectical partner, a horizon within the subject, a horizon beyond the subject, the unconscious, language, the signifier? Could it be that the capital letter is employed to give an untidy *omnium gatherum* a false aura of authority? The charge of intellectual irresponsibility that questions such as these seem about to make against Lacan is to a large extent forestalled if his thought is considered whole, and as a comprehensive system of mutually implying parts.[46] For the *nom-du-père*, the original Other, introduces a gap between desire and its object(s) which the subject is bounded by, and bound to, throughout his life and at all levels of his experience. This primordial estrangement is by its very nature destined to recur, and be converted, ubiquitously; it is the origin of language and the subject alike, and provides an essential precondition for the humanity of man. And just as this first otherness travels freely between all human places and occasions, so the term 'Other' migrates and is converted within Lacan's prose. Lacan would claim no responsibility for the polysemy of his term; nothing could require him to be personally answerable for a fact of life . . .

It will be clear from everything I have said so far that Lacan has given language a role of unprecedented importance within the field of psychoanalytic enquiry. Freud, in his pamphlet on *The Question of Lay Analysis* (1926), insisted that a future 'college of psycho-analysis' would not only teach diciplines already familiar in medical faculties but 'would include branches of knowledge which are remote from medicine and which the doctor does not come across in his practice: the history of civilization, mythology, the psychology of religion and the science of literature. Unless he is well at home in these subjects, an analyst can make nothing of a large amount of his material' (xx, 246). Lacan's additions to this list include not only linguistics, but 'la rhétorique, la dialectique au sens technique que prend ce terme dans les *Topiques* d'Aristote, la grammaire, et, pointe suprême de l'esthétique du langage: la poétique, qui inclurait la technique, laissée dans l'ombre, du mot d'esprit' (288).[47] The analyst who brings these branches of learning to bear upon his work is not departing from tradition but returning to the fertile sources of psychoanalytic thinking. For Freud and his early followers had an exemplary knowledge of, and responsiveness to, literature and the linguistic sciences.

Lacan's debt to linguistics has already been discussed. But three further debts in this area deserve to be mentioned: to rhetoric and stylistics, to critical exegesis, and to the practice of literary production at large. For the imprint that these activities have left on Lacan's work makes it peculiarly and problematically available to adventurers from the world of letters, and gives us a series of major clues in any attempt to understand the extraordinary catalytic role that his thought has developed within the 'human sciences' in contemporary France.

In his references to the figures and tropes of classical rhetoric, Lacan adheres to a mode of speculative comparison much favoured by Freud. In 'The Claims of Psycho-Analysis to Scientific Interest' (1913), for example, Freud, having at some length discussed dreams as being 'like a language', moves on to another abundant and particularised analogy:

> If we reflect that the means of representation in dreams are principally visual images and not words, we shall see that it is even more appropriate to compare dreams with a system of writing than with a language. In fact the interpretation of dreams is completely analogous to the decipherment of an ancient pictographic script such as Egyptian hieroglyphs. In both cases there are certain elements which are not intended to be interpreted (or read, as the case may be) but are only designed to serve as 'determinatives', that is to establish the meaning of some other element. The ambiguity of various elements of dreams finds a parallel in these ancient systems of writing; and so too does the omission of various relations, which have in both cases to be supplied from the context. If this conception of the method of representation in dreams has not yet been followed up, this, as will be readily understood, must be ascribed to the fact that psycho-analysts are entirely ignorant of the attitude and knowledge with which a philologist would approach such a problem as that presented by dreams.
> (XIII, 177)

The relationship between dreams and hieroglyphic script for Freud is analogous to that between the mechanisms of the unconscious and rhetoric for Lacan:

La périphrase, l'hyperbate, l'ellipse, la suspension, l'anticipation, la rétractation, la dénégation, la digression, l'ironie, ce sont les figures de style (*figurae sententiarum* de Quintilien), comme la catachrèse, la litote, l'antonomase, l'hypotypose sont les tropes, dont les termes s'imposent à la plume comme les plus propres à étiqueter ces mécanismes. Peut-on n'y voir qu'une simple manière de dire, quand ce sont les figures mêmes qui sont en acte dans la rhétorique du discours effectivement prononcé par l'analysé?[48] (521)

The luxuriance of these comparisons – so much in excess of the local needs of either writer's argument – suggests that an undeclared fascination is at work in each case. One might conjecture that for Freud and Lacan alike the fascinating thing is not that comparisons of this kind are instructive but that terms apparently so remote from each other should be comparable at all. Hieroglyphics and rhetoric both represent the triumph of calculation and civilised artifice over the brute materials of experience. How strange, therefore, that the unconscious, so easily thought of as brutish and anarchic, should reveal itself to have a perfectly 'civilised' cunning in the ways it manipulates its structures. Beyond this strangeness, a new science of the unconscious is coming into view.

As we have seen, Lacan gives two rhetorical terms – metaphor and metonymy – special duties and privileges in his writing. But although many other terms are proclaimed in lists like the one I have just quoted, they are much more important for the lesson they teach corporately than for any individual uses they might have as analytic tools.[49] The analyst who knows about rhetoric is more likely than a colleague who does not to remain alert both to those inflections of normal usage which comprise the 'style' and the singularity of an individual patient's discourse and to the specific characters of the unconscious discourse that the spoken word allows the analyst to reconstruct. The enduring appeal that comparisons like these hold for both Freud and Lacan stems from their combined universalising and particularising capacities: they serve to enforce a general truth about the unconscious – that it has, or, in Lacan's view, *is* structure – but at the same time allow the informed observer to focus sharply on the manner in which nameable individuals suffer.

Lacan's skill and resourcefulness as an exegete are visible

throughout his writing. His command of the Freudian corpus and his ability to argue on many levels, and on different sides of the question, at once are such that a great deal of exposition and commentary takes place between the lines: possible new senses for Freud's texts emerge in rapid succession as we read, and important reservations about certain of Freud's ideas, whether in their original or derived forms, may be glimpsed behind a sudden turmoil of parentheses, asides or qualifying phrases. (Lacan presupposed a detailed knowledge of Freud in the colleagues or pupils who were his original hearers; the general reader of *Écrits* who is not so equipped will need unusual powers of imagination, or of self-deception, in order to make headway – or to suppose that he is doing so.) Nevertheless there are several occasions in *Écrits* and the *Séminaire* when texts are read and reread with minute explicitness. Of these texts two prove to be especially revealing: a sentence by Freud and a short story by Edgar Allan Poe.

In the final sentences of the third of his *New Introductory Lectures*, Freud speaks of the continuing work of analysis: 'Where id was, there ego shall be. It is a work of culture – not unlike the draining of the Zuider Zee' (XXII, 80). The penultimate sentence, which is 'Wo Es war, soll Ich werden' in the original (*GW*, XV, 86), is given in the standard French translation as 'Le Moi doit déloger le Ça.'[50] Lacan is vehement against this French version because it excludes levels of sense present in the original. Freud's is a gnomic utterance worthy of the Presocratics (585, 801, XI, 45). Lacan points out that Freud, contrary to his usual practice, does not use the forms 'das Es' and 'das Ich', and that by these omissions of the definite article two psychical agencies have become two universal principles; that the sentence is a moral imperative; that its two nouns are not flatly opposed (417); and that it contains an astonishing paradox: '[celui] d'un impératif qui me presse d'assumer ma propre causalité' (865).[51] An entire range of paraphrases and 'improved' translations is provided:

Là où fut ça, il me faut advenir. (524)

là où c'était, là comme sujet dois-je advenir. (864)

Là où c'était, peut-on dire, là où s'était, voudrions-nous faire qu'on entendît, c'est mon devoir que je vienne à être. (417–18)

Ici, dans le champ du rêve, tu es chez toi. (XI, 45)

Ainsi se ferme la voie imaginaire, par où je dois dans l'analyse advenir, là où *s*'était l'inconscient.[52] (816)

Lacan contends in each of these reformulations that the realm of unconscious energy, far from requiring ever firmer custodianship and control from the ego, has unsuspected bounty to offer: it is the proper site for the subject, a repository of truth. The 'I' should take up residence there not as a coercive occupying force but as one who willingly casts aside falsehood and returns home; the prodigal 'I' becomes *subject* to the precise extent that it travels back to the unconscious and adopts its plural structures.

If considered solely in the context of Freud's lecture, Lacan's reading of the sentence would seem improbable: the ego's need for mastery over the id is one of Freud's themes in earlier pages, and the erring French translator has given us the gist of a remark which aptly recapitulates that theme. Yet there is no reason why the remark should simply confirm what has gone before: elsewhere Freud had shown himself surprised and saddened by what he took to be a gratuitous urge to repression within the ego, and had sought ways of persuading it, in therapeutic practice, to relax its damagingly tight grip upon the id. It is quite possible that he was allowing the parting moral assertion of his lecture to echo these doubts.[53] But what Lacan has done to the sentence, for all his talk of gnomic resonance, is to remove its ambiguity by a route opposite to the one taken by the French translator. Despite changes of emphasis and implication from one of his versions to the next, he has replied to a possible range of senses with another, mutually confirming, range of his own. Freud's 'Presocratic' hesitation between alternative destinies for the psychical life has turned to imperturbable advocacy in Lacan's hands: one of those destinies is unfailingly better.

Where Freud's 'Wo Es war, soll Ich werden' comes and goes as a modulated refrain throughout Lacan's later work, Poe's 'The Purloined Letter' achieves its prominence more directly: Lacan's extended discussion of the tale is placed at the start of *Écrits* as a ramifying fable of the analytic process and of the constitutive function of the signifier. In Poe's story an incriminating letter addressed to an 'illustrious personage' (a queen, we are to assume) is stolen by a machinating minister in the presence of the royal couple. The Queen sees everything, and the King nothing. The Queen remains silent as the robbery takes place: to protest would be to incriminate herself. The Prefect of Police is given the task of recovering the letter and, having failed, consults the detective Dupin. The police are well-meaning plodders and the detective is all-seeingly astute. Whereas the police search the minister's apartment inch by inch and find nothing, Dupin, who knows his man and reasons that the safest form of concealment would be to leave the letter in full view of the visitor, finds the letter and steals it back. The contents of the letter are never revealed.

Part of the appeal that the story holds for Lacan will be apparent even from this simplistic summary. The purloined letter is a pure migratory signifier. As it passes from hand to hand, and moves from point to point within a complex web of intersubjective perceptions (Poe speaks of the 'robber's knowledge of the loser's knowledge of the robber'), it attracts different meanings to itself, mediates different kinds of power relationship and determines subjects in what they do and are:

> Notre apologue est fait pour montrer que c'est la lettre et son détour qui régit leurs entrées et leurs rôles. Qu'elle soit en souffrance, c'est eux qui vont en pâtir. A passer sous son ombre, ils deviennent son reflet. A tomber en possession de la lettre, – admirable ambiguïté du langage, – c'est son sens qui les possède.[54]
>
> (30)

Lacan's 'Le séminaire sur "La Lettre volée"' and its many associated documents (9–61), together with the earlier version published in *Séminaire* II (211–44), comprise an exegetical performance of rare subtlety. But is not Lacan's interpretation essentially an allegorical one? After all, the mobile signifier, the *lettre volée* which is also a *feuille volante* ('fly sheet'), has been elicited by close reading and has become an immobile signified in the process: the mobility of the signifier is what Poe's story 'means', what it 'is about'.[55] And is it not odd that allegory, which is metalanguage *in excelsis*, should be written, and held to be illuminating, by one who holds metalanguage to be impossible? Odd, yes; and inconsistent, and disappointing in the same way that Lacan's determined urging of sense upon Freud's 'Wo Es war . . .' is disappointing. But only if one confines one's attention to the broad, programmatic unfolding of Lacan's argument. If one looks at the fine structure of his writing, and the insistent play of ambiguity that permeates it, it becomes plain that even the basic psychoanalytic paradigms, and the habit of psychoanalytic explanation itself, may be called into question from within.

Lacan's practical debt to literature and the self-consciously 'writerly' status of his writing are apparent even to the casual reader. His admirers and his critics often give this writing, and especially the conspicuous presence within it of word-play, paradox and counter-logical thinking, a prominent place in their arguments for and against the general validity of his work. Although an emphasis of this kind is in many ways misleading, and has led to serious misrepresentations of Lacan's achievement, there is no difficulty in seeing how 'mere' questions of style have gained their unwonted importance within a theory of mind. For literature not only owns up more readily than other forms of language to its unconscious origins, but rejoices in the superabundance of sense to which it has access and in doing so offers the psychoanalyst a working model of the unconscious considered as an unstoppable and self-pluralising signifying chain.[56] Poetry in particular is exemplary in this role:

> Mais il suffit d'écouter la poésie . . . pour que s'y fasse entendre une polyphonie et que tout discours s'avère s'aligner sur les plusieurs portées d'une partition.
>
> Nulle chaîne signifiante en effet qui ne soutienne comme appendu à la ponctuation de chacune de ses unités tout ce qui s'articule de contextes attestés, à la verticale, si l'on peut dire, de ce point.[57] (503)

Lacan's theory seems to necessitate a certain kind of literary performance. If the unconscious is 'like poetry' in its over-determined and polyphonic structures, then the writer who chooses to treat the unconscious, and wishes to obey its laws in his writing, must needs become more 'like a poet' the closer he gets to the quick of his subject. The overlapping and knotting together of signifiers within the written chain will show the reader what the unconscious is – and by enacting rather than describing it. Lacan here provides us with yet another pair of interdependent definitions. Poetry and the unconscious are mutually supporting: if you want to understand *a*, first understand *b*; if you want to understand *b*, first understand *a*. Yet on this occasion the entire conceptual construction is not free-floating but firmly planted in Lacan's glamorous and conceited prose: this is the place where theories take on corporeal form and where Lacan's twin definitions prove themselves as *writing*.

Lacan's prose is an elaborate mechanism for multiplying and highlighting the connections between signifiers. Word-play abounds, and is given a great deal of intellectual work to do. Here are some examples with a brief comment on certain implications of each: 'la *politique de l'autruiche*' (15): a policy or a politics which belongs at once to the ostrich (*autruche*), to others (*autrui*), and to Austria (*Autriche*, the birthplace of psychoanalysis); '*faufilosophe*' (233): a false (*faux*) philosopher (*philosophe*) who worms his way in (*se faufile*); '*lettre-l'être-l'autre*' (523): the letter implies being implies the other; '*dansité*' (807): density which dances, 'insideness'; 'A casser l'œuf se fait l'Homme, mais aussi *l'Hommelette*' (845): Man comes from the breaking of an egg, but so does the little man, the feminised man and the scrambled man; 'La loi en effet commanderait-elle: *Jouis*, que le sujet ne pourrait y répondre que par un *J'ouïs*' (821): when ordered to enjoyment, or to orgasm, the subject cannot but answer 'I hear'; '*poubellication*' (xx, 29): to publish something is as good as throwing it in the dustbin (*poubelle*); '*âmour*' (xx, 73): soul-love (*âme-amour*). By these means language may be turned upon itself. Just as Joyce in *Finnegans Wake* creates 'tautaulogically' and in so doing makes the word 'tautologically' become what it describes, so Lacan, by writing '*la langue*' as '*lalangue*' (*Télévision*, 21, 72; xx, 126), inserts several facts of language into the name language bears: it is repetitious; it is an affair of the tongue (*langue* – our tongues beat our palates as we say it); it has a musical tendency (*la* is a note in the tonic sol-fa); it has a capacity to shock or surprise ('Oh là là!') (cf. Gk, *λαλαγέω*, 'to prattle, to babble'). Wherever words collide and fuse in this way an atmosphere of play prevails. But an insistent doctrinal point may be heard in the background on each occasion: if the signifier plays and the signified 'slips beneath', then the unconscious is speaking in its native tongue.

Lacan speaks with approval of Humpty-Dumpty as 'le maître du signifiant' (293)'[58] and in his handling of portmanteau words proves himself a worthy heir of Carroll's aggressive talking egg. But he also speaks with approval of his own reputation as the 'Góngora' of psychoanalysis (467), and this second self-image – as the originator of a convoluted poetic style – is quite as revealing as the first. For Lacan has imagined a new, centrifugal French syntax, as well as a new semantics. He savours the ambiguity of prepositions, for example, and plays relentlessly upon the alternative meanings of *à* and *de*. Earlier we saw him admiring the phrase *en possession de* for meaning at once 'possessed by' and 'possessing'.[59] A similar double meaning occurs in a sentence such as: 'le signifiant est unité d'être unique, n'étant de par sa nature symbole que d'une absence' (24).[60] The signifier is the symbol *of* an absence, and becomes a symbol *by means of* an absence. While in a preposition-laden passage like the following a rapid shimmer of alternative relationships will blur the vision of any reader seeking for a single main sense:

La liberté de l'homme s'inscrit toute dans le triangle constituant de la renonciation qu'il impose au désir de l'autre par la menace de la mort pour la jouissance des fruits de son servage, – du sacrifice consenti de sa vie pour les raisons qui donnent à la vie humaine sa mesure, – et du renoncement suicide du vaincu frustrant de sa victoire le maître qu'il abandonne à son inhumaine solitude.[61] (320)

Each of these prepositions is a knot within the signifying chain; they are the moments of switch-over from one possible relationship to another – moments at which condensation and displacement become palpable textual events. A complete account[62] of the characteristic features, syntactic and other, of Lacan's style would include: the ambiguous *que*, disturbances of conventional word order, literal and metaphorical senses interwoven, periphrasis, ellipsis, leading notions alluded to rather than declared, abstractions personified, persons becoming abstractions, widely different words becoming synonyms, synonyms being given widely different meanings . . . All this keeps the signified as a palely fluttering presence behind the rampaging signifier.

It is plain that a writer who uses these devices so frequently and in such close conjunction is not merely running the risk of writing nonsense but envisaging nonsense as a positive literary goal. For Lacan irony and contradiction are inherent in language, and psychology, in so far as it studies discourse, is 'le domaine de l'insensé' (167).[63] When Lacan's 'truth' – the truth of the unconscious – is personified and allowed to talk in its own voice, as in the lecture 'La Chose freudienne', it makes this point:

Je vagabonde dans ce que vous tenez pour être le moins vrai par essence: dans le rêve, dans le défi au sens de la pointe la plus gongorique et le *nonsense* du calembour le plus grotesque, dans le hasard, et non pas dans sa loi, mais dans sa contingence, et je ne procède jamais plus sûrement à changer la face du monde qu'à lui donner le profil du nez de Cléopâtre.[64] (410)

Lacan was decisively influenced by Surrealism in the late 1920s and early 1930s: he had members of the group among his friends; he contributed articles on paranoia to the review *Minotaure*; he was impressed by the Surrealists' experiments in automatic writing and confirmed by Crevel, Éluard and Joë Bousquet in his view that the writings of 'Aimée', the patient whose case-history formed the basis for his doctoral research on paranoia, showed remarkable poetic power (168). *Écrits* contains countless references and allusions to the movement. There is little doubt that the newcomer to Lacan who already has some experience of Surrealist writing will hear many familiar notes being sounded in his work; and such a reader will be well equipped to understand how it is that nonsense may be thought of as a plenitude rather than an absence of sense and given a special role in exploring and proclaiming the truths of the unconscious.

But the young Lacan learned many lessons other than those of the Surrealists, and in later years wooed the unconscious with wiles and artifices far subtler than theirs. 'Nonsense' appears in the Lacan text now as a heady atmosphere of meanings promised but not given, now as an outrageous intruder into the world of rational argument or oratorical persuasion: the 'Cleopatra's nose' episode at the end of the passage that I have just quoted is clearly of this second kind. But in both cases nonsense is an agent of intellectual provocation rather than a static display of psychical structure or a route towards the Surrealist *merveilleux*. It is a reminder to his own discourse that its responsibility is 'dire toujours Autre-chose' (837).[65] For in Lacan's view the person who speaks and is satisfied with what he says is not simply misguided: he is wrong. Every statement that does not provoke change and strangeness within itself is wrong. Truth that seeks to remove itself from the contradictory process of language becomes falsehood there and then.

How puzzling it is, on first reading this self-proclaiming Freudian loyalist, to find that his works apparently resemble those of the master in no single particular of style, presentation or methodological convention. Where Freud is respected, even by those who reject his ideas or would wish to qualify them severely, as being patient and clear-headed in his expositions, able to give due weight to views other than his own in putting his arguments together, and scrupulous in specifying those areas of thought to which his theory is at present or permanently incapable of contributing, Lacan is irascible, peremptory, scornful of contrary opinions, by turns rhapsodic and assertive in his prose style, and plainly unconvinced that his theory anywhere has limits.[66] Lacan does things in a way so different from Freud's that his enterprise can easily be seen, at first encounter, as an act of publicity-seeking sabotage directed at the very foundations of psychoanalysis. His difference from Freud, and especially the high buffoonery that marks much of his writing, is dwelt on with glee in the many hostile responses to which his thought gives rise. Most published responses of this kind are trivial and written by self-righteous bystanders who have tried and failed, or simply failed, to read what

Lacan writes. But his detractors are not all of this order and charges of, say, obscurantism made against him by intelligent and responsible authors cannot be ignored.

Sebastiano Timpanaro, for example, whose *The Freudian Slip* (1974) is a brilliant critique of *The Psychopathology of Everyday Life* conducted from the combined viewpoints of Marxism and textual criticism, writes in that work:

> I must confess that I am incurably committed to the view that in Lacan's writings charlatanry and exhibitionism largely prevail over any ideas of a comprehensible, even if debatable, nature: behind the smoke-screen, it seems to me, there is nothing of substance; and it is difficult to think of a pioneer in the encounter between psychoanalysis and linguistics who has more frequently demonstrated such an erroneous and confused knowledge of the latter, whether structural or not.[67]

Timpanaro's remarks betray a limited knowledge of Lacan and premature judgment. But the fact that such remarks are possible from one who in other matters knows much and judges well will clearly make us ask whether they might represent the polemical surface of a substantial case against Lacan. It is possible, after all, that critics of Timpanaro's kind, having informed themselves fully, would wish to leave the thrust of their judgment undiminished.

Let me mention some of the simplest and least specialised factors that an informed critique of Lacan might concentrate on. Lacan has taken extreme precautions to prevent his work from being made banal and comfortable in the wake of Freud's, and this striving to impede the facile retransmission of his ideas often appears as a calculated effort to be unreadable.[68] Just as you can gain access to the cave of the unconscious only by being inside already, he seems to be saying, so you can gradually reach towards an understanding of my work only by understanding it in advance. Lacan offers us a new conception both of science and of truth, and, within the science of intersubjective speech that he proclaims psychoanalysis to be, asks us to abandon many of the procedures for verification or falsification on which the credibility of scientific enquiry traditionally rests. Truth-to-the-unconscious is the only truth worth the name. The desiring unconscious, and language which is its structure, are plural, layered, involuted, uncodifiable and unstoppable; arguments directed towards a terminus are falsehoods. But the paradox in all this is precisely that *all* language is the metonymic displacement of desire; there is no metalanguage, as Lacan repeatedly insists, no Other for the Other, no truth about truth (813). Why then is a sumptuously polyvalent language to be preferred to the one-thing-at-a-time languages of logic, or conceptual analysis, or empirical description, or traditional psychoanalytic theory? Is it simply that such a language, having more goals for desire visibly on the move within it, may be thought to maintain a closer, more robust contact with the matrix of desire? But that matrix is everywhere and inescapable. We saw Lacan himself pointing to a version of the same paradox in his discussion of 'Wo Es war, soll Ich werden': by what right, and with what moral goal in view, can one urge man to become what he necessarily and unfailingly is? Why set in motion such an elaborate machinery of persuasion when there is strictly no one to persuade? As we read Lacan, we can feel his arguments being traversed by weighty and unargued personal predilections – in this case an exalted predilection akin to the one that led the Engels of *Anti-Dühring* to see true freedom as residing in the recognition of necessity.

A related set of questions is raised by Lacan's expository manner. His theory disallows any distinction between descriptive and prescriptive writing, or between the practical analysis of cases and the working out of relevant theoretical perspectives. He relies greatly on the convincingness of certain recurrent maxims enshrining crucial points of doctrine. These gnomic formulae are often launched, repeated and modulated without supporting argument. They may be set as sudden pockets of relative clarity within a mystifying tangle of word-games and poetic images; they may appear side by side with vituperative assaults on the alleged falsifiers of psychoanalytic thought. (For Lacan all issues are issues of principle, and all local disagreements reveal the forces of darkness and light in mighty combat.) Argumentative support does of course converge on these sentences from elsewhere, and the reader who is able to think in several directions at once will be at a distinct advantage in fitting these materials together. But a writer's prophecies may be all too neatly self-fulfilling when his ideas are presented to us in this form. One might parody the procedure thus: 'If what I say – about language, the unconscious, the Other, the displacement of desire – were true, one would expect writing of a certain kind to be called forth; my writing exists and is of the expected kind; therefore what I say is true.' Or again: 'Ellipsis is a characteristic mode of unconscious mental functioning; so that if I omit main pieces of evidence in stating my case the rules of the unconscious are being obeyed and the truth is being told.' Circularity and question-begging never appear quite as nakedly as this in Lacan's thinking, but they are the risks that it unashamedly runs. He constantly subjects his thought to tests of his own devising; and his thought invariably passes them. Although many notable conceptual systems are invoked as he proceeds – those of Plato, Hegel and Heidegger, for example – these do not provide any manner of external test for his own system. On the contrary, they provide that system with further dialectical challenge, further Otherness – which means, of course, further impetus and support. As contradiction and irony are inherent in language, and as all language thereby becomes, in some sense, self-critical, no external tests are necessary. And to fail a test is, in any case, also to pass it.

This phantasy of omnipotence does not make Lacan's central contributions to psychoanalysis any the less impressive, although it may at first make them difficult for many readers to isolate. The fact that his published work has a pronounced air of narcissistic ostentation has helped it to acquire its improbable prestige within contemporary French culture. In buying *Écrits* you buy an event and a badge. And as the slogans of *Écrits* are part of the tittle-tattle of a capital city, you have no need to read a word of it in order to appropriate its magic. Future sociologists of knowledge will no doubt study the mechanisms whereby an enfeebled 'Lacanism', resembling the '*fofreudisme*' that Lacan caricatures (527), has come to loom larger within the intellectual life of a society than the original ideas and texts.[69]

But in the meantime it is clear that Lacan's ideas, when situated and evaluated within their proper context, are strong enough to survive the false apotheosis to which fashionable opinion has elevated them. For it is in the psychoanalytic context, which is a practical and collaborative one, that they have already been put to work and stringently tested. Independent-minded followers such as Jean Laplanche, J.-B. Pontalis, Serge Leclaire, Maud Mannoni and Octave Mannoni have extended and refashioned Lacan's concepts without attempting to imitate his literary manner. It is plain from their work that Lacan is the originator of a coherent and continuing tradition of psychoanalytic enquiry.

Lacan has made Freud properly readable for the first time in France. His attention to facts of language as they appear in Freud's thinking, and to the ways in which structural linguistics may be used to reorganise the psychoanalytic account of the unconscious, have had numerous practical and theoretical repercussions within the French centres of the movement.[70] I shall mention two of the most far-reaching of these. First, psychoanalysis has been recalled to an awareness of its intellectual responsibilities:

> Elle ne donnera des fondements scientifiques à sa théorie comme à sa technique qu'en formalisant de façon adéquate ces dimensions essentielles de son expérience qui sont, avec la théorie historique du symbole: la logique intersubjective et la temporalité du sujet.[71] (289)

An ambition of this kind sets Lacan apart from such well-known psychiatric radicals as R. D. Laing, David Cooper and Thomas Szasz. For these writers *ideas* have a limited warrant: they are of use chiefly as a means of exposing the faulty premises on which repressive notions of sanity and madness are based, but contribute weakly if at all to descriptive or analytic accounts of psychical process. For Lacan, on the other hand, the exposure of faulty premises is merely part of a continuous process of psychical model-building in which ideas, gathered from a variety of sources and unstably combined, play a vital role. The attempt to formalise such hazardous areas of enquiry as 'intersubjective logic' and the 'temporality of the subject' is still at a primitive stage. What Lacan has done, drawing primarily on linguistics but also upon formal logic and mathematics, is to suggest ways in which intellectual rigour might become possible in branches of psychology where vagueness and guesswork have reigned until now.

Secondly, in drawing attention to the central importance of linguistic mediation in the human subject and in the analytic dialogue, Lacan has reformulated the goals of psychoanalysis both as a therapeutic method and as a moral discourse: 'L'analyse ne peut avoir pour but que l'avènement d'une parole vraie et la réalisation par le sujet de son histoire dans sa relation à un futur' (302).[72] The 'true speech' that analysis seeks to foster is one in which the subject is brought into full contact with the primary language of desire which is overheard in his accounts of his dreams and symptoms. But this speech is possible only when the subject is able to acknowledge the plain facts of lack and incompleteness within himself. It is upon these facts that the Symbolic order is founded, and to inhabit that order is to accept that one's destiny as a subject is one of indefinite displacement, and death.[73]

The Imaginary alternative is seductive, and seems to promise an entire spectrum of fulfilments: identity, integrity, harmony, tranquillity, maturity, selfhood, reciprocity. . . At moments Lacan treats the Imaginary and its concomitant array of worthy-seeming goals with a dismissive shrug: 'Seek these things if you wish, and if you're prepared to settle for baubles and lies; *truth*, of course, is elsewhere.' But in general his handling of the relations between the Symbolic and the Imaginary is at a much higher level of seriousness and complexity. Indeed his account of the unceasing dialectic between them which is ingrained in human living has given back to psychoanalysis much of the sombre moral resonance to be found in Freud's *Beyond the Pleasure Principle*, *Civilization and its Discontents*, and his late essay 'Analysis Terminable and Interminable' (XXIII, 211–53). Lacan's tone even here is quite unlike Freud's, but his refusal to surrender himself to the comforts of optimism or pessimism, and his steadfastness in the face of the irremediable, are of the same high order.

Lacan is widely influential outside psychoanalysis. One of the main reasons for this is that his writing proposes itself consciously as a critique of all discourses and all ideologies. He provides workers in other fields with a cautionary portrait of thinking-as-it-happens, and of the elements of Utopianism and infantile phantasy that may find their way even into the most austere and lucid operations of mind. 'Builders of conceptual monuments, beware!' is the message of *Écrits* to those who would hear. Psychoanalysis, urged by Lacan towards an unprecedented awareness of its own rhetorical predispositions, has acquired for theorists of other persuasions an enviable self-reflexiveness.[74]

For Lacan, Freud's revolution was 'insaisissable mais radicale' (527).[75] And his own has been of the same kind. As he exposes the forces of repression operating within psychoanalytic systems and institutions, and allows the repressed to return in his own writing, he sets before us an extraordinarily original view of what thinking might be. He is a reader of Freud, but his fidelity to Freud is of a different kind from that of Plotinus to Plato or Maimonides to Aristotle. Freud provides him with a guarantee that all thinking is 'thinking other': there is no stability, no stopping place, no supreme system. The speaking unconscious is a model for the intellectual life. Rather than create a monument and leave time, history or opinion to bring it down, Lacan writes works that displace and deconstruct themselves as they are produced. The thinking he shows us is one that inhabits time, proclaims itself as process, and finds its truth in its refusal to be complete.

5

Lacan and literatur[illegible]

Vorrei e non vorrei . . .

Mozart and [illegible] *Don Giovanni*

I'd like to and I wouldn't like to . . .

In Lacan's scientific papers, works of literature – named, quoted, analysed, eulogised – perform tasks of persuasion quite as complex as those they had performed for Freud. Simple tasks too, of course: in his references to literature Lacan, like Freud, depicts himself as a person of educated seriousness and large cultural ambition, and conjures up from the artistic legacy of Europe prophetic evidence for the truths of the new psychological science. But for both of them literature was too provocatively enviable to be used merely for purposes of corroboration or display. Literature was inside as well as outside the field of science; the experience of literature was an incitement to scientific theorising and a premonition of what a coherent theory might be like; indeed certain literary works seemed not simply to invite but already to *be* theories of mind. Yet despite these shared motives, Freud and Lacan manipulate their literary materials differently and have different theoretical notions of how such material can aid or inform scientific enquiry. Whereas for Freud the supreme extra-scientific model for a dynamic psychology was to be found in the tragic drama of Europe, for Lacan the model most often used, and seemingly most elevated by the repeated tributes paid to it, is that of the literary text itself, considered as inexhaustibly ambiguous and plural.

In placing his emphasis upon literature as polysemantic texture, Lacan was vociferous where Freud had been almost silent, and I shall begin my discussion of this emphasis by summarising briefly those aspects of Freud's account that Lacan chose not to pursue, or to pursue by circuitous paths. In his many quotations from verse Freud calls attention not to the verbal texture of his chosen lines but to their overall formulaic shape, or to the gesture of mind they are held to represent, or, in the case-histories and dream analyses, to the associative paths by which certain of their component words or phrases may be reconnected to the general psychical life of the individual. In *The Interpretation of Dreams*, the text of which is laden with references to poetry, two powerful currents within Freud's argument reduce both the specificity of poetic language and the instructiveness of poetry for the dream interpreter. The first of these currents is Freud's account of natural language as inherently ambiguous:

There is no need to be astonished at the part played by words in dream-formation. Words, since they are the nodal points [*Knotenpunkt(e)*] of numerous ideas, may be regarded as predestined to ambiguity; and the neuroses (e.g. in framing obsessions and phobias), no less than dreams, make unashamed use of the advantages thus offered by words for purposes of condensation and disguise. It is easy to show that dream-distortion too profits from displacement of expression. (*GW*, II/III, 346; V, 340–41)

Poetry dissolves from sight in two distinct but related ways here. Its ambiguities, its nodal points and knotted structures, are no more than local instances of what language at large inveterately supplies; and condensation, disguise and displacement go on relentlessly within the unconscious mind, irrespective of the cues and inducements that language may offer. Poetry is lost to language just as language, in its turn, is lost to the seemingly wordless machinery of unconscious thought. Moreover this defeat of poetry is achieved not just by highlighting those mental mechanisms which surpass it in generality but by presenting the activity of the poet and the effects of his work upon his readers in a caricaturally docile and diluted form. In the preceding paragraph Freud had been discussing the transformational procedures characteristic of dreams and had given the writing of a poem as an example of the 'determinant and selective manner' (*verteilend und auswählend*) in which any one thought may operate upon its successors:

If a poem is to be written in rhymes, the second line of a couplet is limited by two conditions: it must express an appropriate meaning, and the expression of that meaning must rhyme with the first line. No doubt the best poem will be one in which we fail to notice the intention of finding a rhyme, and in which the two thoughts have, by mutual influence, chosen from the very start a verbal expression which will allow a rhyme to emerge with only slight subsequent adjustment. (*GW*, II/III, 345–6; V, 340)

Why does this restatement of a familiar 'classical' view of rhyming sound so officiously sensible? Freud has chosen to present the poet's activity as a quest for 'appropriate' meanings and for rhymes from which all trace of rhyming intention has been eliminated. The poet is a patient and sober entrepreneur: his task is to control rather than exploit ambiguity; to prevent those singular nodal points which are rhyme-words from acquiring an excess of semantic weight; to allow thoughts which from the start exercise upon each other a benign mutual influence to enjoy a final tranquil union. A poet of this kind, having no special interest in ambiguity and being debarred from acts of imaginative provocation, leaves the stage empty for a master-manipulator of ambiguity and supremely resourceful provocateur to re-enter: the unconscious itself. Such is Freud's dramaturgy in *The Interpretation of Dreams*.

The second of the currents that I mentioned a moment ago continues and completes this domestication of poetry. The dreams discussed in Freud's book, together with their accompanying associations, are often – and not surprisingly – permeated with 'literary' material: 'In view of the part played by jokes, quotations, songs and proverbs in the mental life of educated people, it would fully agree with our expectations if disguises of such kinds were used with extreme frequency for representing dream-thoughts' (v, 345).[1] But this is not, sadly, a nascent class explanation of Viennese dream-habits. For the textual fragments that come and go in the minds of that city's educated sleepers offer opportunities to the ever-ingenious dream-work that are available too, in an impeccable egalitarian fashion, to all who have access to language. Quoted words may provide bridges or switches (v, 341n.) within the complex internal economy of the dream, but then so may any word, whatever its rank within the hierarchy of a culture. The third and final phase of Freud's analysis of his own '*Non vixit*' dream (v, 421–5, 480–7, 513) ends upon a quotation from Heine's 'Die Heimkehr' ('The Homecoming'):

> Selten habt Ihr mich verstanden,
> Selten auch verstand ich Euch,
> Nur wenn wir im Koth uns fanden,
> So verstanden wir uns gleich. (LXXVIII)
>
> Seldom did you understand me,
> Nor I you, in all the past;
> Only when in filth we land, we
> Understand each other fast.[2]

which had served, Freud tells us, as a pointer to the 'childhood phantasy which turned out to be an intermediate nodal point in the dream-thoughts' (v, 513). Heine's sardonic and acoustically playful lines are not themselves candidates for discussion, having had no 'nodal' role to perform: they are a bridge leading back to the wit and complexity of what Freud twice calls his *schöne(n) Traum*, his 'fine specimen of a dream' as the Standard Edition has it (*GW*, II/III, 424, 484; v, 421, 480).[3] They bring to its resonant close an interpretation that has already had occasion to employ in a variety of ancillary roles the Bible, Shakespeare's *Julius Caesar* and *Henry IV* (Part II), Schiller's *Die Räuber* (*The Robbers*) and Goethe's *Faust*.[4] Fortunate accidents of upbringing and education have made it possible for Freud to populate his dreams and their associations with the emperors, princes and heroic brigands of literature, and there is no mistaking the pleasure he takes in having them as his familiars. But despite the elitism of Freud's cultural assumptions, and the upward mobility that literature is expected to confer upon his own text, a strong democratic voice is always also to be heard in his accounts of the dreaming mind: the dream-work can consume anything in its path, poetry and prating, cabbages and kings; it can fill its gaps with any 'shreds and patches' that come to hand.[5] The unconscious is the working model of a classless society and poets have no special privileges there. Yet poetry itself is not dishonoured by becoming invisible in Freud's psychology of the unconscious: it is rather, in Lionel Trilling's phrase, made 'indigenous to the very constitution of the mind.'[6] And we need hardly remind ourselves that Freud's general theories of mental functioning have had, by their assiduous attention to the production and transformation of meaning, an extraordinary galvanic influence upon the study of poetic form.

'I am but mad north-north-west; when the wind is southerly I know a hawk from a handsaw': Freud quotes Hamlet with approval (V, 444).[7] For were not the craziest of dreams, rather like the Prince himself in his feigned madness, merely concealing their true sense beneath a 'cloak of wit and unintelligibility'? Shakespeare's text, like Heine's and so many others quoted in *The Interpretation of Dreams*, ushers us back into the stable semantic world that its volatile verbal surface may at first seem intent upon subverting. Listen carefully to Hamlet's mad talk and you will hear an underlying sententious wisdom being spoken. Lacan's ambition, on the contrary, is to be mad with Hamlet and to be self-consciously plural as a writer, whether in imitation or in defiance of the literary texts that he quotes. Where Freud exercises a strenuous control upon the textual power of his quotations, Lacan's teaching often strives to unleash that power again, and in response to the strictest psychoanalytic principles. When Lacan writes in Freud's wake about the ambiguity of natural language and about words as 'nodal points', an invocation to literature in one or several of its many guises often has a prominent place, as if literature alone could offer such discussion a necessary fullness and weight:

Le mot n'est pas signe, mais nœud de signification. Et que je dise le mot "rideau" par exemple, ce n'est pas seulement par convention désigner l'usage d'un objet que peuvent diversifier de mille manières les intentions sous lesquelles il est perçu par l'ouvrier, par le marchand, par le peintre ou par le psychologue gestaltiste, comme travail, valeur d'échange, physionomie colorée ou structure spatiale. C'est par métaphore un rideau d'arbres; par calembour les rides et les ris de l'eau, et mon ami Leiris dominant mieux que moi ces jeux glossolaliques. C'est par décret la limite de mon domaine ou par occasion l'écran de ma méditation dans la chambre que je partage. C'est par miracle l'espace ouvert sur l'infini, l'inconnu sur le seuil ou le départ dans le matin du solitaire. C'est par hantise le mouvement où se trahit la présence d'Agrippine au Conseil de l'Empire ou le regard de Mme de Chasteller sur le passage de Lucien Leuwen. C'est par méprise Polonius que je frappe: "Un rat! un rat! un gros rat!". C'est par interjection, à l'entracte du drame, le cri de mon impatience ou le mot de ma lassitude. Rideau! C'est une image enfin du sens en tant que sens, qui pour se découvrir doit être dévoilé.[8] (166–7)

In this paragraph from 'Propos sur la causalité psychique' (1946), a vehement attack upon certain organicist theories of psychosis reaches its first culminating point. Against those who would wish to marginalise 'mad' mental processes, and who employ exiguous notions of 'truth' in order to convict mad minds of error, Lacan reasserts the dignity of those processes as scientific subject-matter and their capacity to reveal at an appropriate level of complexity the structure of the psychical apparatus at large – sane or mad, normal or pathological. The crucial factor that the organicists choose to ignore is that madness, whatever its origins, is a mode of meaning: 'le phénomène de la folie n'est pas séparable du problème de la signification pour l'être en général, c'est-à-dire du langage pour l'homme' (166). According to Lacan, students of the human mind wishing to grapple with the 'problem of meaning' could not do better than serve an apprenticeship as students of literature. For literature exposes and dramatises the refractory linguistic medium in which all production of meaning takes place. Where the clinicians whom Lacan is here attacking seek to undermine psychotic discourse by underdetermining it, Lacan himself seeks by reference to the luxuriant domain of literary meaning to restore to that discourse the overdetermination that is its inescapable condition.

Lacan despatches Polonius towards the end of this paragraph, but has been a Hamlet of sorts from the start – in his disconsolate humour, his verbal jesting and the abundance of his tirade.[9] The semantic knot that this tirade unties and reties – the word 'rideau' – is, as we would expect of any 'arbitrarily' chosen example, a particularly intricate one, and allows Lacan to make rapid associative journeys between industry, commerce, art, sex, politics and the psychological sciences.

'Literature' is present in two main forms. In the first of these it is an archive of metaphors, images, glossolalic effects[10] and memorable scenes upon which writers and speakers may draw at will. Among these materials the memorable scenes are here given special prominence – not simply because *Britannicus*, *Lucien Leuwen* and *Hamlet* powerfully echo one another in their intrications of sexual and political passion but because Lacan's paper as a whole provides his allusions with an additional level of motivation. In summoning up Agrippine's celebrated lines:

> Non, non, le temps n'est plus que Néron, jeune encore,
> Me renvoyait les vœux d'une cour qui l'adore,
> Lorsqu'il se reposait sur moi de tout l'Etat,
> Que mon ordre au palais assemblait le sénat,
> Et que derrière un voile, invisible et présente,
> J'étais de ce grand corps l'âme toute-puissante.[11] (I, i)

Lacan continues the play of substitutions to which 'rideau' has given rise, provides the first of three emblems for the surreptitious exercise of political power and anticipates that notion of meaning as a continuous unveiling upon which the paragraph ends.[12] But the professions of psychiatry and psychoanalysis, as Lacan insistently reminds us in this paper and throughout *Écrits*, have their politics too, their shifting patterns of patronage, their struggles for succession, their intrigues, factions and clandestine alliances. Racine's Imperial Rome provides the healing professions with a woundingly parodic self-portrait. Similarly Lacan's phantasy of killing Polonius, and his supercharged rendering of Hamlet's cry 'A rat, a rat!', gain a further edge of dark comedy from the immediate political context of the paper as a whole: much of the argument is an *ad hominem* assault upon Henri Ey, a former mentor of Lacan's, a sagacious senior within French psychiatry and a man of many influential words. The passage from Stendhal to which Lacan refers, besides containing the required curtain and concealed political personage (Mme de Chasteller is an 'ultra enragée', the bemused Lucien is told a few pages later), provides advance notification of Lacan's unmistakable literary and professional style:

> La jeune femme ferma sa croisée et regarda, à demi cachée par le rideau de mousseline brodée de sa fenêtre. Elle pouvait avoir vingt-quatre ou vingt-cinq ans. Lucien trouva dans ses yeux une expression singulière; était-ce de l'ironie, de la haine, ou tout simplement de la jeunesse et une certaine disposition à s'amuser de tout?[13]

The original hearers of 'Propos sur la causalité psychique' could easily have asked Lucien's question of Lacan's inscrutable argumentative manner. For this was a manner in which rage, frivolity and what he himself calls 'une ironie, sans doute un peu risquée' (160)[14] already played what would have seemed to many contemporaries a disproportionate and unprofessional role.

The multitude of writers appearing elsewhere in Lacan's paper includes Fontenelle, Flaubert, Schiller, Molière, Montaigne and Plato. Each of them, considered alone, is a multiplier of local meanings, a supplier of knots to Lacan's own discourse. But a procession of writers moving at speed through the text, and striking up unhistorical relationships with each other as they move, creates within the argument strong cross-currents of association that have their own lesson to teach. The associative play that occurs between earlier writers, and between the gathered fragments of earlier texts, indicates among other things that a crucial moral responsibility has been assumed and is being discharged by the psychoanalytic theorist: he has become a guardian of what Lacan was later to name the 'Symbolic order' and an upholder of complexity and critical self-awareness in psychological science. In the service of these goals, the literary tradition itself has become – and was to remain in Lacan's papers of the nineteen-fifties – an inexhaustible store of textual nuclei or 'nodal points'.

I mentioned two roles for literature in this passage. The second is this: Lacan's writing seeks to become what it beholds, to emerge efflorescent from the contemplation of other men's *fleurs de rhétorique*. Long before he begins to use the classical technical terms in his accounts of the 'rhetoric of the unconscious' and to claim Quintilian as an intellectual forbear and sponsor,[15] he is here placing an unusual 'writerly' pressure upon certain figures of speech in the organisation of his ideas. Against the rough principles of entailment and *enchaînement* that the psychoanalytic theorist might ordinarily be expected to observe, Lacan creates an anaphoric refrain ('C'est par . . . C'est par . . .') that removes his text from the time-dimension of consecutive argument. But he does not dissolve an expected logical sequence merely in order to give his text a sprightly forwards movement of its own. Anaphora, the simplest and possibly the commonest of the *schemata verborum*, far from propelling the reader smoothly from the sentence opening towards the substance of each proposition, here develops substance, and counter-logical energy, if its own. Lacan plays upon the preposition 'par' rather as Rimbaud had played upon 'à' in his 'Dévotion' ('A ma sœur . . . Ce soir à Circeto . . . A tout prix'). The *par*-sequence *exemple*, *convention*, *métaphore*, *calembour*, *décret*, *occasion*, *miracle*, *hantise*, *interjection* is governed by a repeated syntactic gesture of the kind often used to create a semblance of commensurability between terms that might otherwise appear disparate. But in this sequence the leaps and swerves between logical categories are so abrupt that syntax alone is powerless to control them. Lacan's discrepant opening phrases redirect attention to the most convention-bound segment of his propositions. For it is here, in the play between openings, that the social order comes into momentary contact with the divine order ('convention' – 'miracle'), linguistic structures with mental acts ('métaphore' – 'méprise'), anarchy with legality ('calembour' – 'décret'), unfocused apprehension with punctual articulation ('hantise' – 'interjection'), necessity with circumstance ('décret' – 'occasion'). And here that ready-made phrases ('par occasion', 'par miracle') acquire by contagion a new surge of semantic power. Using the terms of one familiar distinction within the science of rhetoric, we might describe this process – new to psychoanalysis in 1946, but not new to literature – by saying that the *schemata verborum* have become a privileged site for the *figurae sententiarum*. The syntactic pattern that prepares the reader for the emergence of an idea has been inflected in such a way that it becomes an idea-source in its own right.

Lacan's explosion of the word 'rideau' ends in an archly self-conscious and *en abyme* fashion: what better way of removing this serried catalogue of curtains from view than by bringing down upon it . . . the curtain? Densely accumulating 'literary' effects like these, together with the allusiveness I discussed a moment ago, seem to place entire regions of Lacan's work beneath the sign *littérature* and to give any student of that work who has a literary as distinct from a psychoanalytic or philosophical background a special sense of professional advantage. Later I shall argue that the warrant of the 'literary Lacanian' is a severely limited one. But before doing this I shall present in summary form certain of the further ways in which Lacan flatters and seeks flattery from the man or woman of letters and appears, in the working out of his theory, to be summoning psychoanalysis and literature to a shared apotheosis.

The 'literary scholar' – if I may be allowed so to epitomise the multitude of those who busy themselves in the systematic study of literature – will find, if he or she chooses, many years of employment in examining *Écrits*. Jobs are particularly plentiful for the source-hunter, the genealogist of ideas and the forensic scientist of originality. For beyond Lacan's numerous named antecedents there lies an innumerable company of Lacanians before the event – writers who have in some way anticipated an aspect of his system. Considering 'Propos sur la causalité psychique' for a further moment, we may discover, for example, that one of Lacan's principal contentions – that madness is inherent in human thinking, and that mental scientists who would deny this are behaving in some (other) sense 'madly' – had already been expressed with incomparable lapidary force by Pascal in his *Pensées*: 'Les hommes sont si nécessairement fous, que ce serait être fou par un autre tour de folie, de n'être pas fou.'[16] Similarly, Lacan's (and Freud's) notion of the word as a signifying 'knot' is already to be found in, say, Gracián's treatise *Agudeza y arte de ingenio* (*Subtlety and the Art of Ingenuity*) (1648): 'A word is like a vocal hydra for, in addition to its own and immediate significance, if one cuts or disarranges it, from each syllable is born an ingenious subtlety, and from each accent, a conceit.'[17] Both writers appear by name in later papers: the *pensée* itself is quoted in 'Fonction et champ' (283) and tribute paid to Pascal in 'D'une question préliminaire à tout traitement possible de la psychose' for having isolated the notion of 'social psychosis' (576). An episode from *El criticón* (*The Critic*) is summarised in 'Fonctions de la psychanalyse en criminologie' (147), while in 'La Chose freudienne' Gracián is hailed, together with La Rochefoucauld, Nietzsche and Freud, as a celestial body within the tradition of the European *moralistes* (407).

We do not know the extent of Lacan's debts to Gracián and Pascal in 1946 and there is no reasonable basis on which to decide what contribution, if any, they made to the formulation of his paper. Answers to individual questions such as these are not in any case likely to shed strong light upon the origins, the coherence or the explanatory capacity of a psychoanalytic theory. But this does not mean that the literary scholar has a merely menial task to perform. For general questions about the textual relationship of later to earlier thinkers, even if they are phrased in terms of a naïve antithesis between accidental affinity and deliberate plagiarising choice, take us to the centre of what could be called the drama of indebtedness. Psychoanalysis is of course precisely a *theory* of indebtedness, or 'belatedness' – the only fully-fledged theory of the subject to date – and at the same time, in its own political history, enacts that drama in a series of macabre episodes. The text of *Écrits*, like that of *The Interpretation of Dreams*, is suffused with anxious enquiries of the kind 'how many predecessors can I allow myself to have?' and 'how good can I allow them to be?'. Too many (or too good) and my story will already have been told. Too few and the issues that I address will not seem time-honoured enough to be worth taking seriously. The literary scholar, as the work of Harold Bloom amply and brilliantly demonstrates, is well placed to detect the voice of Freud *agonistes* beneath the condescending catalogue of dream doctrines ancient and modern with which *The Interpretation of Dreams* begins, or to understand the peculiar anguish of a thinker who wishes to be the point of convergence towards which the ideas of Freud, Saussure and Hegel tend yet wishes to remain for ever free from the taint of derivativeness or eclecticism.

A further long-term task awaits the literary scholar who combines competence as an intellectual historian with skill in the critical analysis of texts. This task, which has until now fallen chiefly into fumbling hands, is the description and analysis of Lacan's prose style. His style, 'agaçant dès l'abord' for a majority of readers, according to Georges Mounin,[18] has often been thought of as an offence against some unwritten code of decorum in the human sciences, and much supposed stylistic discussion of Lacan's writing has been devoted to the reinforcement of that code against further attack. Yet indecorousness on the Lacanian scale, once it is perceived within the perspective offered by the history of European prose, begins to have forbears and begins to be analysable. The asymmetry, obscurity and conceitedness of Lacan's writing, still so shocking to certain commentators who have sought and failed to find in it the bland prosaicism of the international psychoanalytic journals, begin indeed to seem like survivals from a lost world of mannerist exuberance. This passage from 'Subversion du sujet et dialectique du désir dans l'inconscient freudien' (1960) contains elaborate figuration derived from Freud's 'Wo Es war, soll Ich werden':[19]

> Énonciation qui se dénonce, énoncé qui se renonce, ignorance qui se dissipe, occasion qui se perd, qu'est-ce qui reste ici sinon la trace de ce qu'il faut bien qui soit pour choir de l'être?
>
> Un rêve rapporté par Freud dans son article: *Formulations sur les deux principes de*

l'événement psychique, nous livre, liée au pathétique dont se soutient la figure d'un père défunt d'y être celle d'un revenant, la phrase: Il ne savait pas qu'il était mort.

Dont nous avons déjà pris prétexte à illustrer la relation du sujet au signifiant, par une énonciation dont l'être tremble de la vacillation qui lui revient de son propre énoncé.

Si la figure ne subsiste que de ce qu'on ne lui dise pas la vérité qu'elle ignore, qu'en est-il donc du *Je* dont cette subsistance dépend?

Il ne savait pas... Un peu plus il savait, ah! que jamais ceci n'arrive! Plutôt qu'il sache, que Je meure. Oui, c'est ainsi que Je viens là, là où c'était: qui donc savait que J'étais mort?

Être de non-étant, c'est ainsi qu'advient Je comme sujet qui se conjugue de la double aporie d'une subsistance véritable qui s'abolit de son savoir et d'un discours où c'est la mort qui soutient l'existence.[20] (801–2)

'Wo Es war...' is here cross-fertilised with the proposition '*his father had really died, only without knowing it*' from 'Formulations on the Two Principles of Mental Functioning' (1911) (XII, 225),[21] and to their emerging hybrid forms a range of supplementary Hegelian tinctures is given.

It might at first seem that secure purchase could be achieved upon these paragraphs simply by examining the interplay between their Freudian and Hegelian 'sources', especially as the paper as a whole advances a concept of desire that by turns conflates and counterposes Hegel's *Begierde* and Freud's *Wunsch*. Where Freud is quoted almost verbatim, Hegel's *Phenomenology* exerts a continuous subterranean pressure upon Lacan's text. His last phrase, for example – 'un discours où c'est la mort qui soutient l'existence' – may be thought of as a twofold remembrance of the *Phenomenology*. Hegel on death, in such passages as:

the life of Spirit is not the life that shrinks from death and keeps itself untouched by devastation, but rather the life that endures it and maintains itself in it. It wins its truth only when, in utter dismemberment, it finds itself.[22]

and Hegel on the unavoidably universalising force of human language:

They *mean* 'this' bit of paper on which I am writing – or rather have written – 'this'; but what they mean is not what they say. If they actually wanted to *say* 'this' bit of paper which they mean, if they wanted to *say* it, then this is impossible, because the sensuous This that is meant *cannot be reached* by language, which belongs to consciousness, i.e. to that which is inherently universal.[23]

have been compressed and refashioned into a characteristic Lacanian representation of the divided human subject: the subject ('Je comme sujet'), which is an effect of – or an event within – language, is by that token as death-haunted as 'Spirit' itself in

Hegel's account. Hegel is selectively adduced to remind psychoanalysis of the scale and the intensity of its first tragic perceptions.

Lacan is by turns a master of two servants and a servant of two masters in the dialogue that he establishes between Freud and Hegel. His insistent play upon 'Je' in the passage as a whole may be thought of as an equivocation between the Freudian ego ('Das Ich') and the speaking 'Ich' with which Hegel often dramatises his descriptions of self-consciousness. The Freudian ego appears here in its familiar role of polemical adversary: the ego is dead but refuses to acknowledge its own demise; it must be persuaded of its own deadness ('que Je meure') and of the delusional thinking upon which it has flourished; it may be resurrected only under the perilous conditions of subjecthood.[24] And, in the process of persuasion, the dialectically mobile artefact that is the Hegelian 'Ich' becomes Lacan's ally against the allegedly inert and alienating ego of psychoanalytic tradition. For Hegel, the speaking 'I' could not escape the destiny of the spoken 'piece of paper':

> The 'I' that utters itself is *heard* or *perceived*; it is an infection in which it has immediately passed into unity with those for whom it is a real existence, and is a universal self-consciousness. That it is *perceived* or *heard* means that its *real existence dies away*; this its otherness has been taken back into itself; and its real existence is just this: that as a self-conscious Now, as a real existence, it is *not* a real existence, and through this vanishing it *is* a real existence ['und eben diß ist sein Daseyn, als selbstbewußtes Jetzt, wie es da ist, nicht da zu seyn, und durch diß Verschwinden da zu seyn'].[25]

We may conjecture that the dialectic between vanishing and reappearing, and between existence real and unreal, to be found in passages like this affected Lacan not simply because it was philosophically congenial to him but because it had been enshrined in pungently 'dialectical' patterns of syntax. And our grasp upon this passage from 'Subversion du sujet' may feel completely firm once the after-shocks of Hegel's *stylistic* achievement have been traced within Lacan's writing. Consider Hegel's closing words, for example, the original text of which I have also quoted. Phases within the dialectic which could easily have been, and elsewhere in the *Phenomenology* often are, divided between separate sentences are here presented as the interdependent members of a single complex proposition. As the sentence is read, states of affairs that might be thought of as mutually exclusive – existing or not existing, being present or being absent – borrow from its grammar a semblance at least of mutual necessity. Syntactic structure here provides not a logical but a dramatic vindication of the dialectician's argumentative procedure. A similar accommodation between argument and syntax is to be found in Lacan's 'qu'est-ce qui reste ici sinon la trace de ce qu'il faut bien qui soit pour choir de l'être?'. We do not of course have to look further than everyday speech to find examples of mimetic syntax put to work for persuasive purposes such as these. And imaginative literature abounds in sentences that enact within themselves, as Lacan's does, the inseparability of living and dying:

> Tousiours, toute heure, ainsi sans cesser
> Fauldra finir ma vie, & commencer
> En ceste mort inutilement viue.[26] Scève: *Délie*, 267

> A Universe of death, which God by curse
> Created evil, for evil onely good,
> Where all life dies, death lives, and Nature breeds,
> Perverse, all monstrous, all prodigious things . . .
> Milton: *Paradise Lost*, II, 622–5

> The smile on your mouth was the deadest thing
> Alive enough to have strength to die . . .
> Hardy, 'Neutral Tones'

Yet despite the fact that syntactic effects of this sort – which allowed the multifarious imprint of unbeing upon being to become visible and audible within discourse – were available to Lacan without his having recourse to Hegel, the stylistic lesson of the *Phenomenology* was a compelling one. For here was a book in which living death and dying life were presented as internal to human consciousness and in which syntax was mobile portraiture of that consciousness at grips with negativity; one which did not shun obscurity and incantation in its pursuit of philosophical goals; and one which seemed to predict with extraordinary clarity a central teaching of psychoanalysis: that the human sense of self is an uneasy fabrication, born under the pressure of others and of the inextirpable otherness that social code and custom embody.

How far does Hegel, whether as conceptual source or as stylistic influence, take us in understanding how to read *Écrits*? Quite far, I would suggest – but only if we consider Lacan's resistances in parallel with his enthusiasm. For Lacan employs a battery of rhetorical devices to deflect and frustrate the 'Hegel effect' in his writing and to repudiate the upwards dialectical spiral by which, in the *Phenomenology*, Spirit approaches the realm of Absolute Knowing.[27] The passage that I have been discussing comprises short, gnomic, quasi-Biblical paragraphs between which the causal connectives are few and weak. Ellipsis, apposition, word-play, paradox and ambiguity concentrate attention upon each of those paragraphs as an individual unit of meaning, and between units certain repeated words (or their cognates and synonyms) may create a flickering pattern of lateral connections: *choir de l'être – défunt – mort – que Je meure – J'étais mort – la mort* and so forth. Exclamations, interrogations, trailing syntax and unmarked 'quotations' from personified mental agencies further interrupt the forwards – and completely forestall the upwards – movement of the argument; formulaic phrases appear in a sudden and seemingly unmotivated fashion. Devices, that is to say, which would ordinarily be expected to have no more than an occasional heightening function in theoretical discourse are here used so intensively that they dominate the textual foreground and make the pursuit of sense indefinitely subject to detour and delay. In the absence both of sustained argument in the Hegelian (or any other) manner and of extended periodic sentences, these devices are the main instruments available to us with which to conduct our thinking. Our thinking takes place discontinuously, in a now obfuscated and now sententiously pointed verbal medium. Prose of this kind may, with all due caution, be called 'baroque' – and 'baroque' in a much stricter definition of the term than Lacan's commentators, who use it frequently, seem mostly to have in mind.

Morris Croll, in his remarkable pioneering essay on 'The Baroque Style in Prose', spoke in qualified praise of a new movement in the prose literature of Europe that for him had reached its apogee in about 1630:

It disdained complacency, suavity, copiousness, emptiness, ease, and in avoiding these qualities sometimes obtained effects of contortion or obscurity, which it was not always willing to regard as faults. It preferred the forms that express the energy and labor of minds seeking the truth, not without dust and heat, to the forms that express a contented sense of the enjoyment and possession of it. In a single word, the motions of souls, not their states of rest, had become the themes of art.[28]

Of passages chosen to illustrate the 'curt style' or *stile coupé*, Croll wrote:

Logically they do not move. At the end they are saying exactly what they were at the beginning. Their advance is wholly in the direction of a more vivid imaginative realization; a metaphor revolves, as it were, displaying its different facets; a series of metaphors flash their lights; or a chain of 'points' and paradoxes reveals the energy of a single apprehension in the writer's mind.[29]

Although it would not be accurate to speak of a 'single apprehension' pursuing its course through the last paragraphs that I quoted from Lacan, Croll's pointed and metaphorical remarks about the cultivation of 'point' and metaphor characterise clearly the kind of thinking that 'baroque' writing encourages Lacan to perform. He abandons the language of tranquil certitude in which his colleagues and contemporaries in psychoanalysis mostly choose to write (even when describing their uncertainties), and uses instead an enraged, risk-taking language of scepticism. His writing is propelled not simply by an urge to be difficult and discontinuous, but by an urge, transmuted into a moral imperative, to be surprising.[30]

If we consider the baroque writers whom Lacan chose to name as ancestors, we find that his enthusiasm for Gracián is matched and to some extent offset by his enthusiasm for Góngora: the traditions of *conceptismo* and *culteranismo* that clashed so vigorously in early seventeenth-century Spain clash again in Lacan's writing.[31] Both traditions are valued by him for the difficulty they promote and for their seeming hostility to the intellectual vice of 'good sense'. Lacan hands the burden of difficulty back and forth between syntax and sound, between tropes and schemes, between conceited thinking and opulently allusive verbal textures. He is by temperament a Senecan in his handling of syntax, but will turn his hand to a Ciceronian sentence when the injunction 'dire toujours Autre-chose' (837) requires it.[32] These comparisons should not of course be pressed too far, especially as Lacan's self-identification with the dead geniuses of Europe has on occasion a shallow grandiosity about it, quite untouched by his otherwise pervasive irony. His writing is not always good, even by his own unusual criteria. His euphuistic contrivances sometimes smack of the school literary magazine and his conceits of the undergraduate debating society; his puns and quibbles sometimes approach inanity. And a time-travelling Quintilian, coming upon declamatory lists of his own rhetorical figures in *Écrits*, might wish to caution Lacan with a list of those vices into which devices may dwindle: Lacan's *accismus*, *metonymy*, *catachresis*, *antiphrasis*, *hypallage* and *litotes* (466) might be countered, after an inspection of his writing, by *anoiconometon*, *cacosyntheton*, *cumulatio*, *nugatio*, *periergia* and *scurra*.[33]

The literary scholar for whom I have been compiling an agenda might take on as a worthwhile lesser task an analysis of the ways in which Lacan's writing goes wrong, disserves his ideas and falls short of the complex psychoanalytic notion of *vérité* that his teaching propounds.[34] But the major task that falls to such a scholar, and in particular to the stylistician, is that of saying what kind of writing Lacan's is and of analysing in detail its sense-making procedures. Such analysis cannot of itself provide any manner of test for the coherence of Lacan's theory. But an understanding of those procedures – and an ability to tell the difference between consecutive and conscientiously anti-consecutive styles of argumentation – are prerequisites for anyone who would devise for that theory an appropriate range of tests.

Work of this kind could be thought to provide the literary scholar with his or her crowning role in the psychoanalytic domain. But Lacan can be even more seductive than this. His designs upon literature and its custodians may be seen at their most guileful in this passage from 'Fonction et champ', which has been much discussed and now enjoys something approaching canonical status:

> L'inconscient est ce chapitre de mon histoire qui est marqué par un blanc ou occupé par un mensonge: c'est le chapitre censuré. Mais la vérité peut être retrouvée; le plus souvent déjà elle est écrite ailleurs. A savoir:
>
> — dans les monuments: et ceci est mon corps, c'est-à-dire le noyau hystérique de la névrose où le symptôme hystérique montre la structure d'un langage et se déchiffre comme une inscription qui, une fois recueillie, peut sans perte grave être détruite;
> — dans les documents d'archives aussi: et ce sont les souvenirs de mon enfance, impénétrables aussi bien qu'eux, quand je n'en connais pas la provenance;
> — dans l'évolution sémantique: et ceci répond au stock et aux acceptions du vocabulaire qui m'est particulier, comme au style de ma vie et à mon caractère;
> — dans les traditions aussi, voire dans les légendes qui sous une forme héroïsée véhiculent mon histoire;
> — dans les traces, enfin, qu'en conservent inévitablement les distorsions, nécessitées par le raccord du chapitre adultéré dans les chapitres qui l'encadrent, et dont mon exégèse rétablira le sens.[35] (259)

Lacan's manner here may at first seem ingenuously catechistical, as if the question 'what is the unconscious and where can I find it?' had long ago ceased to be a vexatious one and could henceforth be answered in a string of simple doctrinal propositions. But the passage is in fact an ingenious summary of certain major Freudian metaphors for the unconscious, executed in such a way that Lacan is able to pinpoint a recurrent hesitation in Freud's own thinking.

The two metaphorical orders that Lacan ranges against each other are, roughly, the 'archaeological' and the 'semiotic', each of which made a precociously elaborate appearance in Freud's pre-psychoanalytic writings and was to be drawn upon and modified throughout his career as a theorist.[36]

Freud often spoke of such mental activities as perception, repression and remembering in 'writerly' terms. Movements from one psychical system or level to another could easily be represented as processes undergone by written characters – translations, transcriptions, inscriptions, re-inscriptions, imprintings, paraphrases – and the meanings that these characters bore were often held to be vulnerable to distortion during transmission. Whereas the 'lower' psychical levels had to varying degrees a retentive capacity, the uppermost level, consciousness itself, was a writing surface on which no permanent trace could be formed (XIX, 230). Over and against these endlessly retranscribable written messages, archaeology offered its stable and durable relics as an alternative order of meaning: despite the hazards of burial and excavation, what had once existed in the mind existed still and could be recovered intact. The only writerly art to retain its power within this archaeological dimension was that of Champollion and his fellow code-breakers – those who retrieve whole meanings or whole meaning-producing systems from material remains.[37] If this Freudian background is taken into account, Lacan's manœuvre in the passage seems straightforward enough. For he reinterprets Freud's archaeological objects, his 'monuments', as mobile creatures of language upon which – we may suspect – equally mobile acts of interpretation could play indefinitely. Are we not witnessing one of those corrections of Freud at the hands of Freud in which Lacan became so expert? Is not the semiotic strain in psychoanalysis being talked to victory over the archaeological?

I think not. For Lacan's thoroughgoing attempt to cocoon mental processes in linguistic imagery leads in the final cadence of the final paragraph to a remarkably simple hermeneutic lesson: by informed exegesis gaps in the material may be filled, barriers to understanding circumvented and an original plenitude of sense re-established. The archaeological mode, so comprehensively repudiated on the metaphorical surface of this litany, has behaved in character: it has gone underground and survived intact. From this point of view Lacan's account of censorship is particularly revealing. He alludes of course to Freud's celebrated comparison of certain inhibiting mental agencies with the 'Russian censorship' through which foreign newspapers crossing the frontier had to pass (I, 273, V, 529), and does not in any fundamental way alter the force of Freud's account. The unconscious 'chapter' was complete and coherent before the censor's blanking device was applied to it, and will become so again, once censorship has been lifted. Derrida has shown what difficulties may arise if 'semiotic' metaphors in psychoanalysis are incompletely followed through. He writes of the layers within Freud's 'mystic writing pad' (XIX, 227–32) and within his stratified mental models at large:

> L'écriture est impensable sans le refoulement. Sa condition, c'est qu'il n'y ait ni un contact permanent ni une rupture absolue entre les couches. Vigilance et échec de la censure. Que la métaphore de la censure soit issue de ce qui, dans le politique, regarde l'écriture en ses ratures, blancs et déguisements, ce n'est pas un hasard, même si Freud, au début de la *Traumdeutung*, semble y faire une référence conventionnelle et didactique. L'apparente extériorité de la censure politique renvoie à une censure essentielle qui lie l'écrivain à sa propre écriture.[38]

The erasures, blanks and disguises that are the stock-in-trade of the political censor are features too of the very writing upon which he exercises his vigilance . . . and of all other writing too. What Lacan has done by way of his compacted linguistic metaphors is restore to the unconscious materials upon which psychoanalysis operates an Edenic continuity and fullness quite belied by other elements of his argument in 'Fonction et champ'. He has deprived both writing and the unconscious considered as writing of their endemic blanks and has alluded neither to the psychoanalytic dialogue nor to the silences that punctuate and propel it. During a half-page interlude, psychoanalysis has become a simple art of memory, a self-help device with which to procure by introspection knowledge of one's own past. This is the game that the literary scholar is invited to join. And the sentimental inducements that accompany the invitation are powerful ones.

Such a scholar will already know how heterogeneous and unruly his chosen 'discipline' often is. He will know that in order to get his texts right, or to approach with due circumspection the difficulty or undecidability of those texts, a number of separate professional skills must already be at his command. Before becoming the interpreter of his text – if such is his ambition – he will have had to discover, isolate and peruse it. These preliminary activities may already have demanded of him a variety of editorial, bibliographical, historical or lexicographical capacities. Interpretation proper demands many more. The self-esteem of such a scholar will be greatly fortified by Lacan's portrait gallery of virtuous academic practitioners. The exegete upon whom the responsibility for 're-establishing sense' finally falls has already been an epigrapher, an archivist, a stylistician, a student of oral culture, a detective, and must always be prepared to exploit in new ways his many-sided expertise. The psychoanalyst and the literary scholar each offer the other a flattering mirror in which a quality of their performances that might otherwise seem shallow technical address emits a halo of moral worth. Both are campaigners against inaccuracy and lies, and a strong sense of professional uprightness unites them. Their moral horizon is unclouded by low motives, just as their hermeneutic activities are unhindered by ignorance or partial sight. In purely psychoanalytic terms the price to be paid for these moments of euphoric fellow-feeling is a dangerously high one: in the pursuit of such moments, psychoanalysis, whether as a distinctive mode of remembrance or as a distinctive method for studying the intersubjective dialectic of human speech, has to be abandoned.

It might be objected against objections such as these that they are far too ponderous and literal-minded; that Lacan is seeking simply to civilise his colleagues by reminding them of the humane arts that adjoin their own; that he is sketching an extra-medical curriculum for the 'college of psycho-analysis' that Freud had once foretold (XX, 246);[39] and that a strict psychoanalytic account of human communication, being amply present elsewhere in 'Fonction et champ', has no need to be here too. If the overall coherence of Lacan's paper and that alone were at stake these objections would indeed have considerable weight. For the paper has, as it proceeds, an outstanding capacity to answer its own questions and redistribute its own emphases. But the paper is also so intricate and opaque in the detailed working out of its argument that its plain hortatory passages, when they occur, are likely to become disconnected from that argument and present themselves as textual outliers – blocks of safe and serviceable meaning. Such blocks, of which I have been examining perhaps the most monumental example, may be gravely misleading. They may mislead to the point of suggesting that Lacan's version of psychoanalysis is no more than conventional literary study fancily redescribed. While Lacan is to a considerable degree responsible for the over-valuing of letters that his work has often seemed to encourage (he could have written differently about literature at certain exposed moments in his papers – less fulsomely, less obligingly), he has also protested vigorously against the 'inflation littéraire'[40] to which psychoanalysis at large has been subjected. For Lacan the credentials of literature, both as a cultural edifice and as a source of instruction for psychoanalysis, are too impressive not to be suspect.

It would be convenient to see the relationship between Lacanian theory and literary studies as one of reciprocal support and enhancement. Many critics writing in the penumbra of that theory have derived special advantages from it: they have been alerted once again to the implicitness, mobility and ambiguity of much literary meaning; they have been given – by the 'Séminaire sur "La Lettre volée"' (11–61) and by much else in the Lacanian corpus – new ways of looking at plot, figurality and embeddedness in prose fiction; they have been shown the vein of commodity fetishism that runs through the modern notion of 'text' quite as damagingly as it once ran through the antiquated notions of 'masterpiece' and 'great work' and have been invited to become suspicious of literary criticism itself as a ritual of obeisance before certain sanctified verbal artefacts; they have been given tools with which to think incisively about literary works as productions of desire, and about the desire-ladenness of the dealings that they themselves have with the works they write about and the readers they address. Lacan's theory has held out the promise of a new style of materialist social criticism – one that is able to make coherent connections between the structure of the unconscious and the interactive signifying practices that constitute a given culture.[41] Critics who have debts such as these are perhaps especially likely to believe that Lacan's psychoanalysis has equal and opposite debts to literature. But the relationship is in fact an asymmetrical one, and for reasons that I shall now discuss.

We have already seen that literature, for Lacan, is a Protean object of desire and that his theoretical texts sometimes become overwrought in their attempts to trap and devour it. Literary texts even when enlisted for simple-seeming didactic purposes may provoke a series of anxious manœuvrings in Lacan's own writing, as if envy and suspicion were making any one focal point impossible to maintain. In 'Propos sur la causalité psychique', for example, Lacan discusses Molière's Alceste as a prophetic instance of the Hegelian 'beautiful soul' (*schöne Seele, belle âme*)[42] who, falsely identifying the law of his own heart with the law of Nature, is driven by the spectacle of his flawed fellow humans into one of two equally unsatisfactory postures – frenzied conceit or languid self-absorption.[43] According to Hegel both postures betokened derangement or madness.[44] This Hegelian account of the madness that resides in claiming peerless sanity for oneself suits Lacan's argument well: Hegel's strictures on the 'beautiful soul' anticipate but do not pre-empt Lacan's critique of the delusional diagnostic procedures held to underlie much contemporary psychiatry; and the relationship between the beautiful soul and his fellows resembles but does not over-resemble the paranoid relationship between individual and 'other' that Lacan's paper characterises at length. Lacan at first simply replaces Hegel's favourite literary instance (Karl Moor in Schiller's *Die Räuber*) with a character who is more accessible to a French audience and more attuned to his personal taste (173) and then reiterates Hegel's point: 'Alceste est fou et . . . Molière le montre comme tel – très justement en ceci que dans sa belle âme il ne reconnaît pas qu'il concourt lui-même au désordre contre lequel il s'insurge' (173).[45]

It is in the ensuing analysis of *Le Misanthrope* that the psychoanalytic mode is superimposed upon the phenomenological, and that the evidential value of literature in either of these modes begins to dissolve. Alceste discovers and despises in the social world around him not just an oppressive otherness that thwarts his own would-be independence of mind but a series of narcissistic reflections in which his own narcissism is mirrored:

> Je précise qu'il est fou, non pas pour aimer une femme qui soit coquette ou le trahisse, ce que nos doctes de tout-à-l'heure rapporteraient sans doute à son inadaptation vitale, – mais pour être pris, sous le pavillon de l'Amour, par le sentiment même qui mène le bal de cet art des mirages où triomphe la belle Célimène: à savoir ce narcissisme des oisifs qui donne la structure psychologique du 'monde' à toutes les époques, doublé ici de cet autre narcissisme, qui se manifeste plus spécialement dans certaines par l'idéalisation collective du sentiment amoureux.[46] (173)

Despite Alceste's vituperations against society, society is no more than a resistant surface by way of which his aggression rebounds upon its appointed target – himself. Lacan relates Alceste's self-destructive impulse – 'l'*agression suicidaire du narcissisme*' (174)[47] – to recent psychiatric studies of paranoia, including his own doctoral dissertation. But this recourse to Molière is more than an attempt to draw ready-made case-material from the public domain of letters, and Lacan's analysis does not seek merely to test the explanatory power of his own recently introduced concept of the mirror phase. For his discussion ends upon a melodramatic inflection of the entire preceding argument:

> J'eusse pu, au lieu d'Alceste, rechercher le jeu de la loi du cœur dans le destin qui conduit le vieux révolutionnaire de 1917 au banc des accusés des procès de Moscou. Mais ce qui se démontre dans l'espace imaginaire du poète, vaut métaphysiquement ce qui se passe de plus sanglant dans le monde, car c'est cela qui dans le monde fait couler le sang.[48] (175)

Hegel had paid his tribute to the versatile instructiveness of Schiller's Karl Moor by refraining from naming author, character or play anywhere in the *Phenomenology* and by avoiding direct quotation: Karl Moor is an immanence within the text and perceptible only through a veil of allusions.[49] Lacan's tribute to his corresponding literary instance, on the other hand, is paid in a violent switch of focus: he could be writing about the show trials of the Stalin era or about the broad spectacle of human slaughter, but in obedience to some unspecified scruple has chosen instead to discuss the 'metaphysical' equivalent of these events, a work of literature in which a fundamental structure of human awareness is attested. Alceste is threatened with dismissal – what can we expect a mere fiction to tell us about paranoid aggression when historical facts speak of it with such loud eloquence? – and then pompously rehabilitated.

But it is not made clear why Molière's misanthrope possesses a paradigmatic value superior to that of the self-accusing Bolshevik. Indeed the overwhelmingly intricate cultural mediations through which the underlying psychical mechanism has passed in each of these illustrative cases make both of them markedly less tractable than the clinical case-material that Lacan adduces elsewhere in the paper. The epistemic claims of imaginative literature are thus asserted, denied, forcibly re-asserted and equally forcibly re-denied as the paper proceeds. The psychoanalytic paradigm visible in the literary text must by definition be visible elsewhere too, and literature must be reminded that it has no enduring prerogatives. That paradigm derives its authority not from any one discursive convention or any one pre-existing observational record, but from its capacity to migrate indefinitely among a variety of associated discourses – clinical, historical, philosophical, dramatic, poetic – and to attract suitable observational materials to itself as it travels. Literature may contribute to a public demonstration of the fact that psychoanalytic concepts are overdetermined, but that demonstration will convince only if literature follows the destiny of all other modelling devices and is, in its turn, supplanted.

The full story of Lacan's disaffection from literature and from literary models within psychoanalytic theory cannot be recounted here. But the rhythm of admiration, envy and aggression that marks his handling of literary materials produces an unstable and all but unlearnable lesson for the literary scholar who comes to Lacan's work in search of instruction. On the one hand, as we have seen, Lacan is very different from Freud in the elaborate tribute that he pays to the literary text: it is opaque, involved, self-referring, heavy with the promise of meaning, and offers not simply a theoretical model for the unconscious but a practical model for the psychoanalyst as verbal performer. At moments literature is the royal road to psychoanalytic understanding, and the literary scholar an honoured travelling companion, a fellow adventurer on polysemic seas and a fellow seeker after a buried, 'original' order of meaning. But on the other hand, and at other moments, literature is nothing much – a passing instance of self-replicating structure in a world where all other mental productions are such structure too. Lacan's most expansive tribute to poetry in 'L'instance de la lettre dans l'inconscient' contains a characteristic vacillation:

> Mais il suffit d'écouter la poésie . . . pour que s'y fasse entendre une polyphonie et que tout discours s'avère s'aligner sur les plusieurs portées d'une partition.
>
> Nulle chaîne signifiante en effet qui ne soutienne comme appendu à la ponctuation de chacune de ses unités tout ce qui s'articule de contextes attestés, à la verticale, si l'on peut dire, de ce point.[50] (503)

If you want to understand the unconscious as a signifying chain, poetry will help you figure it; and if you want to understand the signifying power of poetry, polyphonic music will help you figure that . . . The play of substitutions between different structural orders that can be observed in miniature here is a major feature of Lacan's later thinking. The *Knotenpunkte* of the literary text give way to Borromean knots, Moebius strips, algorithms, mathemes. And the quest for higher-order formal systems in which to articulate the logic of the signifier may itself be abandoned in ways that overshoot or undershoot the profession of letters altogether. As Lacan celebratedly said at a conference in Johns Hopkins University in the late 1960s: 'The best image to sum up the unconscious is Baltimore in the early morning.'[51] Such gestures from Lacan, of which there are many, hold out little hope or encouragement to the profession of letters, even in Baltimore.

The best hope to be had from Lacan for the relationship between psychoanalysis and literary studies seems to me this: that the resurgent science of rhetoric, as applied to literary texts, might eventually find a psychodynamic theory that is appropriate to it in complexity and explanatory range. Even this hope, which is of necessity a qualified one, has to be worked for, and extricated from the false promises and premature solutions that Lacan's literary manner has held out to criticism. A major teaching of psychoanalysis for Lacan is that the unconscious has a 'style' of its own, and in a number of his programmatic statements on the transmission of psychoanalytic doctrine he may easily suggest to the unwary that this style can, by mere exposure to its benign contagion, be 'caught':

> Tout retour à Freud qui donne matière à un enseignement digne de ce nom, ne se produira que par la voie, par où la vérité la plus cachée se manifeste dans les révolutions de la culture. Cette voie est la seule formation que nous puissions prétendre à transmettre à ceux qui nous suivent. Elle s'appelle: un style.[52] (458)

There are of course taut and slack ways of reading pronouncements like this. The slackest reading of all would perhaps be the one which concluded that the style of the unconscious, a recommended style of psychoanalytic theorising and Lacan's own literary style were in some obscure fashion coterminous, and that an on-the-cheap understanding of the unconscious could be had by the cultivation of Lacanian verbal mannerisms. It would seem that Lacan has often been understood in this way, if we may conjecture from the numerous dismal exercises in Lacanobabble that have already found their way into print. Here a pun, there a portent, a paradox for all occasions, everywhere a carefree dance to the beguiling music of the signifier . . . I hesitate to spoil such sport, or to recommend slowness and exigency to those literary scholars who have felt a thrill of emancipation run through their own writing after exposure to Lacan's charismatic touch. But it makes little sense for literary scholarship, traditionally so poorly furnished with theoretical self-awareness, to be content with quibbles, conceits and conundrums when a powerful new theory of the *res literaria* is at hand.

The new theory that I am referring to here is not psychoanalysis at large so much as the psychoanalytic account of discourse announced by Freud in *The Interpretation of Dreams*, *The Psycho-*

pathology of Everyday Life and *Jokes and their Relation to the Unconscious* and re-articulated by Lacan. This account is extraordinarily adept at providing coherent and mobile interrelationships between moments and levels within discourse that are often –'for convenience', it is said – partitioned off from one another by analysts of literary texts. It allows individual utterances simultaneously their syntactic and their counter-syntactic modes of connection, their directedness towards a propositional goal and their accumulating cargo of associations. It allows that undeclared meanings may trace their paths both in plain-spoken declarations and in oblique refusals to declare. But perhaps most provocatively of all it insists on giving an intentional past and an intentional future to utterances that present themselves as inhabiting the imperishable *now* of right-minded self-expression. For Freud the psychical life of the human individual was organised in such a way that, far from simply hovering in Romantic languor between the irrecoverable and the unattainable, its every present moment was doubly pressurised: the individual in his speech was actively revising and restructuring his past[53] in view of an actively desired future, and any understanding of what individuals meant when they said what they said – inside or outside the analytic dialogue – was a matter of holding a proper interpretative balance between these retroactive and anticipatory forces.

Lacan's contribution to the closer study of these forces takes a number of distinct forms. He constructs logical models for the processes of mental restructuration and prestructuration that underlie human conduct. He relates those models to linguistics and linguistics itself to the temporality of intersubjective speech. And he pays his writerly tribute to the concepts of retroaction and anticipation by creating an elaborate interplay between tenses and between time-levels in his own syntax. The extent to which these distinct goals may be pursued conjointly will be apparent from this retrospective summary, in 'Fonction et champ' (1953), of Lacan's earlier paper 'Le Temps logique' (1945):

> L'auteur de ces lignes a tenté de démontrer en la logique d'un sophisme les ressorts de temps par où l'action humaine, en tant qu'elle s'ordonne à l'action de l'autre, trouve dans la scansion de ses hésitations l'avènement de sa certitude, et dans la décision qui la conclut donne à l'action de l'autre qu'elle inclut désormais, avec sa sanction quant au passé, son sens à venir.
>
> On y démontre que c'est la certitude anticipée par le sujet dans le *temps pour comprendre* qui, par la hâte précipitant le *moment de conclure*, détermine chez l'autre la décision qui fait du propre mouvement du sujet erreur ou vérité.[54] (287)

In these two paragraphs, each of which is also a single sentence of some complexity, Lacan's logical model makes its return journey to syntax and to the local determinations of the signifying chain: the new sense of temporality and causality that psychoanalysis fosters, having earlier been formalised as a silent drama of consecutive logical operations, now again becomes psychoanalytic raw-material *par excellence* – backward- and forward-looking speech.

I spoke a moment ago about a possible new relationship between rhetoric and the psychodynamic theory elaborated by psychoanalysis. But students of rhetoric might with some justice protest at this point that rhetoric *already knows* about temporal and causal mechanisms like these as they occur in discourse, that rhetoric *already is* a sufficiently versatile dynamics of speech and that any attempt to introduce it to an extraneous psychological theory will cause occult qualities to run riot amongst a set of well-organised and well-tested analytic conventions. If psychoanalysis, they might add, is to constitute itself belatedly as an alternative dynamics of speech, then let it at least learn a lesson in strictness from the speech-science of antiquity and its modern continuators. One of our most distinguished new rhetoricians, Gérard Genette, whose cult of strictness by no means excludes play from his own writing, becomes notably impatient when play takes a 'psychological' turn and seeks in his 'Discours du récit' to reclaim for rhetoric precisely the notions of 'anticipation' and 'retrospection'; he does this in part by depsychologising their names:

pour éviter les connotations psychologiques attachées à l'emploi de termes comme 'anticipation' ou 'rétrospection', qui évoquent spontanément des phénomènes subjectifs, nous les éliminerons le plus souvent au profit de deux termes plus neutres: désignant par *prolepse* toute manœuvre narrative consistant à raconter ou évoquer d'avance un événement ultérieur, et par *analepse* toute évocation après coup d'un événement antérieur au point de l'histoire où l'on se trouve . . .[55]

Prolepsis and *analepsis* are to be joined later in this seminal essay by *syllepsis*, *metalepsis* and *paralepsis*, all similarly decontaminated; each technical term is given clear contours by Genette and retains them even when the literary texts under discussion become dauntingly embroiled (other critics retreat from the rhetorical imbroglio of Proust's *A la recherche*: Genette does not); and 'psychology' would indeed be the enemy of such a rhetorical system if it brought into the discussion arbitrary consignments of affectivity and subjectivity rather than system of its own.

But psychoanalysis is a system of a peculiarly obdurate and resourceful kind. It has had of course its misfortunes in promulgating itself as such. Its central object of concern – desire – still sounds to many ears like the quintessence of the unsystematisable. It has had to borrow names for its method of studying desire from existing systematic disciplines: it has been a hydraulics, an economics, a topography, a semantics, a poetics and a rhetoric of desire – and many odder things besides – and while gaining from these disciplines an air of conceptual and terminological integration has come in the process to seem parasitical upon them. And certain of its concepts – 'repression', 'sublimation', the 'ego', the 'Freudian slip' – have been assimilated so readily by the psychological vernacular of twentieth-century Europe and North America that it has become possible, though unwise, to claim against psychoanalysis that common sense must have known *ab initio* what Freud presented as discoveries of his own. But despite these misfortunes psychoanalysis has pursued its systematic calling, and nowhere more plainly than in its major theoretical mutations: in Freud's revisions of his own theory and in Lacan's retelling of their history, psychoanalysis has been intent both upon the removal of systemic dissonances from within itself and upon the extension of its systematising reach. The rhetorician who looks beyond his minutely differentiated tropes and figures into the desire-laden world of an unspecified 'psychology' is indeed likely to feel that his analytic categories are being threatened by a resurrected vitalism, or by an encroaching tide of mere animal energy. But if he looks into the desiring system postulated by psychoanalysis he will find another rhetoric – of anxiety, obsession, pleasure and unpleasure, fore-pleasure and after-pleasure, repression and remembrance – strikingly similar to his own in its capacity to multiply, separate and interconnect its categories. This rhetoric, which in Lacan's texts often calls itself by that name, still has an insolent habit of calling itself by other names too, and of presenting itself both as a science of language and as a science of the unnameable propellent forces in human living. But rhetoric proper will find a refracted version of itself in the improper psychoanalytic domain. Psychoanalysis is a rhetoric under construction; one that takes risks; one that creates categories in the thick of its own appetites. And it is perhaps in this sense of obstructed and exacerbated kinship betwen the two intellectual disciplines that their value to each other resides.[56]

During the composition of *The Interpretation of Dreams*, Freud was galvanised by an idea of G. T. Fechner's in his *Elements of Psychophysics*, and he warmly acknowledged his debt to Fechner on a number of later occasions.[57] This idea, as Freud reported it to Fliess in 1898, was that 'the dream process is played out in a different psychic territory' (Freud/Fliess, 299; *Origins*, 244–5). Here were the beginnings of Freud's career as a mental topographer. Although there were dangers and limitations in imagining the mind as spatially extended, the representation of the unconscious and the preconscious–conscious systems as alternative 'psychic territories' had a singular expressive advantage: it reminded the mental scientist as he set out to construct further and more inflected mental models that the mind was incurably self-divided and that between its inner territories no permanent bridges could be built. The expressive power of Fechner's idea, which was exploited by Lacan on numerous occasions, can be further exploited in summarising the 'best hope' that Lacan allows for a relationship between psychoanalysis and literary studies: let each of them be for the other not an obliging mirror or a casual adornment, but an *anderer Schauplatz*,[58] an insistent and disobliging 'other scene'.

Epilogue

Je n'ay presque plus rien de ma forme première,
Ma parole n'est plus qu'une confuse voix

Marc-Antoine Charpentier: *Actéon*

Almost nothing remains of my original form;
My speech is no longer anything but a confused voice

IT WOULD BE CONVENIENT to assume that Freud's *Wißtrieb*, his instinct for knowledge, exerted a continuous daily pressure upon those for whom it was an avidity of mind. Upon, say, Freud, Proust and Lacan. Just as it would be convenient to assume that the knowledge-seeker's working fictions and hypotheses – the mental constructions by which he experimentally produces the pleasures of knowledge as fine gradations of fore-pleasure – exerted a continuous counter-pressure upon the world. The convenience here would be more than a matter simply of providing him with a heroic emblem of himself at work, a flattering fiction with which to re-energise him for the later stages of his task. For this double image could also serve as an embryonic explanation of explanation itself, and one for which the widely admired virtues of economy and elegance could be claimed. A world to be known, a desire to know, a perceptive and adroitly manipulative mental apparatus at the ready . . . from a promisingly simple conjunction such as this, the pursuit of knowledge could scarcely emerge as other than wholesome, progressive and encouraging.

But if Freud, Proust and Lacan are to be thought of as exemplary figures in the recent history of the *Wißtrieb*, and as theorists of indefinitely self-replenishing zeal – it will be plain that both descriptions seem to me deserved – we should perhaps pause to ask whether economy and elegance are in fact prominent among the virtues that their works possess. Each of these writers provides us, of course, with impressive moments of adequation or commensurability between his report on experience and his report on the theory-making that experience prompts: such theoretical contrivances as the Oedipus complex, involuntary memory and the mirror phase, to name only the best publicised, have a still extraordinary capacity to organise the teeming observational materials with which each writer surrounds them, and this capacity is no less extraordinary when we have reminded ourselves of the sleight-of-hand by which adequation is achieved in each case. Yet each writer is also inhabited by a demon, an imp of the perverse, who seeks to wreck the persuasive correspondence between experience and theory by driving theory into surplus. A benevolent account of this process would say that such is the propensity of fertile minds, 'invent or perish' being their slogan. But Freud, Proust and Lacan have each a much stronger destructive appetite than this suggests: theories, even the most cherished, must be shown to be mutable or destructible lest further theories cease to be worth contriving. Where other people's theories are often unmade by thinkers of this kind as a simple preliminary to the establishment of their own, the aggressive energy directed against their own theories once these have been established has an altogether more intimate purpose: it is a way of achieving longevity for one's desires. As theory and experience reach their moment of certain-seeming correspondence, uncertainty becomes an emotional imperative.

Freud speaks in the closing pages of his 'Notes upon a Case of Obsessional Neurosis' (1909) of the neurotic patient's need for uncertainty and doubt and of the elaborate manœuvres that he is often compelled to adopt in order to remain uncertain in a world where accurate measuring devices and reliable sources of information exist (x, 232). Secure knowledge would bring him unspeakable terror. But this passage is so drained of precise clinical reference, and so infused with allusions of a general epistemological kind, that it becomes a miniature portrait of everyman as thinker. Freud has clearly known, and expects his reader to recognise, that tendency of thought – at large, in neurosis and beyond it – by which the cult of self-preservation by uncertainty may be taken to a self-destructive extreme. Obsessional neurosis as discussed by Freud here is a mental affliction for which 'philosophising', 'theorising' and 'metaphysical questioning' could easily be thought appropriate alternative names. Psychoanalysis was, after all, 'a mental science which makes it possible to understand both normal and pathological processes as parts of the same natural course of events' ('Goethe Prize Address' (1930), XXI, 208). Yet it would make only very weak sense for me to say at this stage in my enquiry that Freud's account is 'like Proust's' or 'like Lacan's' in its ready assimilation of 'pathological' to 'normal' or 'neurotic' to 'theoretical' mental performances. A much stronger point of comparison is at hand, however, as soon as the self-destructiveness of the theorising mind is considered, and it is Lacan, in the tragical jesting of 'La Chose freudienne', who offers the most compelling image of the speculative extremities to which each of these writers finds himself driven.

In the face of Freud's militant self-portraits as Moses, Hannibal,

Alexander and Napoleon, Lacan depicts him as Actaeon, hunted and devoured, in a passage that I referred to earlier[1] and shall now quote in full:

> Mais si une métaphore plus grave convient au protagoniste, c'est celle qui nous montrerait en Freud un Actéon perpétuellement lâché par des chiens dès l'abord dépistés, et qu'il s'acharne à relancer à sa poursuite, sans pouvoir ralentir la course où seule sa passion pour la déesse le mène. Le mène si loin qu'il ne peut s'arrêter qu'aux grottes où la Diane chtonienne dans l'ombre humide qui les confond avec le gîte emblématique de la vérité, offre à sa soif, avec la nappe égale de la mort, la limite quasi mystique du discours le plus rationnel qui ait été au monde, pour que nous y reconnaissions le lieu où le symbole se substitue à la mort pour s'emparer de la première boursouflure de la vie.
>
> Cette limite et ce lieu, on le sait, sont loin encore d'être atteints pour ses disciples, si tant est qu'ils ne refusent pas de l'y suivre, et l'Actéon donc qui ici est dépecé, n'est pas Freud, mais bien chaque analyste à la mesure de la passion qui l'enflamma et qui a fait, selon la signification qu'un Giordano Bruno dans ses *Fureurs héroïques* sut tirer de ce mythe, de lui la proie des chiens de ses pensées.[2]
>
> (412)

The historical content of this Ovidian parable is plain enough: in the works of Freud the rational discourse and the rational scientific ambitions of the nineteenth century reached a culminating point, but they overreached themselves in the process and began to disintegrate irreversibly. Diana, who in the play of this augustly facetious text is both the underground divinity of the unconscious mind and a temporary resident of Plato's cave, has given thinking an intolerable burden of risk and futility. In the well-known tale that Freud himself had told about the destruction of modern European man's self-esteem, psychoanalysis had come as a blow of millennial proportions: it was the psychological counterpart to the cosmological and biological blows already administered by Copernicus and Darwin (XVII, 140–1, XIX, 221).[3] But although the damage inflicted upon the narcissism of the human species during the psychoanalytic epoch could be expected to be qualitatively distinct from that caused by earlier scientific revolutions – in that psychoanalysis proclaimed the human mind inherently and irreparably self-divided – Freud often presented his own doctrine as an edifice bizarrely untouched by the cataclysm that it had provoked. The scientific rationality that had (we are to suppose) actuated Copernicus and Darwin, far from surviving into the new epoch in the tenuous and imperilled form that psychoanalysis seemed to predict, had found in Freud a fearless new upholder.

In Lacan's even more overtly mythicised version of the same story, on the other hand, psychoanalysis is thought not simply imperilled but permanently in flight and with no hope of refuge other than the end of thought. There is nothing surprising about such mentalising and moralising elaborations of Ovid, even in the twentieth century when they are no longer in vogue. Indeed Lacan is here inserting himself with unusual straightforwardness into an ancient tradition. Behind Lacan's Actaeon, there is Bruno's, duly acknowledged:

> I' allargo i miei pensieri
> Ad alta preda, ed essi a me rivolti
> Morte mi dàn con morsi crudi e fieri
>
> I stretch my thoughts to the sublime prey,
> and these springing back upon me, bring me death
> by their hard and cruel gnawing.[4]

just as, behind Bruno's, there are Boccaccio's and Petrarch's (and many others):

> Vero dirò; forse e' parrà menzogna:
> ch'i' senti' trarmi de la propria imago
> et in un cervo solitario et vago
> di selva in selva ratto mi trasformo,
> et ancor de' miei can fuggo lo stormo.
>
> I shall speak the truth, perhaps it will appear a lie,
> for I felt myself drawn from my own image
> and into a solitary wandering stag
> from wood to wood quickly I am transformed
> and still I flee the belling of my hounds.[5]

Lacan resembles Bruno and Petrarch in particular among his many distinguished predecessors – in his presentation of death as self-chosen by the desiring mind. The mind, by allowing its passion to pursue certain goals at all – Laura, the beauty of the Divine, the unconscious – conduces to its own ruin; the imagery of all three writers fuses the sexual and intellectual modes of desire into a unitary portrait of mind as enthusiastic, rapacious and self-consuming in all its pursuits. Lacan is at a far remove from the hyper-virginal, epistemic Diana that Kierkegaard's narrator constructs for himself in *Diary of the Seducer*: 'I am not interested in spying on her in her bath, not at all, but I would like to spy on her with my questions.'[6] Again there is little to surprise us in the willingness of Lacan's Freud to spy upon the goddess with eyes and questions at once – Freud himself had familiarly linked the *Wißtrieb* with the *Schautrieb* and portrayed the knowledge-seeker as an infant *voyeur* newly come of age. Similarly the Hegelian deathhauntedness of the Symbolic order over which the modern Diana presides will be quite the expected thing for any experienced reader of *Écrits*. But what seems to me distinctly surprising is that Lacan's emblematic Freud, hounded by thoughts that are the death of thought, propelled by desires that would extinguish desire if allowed to run their course, should be offered as a model of rectitude to the psychoanalytic profession. In its earliest form 'La Chose freudienne' was a commemorative oration delivered at the Viennese neuro-psychiatric clinic, and Lacan repeatedly taunts his clinical audience with a contrast between Freud's intellectual heroism and the alleged pusillanimity of most clinicians, Freudian or not. Their failure of moral nerve and energy lies in their reluctance to be inflamed by their thinking, and in their refusal, once inflamed, to be devoured.[7] Strong medicine indeed.

In the closing paragraph of the paper, which recapitulates and further amplifies the fateful encounter between Actaeon and Diana, sarcasm and moral exhortation are transmuted into grandiose prophetic utterance:

> Car la vérité s'y avère complexe par essence, humble en ses offices et étrangère à la réalité, insoumise au choix du sexe, parente de la mort et, à tout prendre, plutôt inhumaine, Diane peut-être . . . Actéon trop coupable à courre la déesse, proie où se prend, veneur, l'ombre que tu deviens, laisse la meute aller sans que ton pas se presse, Diane à ce qu'ils vaudront reconnaître les chiens . . .[8] (436)

The unconscious is again the unthinkable extremity towards which the analyst is driven and from which he flees, although this later passage has a new focal point: it is an attempt to represent the horrified moment between advance and recoil, between the vivifying and mortifying phases of the hunt for truth. Devices of style that elsewhere in *Écrits* often inject an air of distraction into Lacan's writing are here used to supply a set of triumphantly apposite ambiguities. Who is the prey, Actaeon or Diana? Lacan's appositional syntax allows both readings. Is Actaeon a live exponent of venery or a dying stag? The tenses make him both, by placing him at an uncertain moment of present futurity or future anteriority – just as Titian, in the superb *Diana and Actaeon* now in Edinburgh (Plate 4), sends the young huntsman's astonished glance both towards the goddess and towards the stag's skull that is an emblem of his posthumous fate. Does Actaeon's guilt come from having hunted the goddess in the first place or from some other, unspecified, source that now prevents him from hunting her further? 'Trop coupable à courre la déesse' contains an incongru-

4 Titian, *Diana and Actaeon*; Edinburgh, National Gallery of Scotland

ous preposition – as if *à* were the resultant when the semantic forces of the permissible prepositions (*pour* and *de*) converged – and this makes both kinds of guilt equally probable; 'à courre' also introduces an echo both of *chasse à courre* ('hunting') and of *être à court de* ('to be short of'): Actaeon, we are invited to surmise, has taken to the woods and fields because he is short of a goddess. And what of the dogs upon which the paper closes? They are Freud's thoughts, enchanted by the unconscious, turning murderously upon their author. But the central thrust of Lacan's invective in 'La Chose freudienne' would suggest that they are Freud's thoughts in another guise too – codified and professionalised by an international organisation and thereby fated to dissipate their native strength. In this second reading, the baying pack would be latterday psychoanalysts, recognised by 'Diana' as worthless. Ambiguities of this kind produce a psychology of thinking that is at the same time an ecstatic vision of undifferentiated mental process. A parting sarcasm gives Lacan's trance its last characteristic savour of wilfulness and aggression.

'Toute pulsion est virtuellement pulsion de mort' (848), Lacan writes in 'Position de l'inconscient' (1960).[9] By thus seeming to place a major element of his professional creed under the sign of Thanatos, Lacan will simply have confirmed for certain of his readers what they have long darkly suspected: that psychoanalysis is indeed an 'impossible' profession, a science of the unthinkable, a symptom of the malady that it claims to diagnose, at best a modern version of homeopathic magic. But Lacan's hyperbolising of the Actaeon myth, and his insistence that the theme of death both must be addressed and cannot not be addressed in the psychoanalytic dialogue, draw attention to a feature of Freud's thinking that its detractors energetically ignore. Freud is often accused of having given his psychodynamic systems a self-fulfilling circularity that immunises them against rational criticism. And certainly in his periodic accounts of 'resistance to psychoanalysis' as a symptom that psychoanalysis alone is equipped to explain he is serenely unconcerned to conceal the indigent logic that underlies them: 'if you object to what I say I must be right'.[10] Against the complacency of this, and against the arrogance and dogmatism that are clearly visible elsewhere in Freud's works, Lacan gives us a version of Freudian thinking that is remarkable for its negative capability – its power to endure amid the disasters that the theorising mind inflicts upon itself. Lacan looks from book to book in the Freudian corpus, attends both to the areas of irresolution within a theory at a given moment and to its mutations over time, and points, not with condescension or *Schadenfreude* but with a sense of rightness being rediscovered in the world, to the tendency of psychoanalytic theories to collapse or implode.

Lacan's vision of these theories *in statu moriendi* – achieving their rightness by refusing to be right – brings with it, as I have already suggested in an earlier chapter, its own dangers of circularity and complacency ('the more ragged, desiring, intentional, over-determined, uncircumscribable and unfinishable my theorising becomes the more it resembles the unconscious that my theorising postulates').[11] Yet Lacan's redescription of the Freudian unconscious captures one dimension of the psychoanalytic project with uncanny lucidity. That project re-emerges in Lacan's account as a set of strict therapeutic and hygienic measures for the theoretical intelligence and a prolegomenon, scrupulous but of indefinite duration, to any future epistemology. The unconscious is at once the supreme object of knowledge and the overriding (liberating and disabling) condition under which knowledge is pursued. Ever-present yet elusive, monumental yet made out of impalpable desire, systematic yet destructive of system, plain-spoken yet incurably ironic . . . the unconscious constructed by Lacan from a disparate mass of Freudian and other materials offers one cogent overview of Freud's entire theoretical production. In this perspective the history of Freud's theories is the history of a lost innocence and an insatiable intellectual jealousy. His explanations perpetually fall short of their *explicanda*, or exceed them, or circumvent them. The unconscious is Freud's Diana, his Laura, his Albertine – the force that by refusing to be known sets in motion an unstoppable theoretical machine.

Psychoanalysis redefined in these terms continually reminds the theoretical intelligence that it is embodied and mortal and re-introduces a disorganising sense of flux into its models of itself. The future epistemology that this psychoanalysis now promises is one that is able to tailor itself to the endemic discontinuities of the human mind, to hear and speak the crazed, irresolute language of mind-in-process. But the self-inflicted wounds of psychoanalysis are not all of this salutary kind, and I shall now summarise some of the more damaging features of the psychoanalytic style of thinking, in what seems to me an ascending order of gravity.

First, the opportunities for self-criticism that Freud derived from his own consecutive models of the mental life and made available as a general problematics to model-builders at large have often been calamitously wasted within the profession of psychoanalysis. Proponents of Freudian theory who have received their main lesson from Freud's own writings – as distinct from psychoanalytic textbooks and manuals – might be expected to possess an uncommonly acute sense of theory in its local cultural determinations and to grant with exemplary candour that theories, like dreams and phantasies, have among many other notable qualities that of fulfilling the theorist's wishes. They might be expected to grant also that psychoanalytic concepts and paradigms, even when they have to a large extent been purged of those wishes, are transient conventions, destined to be displaced by others that have higher explanatory power – or that are just other. But, although the senior scientific disciplines upon which psychoanalysis modelled itself in its formative years have plainly continued to alter in this way, psychoanalysis has protected its founding concepts with jealous vigilance. It could well be that precisely the negativity directed by Freud against his own theories at certain 'heroic' moments of doubt has seemed to remove the need for sustained self-criticism and conceptual innovation within the profession that he inaugurated. Freud was the founder both of a self-reflexive theoretical style and of a doctrine. For a majority of his successors it has proved easier to replicate the doctrine than to emulate the style. The politics of psychoanalytic knowledge are marked by two complementary restrictions: in the domestic sphere, a supererogatory adherence to the original paradigms and, in the sphere of external relations, a refusal to enter into serious preliminary discussion, let alone collaboration or declared rivalry, with adjacent conceptual systems. Emancipatory lessons are still to be learnt from the works of Freud by those who willingly enclose themselves in the authoritarian professional system that he created for the transmission of his concepts.

Secondly, psychoanalysis, by severing mind from society and from history and by nominating a timeless, asocial *seelischer Apparat* as its prime object of study, has made itself into a passive recipient of disguised messages from the excluded public world. While cautiously adjusting its theoretical apparatus to the fluctuating needs of 'soul' and vigorously safeguarding its therapeutic procedures, it has become all unknowingly (it would seem) imprinted with an astonishing variety of reactionary social practices. At its worst, it has become a combined unguent and astringent for the psyche under consumer capitalism. And this would-be bastion of enlightenment, this mind-made source of illumination turned proudly back upon the mind, has entered into complicity with *l'infâme*; its delicate inscriptions and re-inscriptions of the unconscious mind have become a *tabula rasa* upon which certain dominant myths of the age may be rewritten without being subjected to any form of critical scrutiny.

But thirdly, and more damagingly still, psychoanalysis has actively trivialised those social determinants of mental structure that it has felt obliged, however reluctantly, to take into account. Freud spoke often about the interface between individual and society, and did so in a memorably programmatic way at the start of *Group Psychology and the Analysis of the Ego* (1921):

> The contrast between individual psychology and social or group psychology, which at a first glance may seem to be full of significance, loses a great deal of its sharpness when it is examined more closely. It is true that individual psychology is concerned with the individual man and explores the paths by which he seeks to find satisfaction for his instinctual impulses; but only rarely and under certain exceptional conditions is individual psychology in a position to disregard the relations of this individual to others. In the individual's mental life someone else is invariably involved, as a model, as an object, as a helper, as an opponent; and so from the very first individual psychology, in this extended but entirely justifiable sense of the words, is at the same time social psychology as well. (XVIII, 69)

But this programme has not been fulfilled, and the variety of interactions and reciprocal determinations that Freud sketches here have not been pursued with anything approaching theoretical seriousness by his followers. The history of human culture is often, for psychoanalysis today, the history merely of repression and its vicissitudes; and repression – like the desire that it acts upon – is often a mere psychological datum, a mere fact of the inward life. As all societies and social groups are agencies for the control of human desire, the specific pathogenic pressures exerted by this collectivity rather than that have seemed to lack force and coherence as scientific or clinical subject-matter. Apathy and disenchantment seem the inevitable lot of any theorist who looks upon society through this sort of lens. Why look, therefore? Freud's resigned turning inwards to the mind conceived of as a quasi-autonomous system of interrelated forces is not markedly improved upon by Lacan, for all his insistence that language is the inevitable bearer of social meanings into the mental interior. Lacan's 'chain of signifiers' cannot do otherwise than bind the individual mind to the ambient social world in which the chain has been forged, but this does not mean – *pace* many Lacanian disciples – that psychoanalysis has come of age as a social theory. Lacan's theory, like Freud's, does of course already allow social forces to be seen at work in the production of certain relatively stable configurations or propensities of desire – 'mind-types', we might call them – and that theory is at moments extraordinarily instructive in studying such social and political materials as authoritarianism, psychopathic crime, the policing of sexual minorities, sexual and racial prejudice. But detailed work on the interpenetration of social structure on the one hand and psychical structure of the kind that psychoanalysis describes on the other has still to be done – and in the meantime magical political slogans of a *psychanalysant* kind are a poor substitute for it.

The problem is twofold: psychoanalysis has to a large extent failed to develop its own early social insights, but it has also, and more completely, failed to answer the most searching of the early critiques that were directed at it. Such works as V. N. Vološinov's *Freudianism. A Marxist Critique* (1927)[12] or Georges Politzer's *Critique des fondements de la psychologie* (1928), for all their pamphleteering exuberance and overstatement, raise crucial difficulties that, fully considered, could have been of major benefit to psychoanalysis in refining and expanding its theory. A collaborative research programme between psychoanalysis and sociology has been called for regularly since the early thirties, and perhaps most challengingly by writers associated with the Frankfurt Institute for Social Research: by the young Erich Fromm in his paper 'The Method and Function of an Analytic Social Psychology' (1932) and by Adorno and Habermas on numerous occasions.[13] But 'official' institutional psychoanalysis, though committed to dialogue in its clinical and scientific procedures, has firmly refused these invitations to dialogue with its most eligible neighbour among the human sciences.

In my preface, I said that this book was not to be a work of theory and I do not intend to turn it into one at this late stage, although the need for a fully interactive theory of social and psychical structure is an urgent one. The best that I can do to promote this goal at the end of a study that has, in part, sought to align psychoanalysis with a monumental work of prose fiction is perhaps simply to remind my reader of Proust's capacity, in describing feeling and behaviour, to work productively on the borders of society and the individual mind. Explanations of the interactive kind that psychoanalysis all too often eschews are of course the copper coinage of Proust's novel. As a concrete reminder of this dimension, I shall return briefly to the myth of Actaeon, and set against the mentalising pathos of Lacan's vision the thoroughly socialised eroticism of Proust's. In this passage from the opening of *Sodome et Gomorrhe*, Charlus is addressing Jupien on his sexual tastes and tactics and being overheard by the narrator:

> Un des garçons d'étage m'était connu, je lui désignai un curieux petit 'chasseur', qui fermait les portières et qui resta réfractaire à mes propositions. A la fin, exaspéré, pour lui prouver que mes intentions étaient pures, je lui fis offrir une somme ridiculement élevée pour monter seulement me parler cinq minutes dans ma chambre. Je l'attendis inutilement. Je le pris alors en un tel dégoût que je sortais par la porte de service pour ne pas apercevoir la frimousse de ce vilain petit drôle. J'ai su depuis qu'il n'avait jamais eu aucune de mes lettres, qui avaient été interceptées, la première par le garçon d'étage qui était envieux, la seconde par le concierge de jour qui était vertueux, la troisième par le concierge de nuit qui aimait le jeune chasseur et couchait avec lui à l'heure où Diane se levait. Mais mon dégoût n'en a pas moins persisté et, m'apporterait-on le chasseur comme un simple gibier de chasse sur un plat d'argent, je le repousserais avec un vomissement.[14] (612–13)

This Actaeon is a creature of social history as well as of myth: the *chasseur* ('page-boy', 'huntsman') who has been the momentary object of Charlus's sexual curiosity is so named because his hotel uniform is a reminiscence at least of hunting livery. His predecessors wearing this attire will have had outdoor work as grooms, and their predecessors in turn will have been real, low-ranking participants in the hunt. Proust's play on *chasseur* takes us back through historical time into the world of myth and legend, and his Diana is doubly determined in the same way: she is the divine patroness of the lubricious male *concierge* but also Diane de Poitiers, mentioned by Charlus earlier in the same paragraph. The euhemerism here sardonically applied by Charlus to the lower orders in their amorous sport is elsewhere in the novel often applied by members of the aristocratic caste to themselves: self-divinisation is one prominent technique by which Proust's decaying aristocracy buys itself time. But Proust threads into the farcical politics of Charlus's monologue an equally farcical portrait of predatory sexuality. Charlus remembers that in becoming a stag Actaeon becomes edible, and duly imagines his *chasseur* killed, cooked and served at table. Proust relishes here not only the plasticity of libido, the transformation of one incorporative appetite into another, but also the libidinal basis of social conduct – Charlus's perceptions of class are bathed in sexual phantasy and his absurdly over-ripe disgust at the unresponsive *chasseur* has its simultaneous social, emotional and physical causes. Proust's inglorious Actaeon, unlike Lacan's, is gloriously overdetermined; and in his fluid movements between history and myth, between sex and society, between mental and physical appetite, he offers a far richer emblem than Lacan's dismembered huntsman of the unfinished task that awaits psychoanalytic theory.

My theme in these pages has been theory's intermittent self-awareness as passion. A large part of this awareness, for the three writers that I have discussed, stems from the repeated discovery that theories and their authors are destructible. All three writers cast themselves adrift upon that mental ocean where the spectacle of theory without end turns thought deathwards. Sooner death than this interminable play of fictions . . . But all three have a contrary passion too. Against theory as fiction they set theory as anticipated certitude. Freud in his archaeology, Proust's jealous narrator in his unwilled rememberings and Lacan in his mute encounters with the *réel* which forever lies beyond the reach of language, all have access to that 'joy resembling certainty' of which the narrator speaks. It is in the self-declaring play of desire between certainty and extinction, between bedrock and deadlock, that their new science begins.

Notes

INTRODUCTION

1 Max Schur describes the early audiences for these lectures (delivered 1915–17) as comprising for the most part 'Freud's students, "intellectuals" and curiosity seekers' (*Freud. Living and Dying*, 1).

2 See, for example, *L'Usage des plaisirs*, 10, where Foucault speaks of a now superseded mode of thought which had had the following goal: 'faire de la sexualité un invariant, et supposer que, si elle prend, dans ses manifestations, des formes historiquement singulières, c'est par l'effet des mécanismes divers de répression, auxquels, en toute société, elle se trouve exposée; ce qui revient à mettre hors champ historique le désir et le sujet du désir, et à demander à la forme générale de l'interdit de rendre compte de ce qu'il peut y avoir d'historique dans la sexualité'. A powerful alternative view of the Freudian concept of repression, and of its heuristic value to historians, is to be found in Peter Gay's *Freud for Historians*.

3 Feminist initiatives within, around and against psychoanalytic theory are among the most crucial of the many assorted initiatives at present taking place in this area. I am thinking in particular of Juliet Mitchell's *Psychoanalysis and Feminism* (1974), Luce Irigaray's *Ce sexe qui n'en est pas un* (1977), *Éthique de la différence sexuelle* (1984) and *Parler n'est jamais neutre* (1985), Jane Gallop's *Feminism and Psychoanalysis. The Daughter's Seduction* (1982) and Juliet Mitchell's and Jacqueline Rose's *Feminine Sexuality* (1982).

4 On Freud's reading of Vaihinger's 'philosophy of "as if"', see below n. 5.

5 Freud often had recourse to the notion of 'fiction' in discussing the uncertain margins towards which a given theory seemed to be propelling him, or the supplementary hypotheses that it seemed to invite (see, for example, XII, 220 n., XIV, 231, XXIII, 235, 239). From 1926, his reading of Kurt Vaihinger's *Die Philosophie des Als Ob* (1911) (*The Philosophy of 'As if'*) is likely to have reinforced his attachment to the notion (see XX, 194 and XXI, 28–9). Two works, very different from each other in aim and scope, which memorably dramatise and problematise 'fiction' as a psychoanalytic category are Octave Mannoni's *Fictions freudiennes* and Maud Mannoni's *La théorie comme fiction* (to which I am indebted for my own sub-title).

6 'truth here reveals its fictive arrangement' (*French Freud*, 46).

7 I should also make it plain that this work does not comprise an introduction to, or a review of, psychoanalytic criticism at large. Such a book now exists: Elizabeth Wright's *Psychoanalytic Criticism. Theory in Practice*. This remarkable work provides not only a comprehensive survey of schools and tendencies – from Freud himself, through Jung, the object-relations theorists and Lacan to Bloom, Derrida, Kristeva and Deleuze and Guattari – but the spectacle of an engaged critical intelligence at work upon live theoretical issues. Max Milner's *Freud et l'interprétation de la littérature* is a lucid introductory survey of those aspects of the Freudian corpus which offer

material for literary critical reflection. The relationship between psychoanalysis and the practice of writing is discussed from a variety of angles in *Écrire la psychanalyse* (*Nouvelle revue de psychanalyse*, 16): see in particular André Green's brilliant essay 'Transcription d'origine inconnue' (27–63).

1. FREUD'S DREAMS OF KNOWLEDGE

1 'Theory is good, but it doesn't prevent things from existing.' For Freud's anecdote, see his obituary of Charcot (III, 13). In the earliest version of the anecdote (I, 139), Charcot's remark was addressed to Freud himself, who had raised a theoretical doubt about one of Charcot's clinical observations (see also VII, 115). The Freud/Charcot relationship has been much discussed, although nowhere, in my experience, with more insight than by J.-B. Pontalis in his *Entre le rêve et la douleur* (11–17).

2 These models are listed below, 101–02.

3 These are to be found in 'On Narcissism: an Introduction' (XIV, 73–102) and *The Ego and the Id* (XIX, 13–66: see in particular, 30, 46).

4 The two instinct theories are summarised briefly below, 38–9. Elsewhere Freud described the coming-into-being of his instinct theory in altogether less dubitative terms than those used in the celebrated remarks that I here quote from the *New Introductory Lectures*. In *Beyond the Pleasure Principle* (1920), for example, the first two of his innovations in this area (the concept of sexuality and the hypothesis of narcissism) 'were a direct translation of observation into theory and were no more open to sources of error than is inevitable in all such cases' (XVIII, 59).

5 Certain writers would contest this 'untestable'. C. R. Badcock, for example, in his *The Psychoanalysis of Culture*, seeks to demonstrate that the theory of culture outlined in *Totem and Taboo* can be tested, and shown to be substantially correct, provided that the observational and experimental purview adopted is suitably large – large enough to include within its panoramic sweep the entire 'case-history' of human religion and society.

6 Stanley Edgar Hyman has provided, in his *The Tangled Bank*, a useful basis for comparison between Freud and Frazer as imaginative writers, although his extreme impatience with *Moses and Monotheism* (see 421–2) causes him to remove this work to the margins of his comparative portrait.

7 For a perceptive brief account of what Freud himself called his 'predilection for the prehistoric in all its human forms' (Freud/Fliess, 342; *Origins*, 275), see Peter Gay, *Freud, Jews and Other Germans*, 39–46; see also J, I, 363.

8 Freud wrote to Fliess on May 28, 1899: 'I gave myself a present, Schliemann's *Ilios*, and greatly enjoyed the account of his childhood. The man was happy when he found Priam's treasure, because happiness comes only with the fulfillment of a childhood wish' (Freud/Fliess, 353; *Origins*, 282); and on December 21 of the same year (describing a patient): 'Buried deep beneath all his fantasies, we found a scene from his primal period (before twenty-two months) which meets all the requirements and in which all the remaining puzzles converge. It is everything at the same time – sexual, innocent, natural, and the rest. I scarcely dare believe it yet. It is as if Schliemann had once more excavated Troy, which had hitherto been deemed a fable' (Freud/Fliess, 391–92; *Origins*, 305).

9 Freud's reaction to this discovery ('annoyance at not being able to be there') is recorded by Max Schur in *Freud. Living and Dying*, 348–9.

10 'The theme of the anterior is its own obsession' (*De l'interprétation*, 426). Ricœur's chapters 'Une archéologie du sujet' and 'Archéologie et téléologie' (407–43, 444–75) are by far the most impressive philosophical reflection that we yet possess on Freud's cult of pastness in psychoanalytic explanation.

11 A magnificent photographic record of Freud's collection is to be found in Edmund Engelman's *Berggasse 19. Sigmund Freud's Home and Offices, Vienna 1938*. Other aspects of Freud's archaeological passion are illustrated in the pictorial biography edited by Ernst Freud and others.

12 Jack Spector, in his invaluable *The Aesthetics of Freud*, surveys Freud's complex self-identification with the figure of Moses and relates convincingly the phantasy-structure of *Moses and Monotheism* to that of the 1914 essay 'The Moses of Michelangelo' (XIII, 211–36). The essential study of Freud's ambivalences towards Jewish tradition is still Marthe Robert's *D'Œdipe à Moïse*.

13 Freud made it plain that 'primal scenes' (*Urszenen*) and other 'primal phantasies' (*Urphantasien*), while having their basis firmly in the material world, could be recreated only by construction and conjecture. A main difficulty in the path of such recreation was the human capacity for 'retrospective phantasy' (*Zurückphantasie*: see *GW*, II/III, 294 and XII, 137n.; IV, 288 and XVII, 103n.), by which later events were projected back upon an earlier past. Analytic 'constructions', Freud is prepared to grant, may have their share of such phantasy (XVI, 336, XVII, 103n.). On Freud's notion of primal phantasy, and on the interplay between the phantasmatic quest for explanatory 'origins' as observed in psychoanalytic patients and the same quest in psychoanalytic theory itself, see Jean Laplanche's and J.-B. Pontalis's classic article 'Fantasme originaire, fantasmes des origines, origine du fantasme'. The stubbornly problematic character of the Freudian quest for the primal or the 'originary' is briefly described by Laplanche in *Vie et mort en psychanalyse*, 209, 218–20 (123, 127–9 in Mehlman's translation). On Freud's recourse to the prefix *Ur-* to signal that which is required to put a stop 'to the sliding of meaning that continually threatens to erupt from the unconscious', see John Forrester, *Language and the Origins of Psychoanalysis*, 130. Wittgenstein remarked of the *Urszene*: 'There is of course the difficulty of determining what scene is the primal scene – whether it is the scene which the patient recognises as such, or whether it is the one whose recollection effects the cure. In practice these criteria are mingled together' (*Lectures and Conversations*, 51).

14 Edward Said, in his admirably problematising collection *Beginnings*, has written of Freud's actual interpretative procedures: 'the interpretation as a whole cannot be visualized at all as having a linear trajectory from birth to maturity, or from ignorance to knowledge, or from absolute terminal to absolute terminal. Neither can one assume that the more antecedent a beginning point, the more certain and the greater the amount of sense. Interpretation is a field of understanding in which statements are dispersed but whose positions can be determined with regard only to certain (but not all) other statements. Not every statement is connected intelligibly with every other one' (169).

15 Freud's identification with Don Giovanni was a conscious one (as Lacan's was to be): 'I send you herewith *il catalogo delle belle*, etc.', he wrote to Fliess on

May 25, 1897 in a note accompanying a bibliography of his scientific publications (*Origins*, 202; Freud/Fliess, 245).

16 Freud constructed an entire 'family romance' around himself as Hannibal, his brother as Hasdrubal and his father as Hamilcar. Having referred to Hamilcar as Hasdrubal in the first edition of *The Interpretation of Dreams* (IV, 197), he corrrected and interpreted the error in *The Psychopathology of Everyday Life* (VI, 217–20), explaining that such an error was especially worthy of note because 'few readers of my book . . . are better acquainted with the history of the house of Barca than its author' (218). In reality Freud's brother was called Alexander – the ten-year-old Freud could well have suggested the name (J, I, 21) –, was the performer of exploits that were disturbing in so far as they rivalled Freud's own (VI, 107–9) and was to be Freud's companion during his conquest of Athens (see below, 31–5).

17 This phantasy of peaceful co-existence between different architectural epochs contrasts sharply with an earlier Roman analogy of Freud's (in *The Interpretation of Dreams*): 'They [day-time phantasies] stand in much the same relation to the childhood memories from which they are derived as do some of the Baroque palaces of Rome to the ancient ruins whose pavements and columns have provided the material for the more recent structures' (V, 492).

18 On aggression and the 'oceanic feeling' in *Civilization and its Discontents*, see Leo Bersani, 'Theory and Violence', 66–70.

19 On the proper translation of *Seele* ('soul') and its cognates as used by Freud, see Bruno Bettelheim, *Freud and Man's Soul*, 70–78. On *seelischer Apparat*, Jean Laplanche comments (*Vie et mort en psychanalyse*, 93n.): 'L'alliance insolite de ces mots vient souligner toute l'originalité du "réalisme" freudien'.

20 On the elaborate personal mythology – 'neurosis', 'phobia' – constructed by Freud from Roman materials, see Alexander Grinstein, *Sigmund Freud's Dreams*, 69–91, Carl E. Schorske, 'Politics and Patricide', 189–93, Sebastiano Timpanaro, 'Freud's "Roman Phobia"'.

21 Freud described his giving of the name Oliver to his second son as a way of transferring to the child his own suppressed megalomania (V, 447–48) and recommended to Ernest Jones, at a time when the first signs of dissension between himself and Jung were beginning to appear, that we 'be kind and patient with Jung and, as old Oliver said, keep our powder dry' (J, I, 348); he identified himself both with Napoleon (see below, 32–5) and with Masséna, who was thought by Freud to be a Jew and for that reason the most fascinating of Napoleon's marshals (IV, 197–98).

22 The motto had already been used for purposes of self-exhortation in Freud's letters to Fliess (Freud/Fliess 374, 441; *Origins*, 298, 330). Peter Gay has discussed trenchantly the rhetoric of 'exploration' in Freud's literary manner: 'Freud's strategies of persuasion all come back to Freud presenting himself as an explorer retracing his steps for the benefit of an intelligent and sympathetic, if inadequately informed, listener. His strenuous voyage, he implies, has more than repaid the strains it imposed with the unexpected and unexampled discoveries that have come along the way and that have culminated in the historic solution of an ancient mystery, the riddle of the Sphinx' (*Freud, Jews and Other Germans*, 57). The entire essay from which this judgment comes ('Sigmund Freud: a German and his Discontents', 29–92) is a model of imaginative generosity and demythologising rigour.

23 In a grandly self-disparaging remark to Marie Bonaparte, Freud is reported to have said: 'Great discoverers are not necessarily great men [*grosse Geister*]. Who changed the world more than Columbus? What was he? An adventurer. He had character, it is true, but he was not a great man' (J, II, 461–2).

24 The myth of the hero (his deeds and historical mission as well as his birth) has now of course passed into the custodianship of the international psychoanalytic movement. Frank J. Sulloway is outstanding among Freudian mythographers and demythologisers for his capacity to combine a sustaining polemical animus with seriousness and responsibility as an intellectual historian (see, in particular, his chapter on 'The Myth of the Hero in the Psychoanalytic Movement', *Freud, Biologist of the Mind*, 445–95). As sustained, serious and responsible critiques of Freud are still so rare, I shall mention here what seems to me the outstanding work to have appeared since Sulloway's: Adolf Grünbaum's *The Foundations of Psychoanalysis*.

25 For Freud's remarks on Schliemann's wish, see above 180n.8. That the spectre of Schliemann is likely to have accompanied Freud to Athens is suggested by the following anecdote recounted by Ernest Jones: 'at half-past ten the next morning, August 30, they sailed for Brindisi, a twenty-four hours' trip. Among the passengers was Professor Dörpfeld, the assistant of the famous archaeologist Schliemann. Freud gazed with awe at the man who had helped to discover ancient Troy, but he was too shy to approach him . . . on September 3 they were in Athens' (J, II, 26).

26 As this paper is among Freud's shortest, I shall not give page references for subsequent quotations from it.

27 Napoleon's bellicosity, for Freud, was intimately connected with the pangs of being a second son. 'To eliminate Joseph', Freud wrote later in 1936 to Thomas Mann, the author of the recently published *Josef in Ägypten*, 'to take his place, to become Joseph himself, must have been Napoleon's strongest emotion as a small child' (*Letters*, 428). Napoleon's coronation as evoked by Freud in the crowning paragraph of his 'Acropolis' essay was a victory at once over father and elder brother – over a brother who was the namesake, as Freud reminds Mann, of the most celebrated Biblical dreamer and dream-interpreter. Thus Freud's self-comparison with Napoleon, having faltered during the early stages of his letter to Mann (Freud was not a second son), re-asserts itself in the end: both were in competition with Joseph (see also Freud/Zweig, 96–7). On the Biblical Joseph as dream-interpreter, see IV, 97, 334, V, 484n. Jack Spector reviews this 'Joseph' motif in *The Aesthetics of Freud*, 47–8. (Proust's narrator not only refers to the Biblical Joseph in this role – 'A la fois Joseph et Pharaon, je me mis à interpréter mon rêve' (I, 629) – but proceeds to describe in his own terms exactly the dream-mechanisms that Freud had recently named condensation and displacement (629–30).)

28 For a fuller account of these events, see J, II, 26–7 and Max Schur (*Freud. Living and Dying*, 225–42), who discusses the superstitious death-fears that accompanied Freud to Athens. Recent studies of the background to Freud's 'disturbance' on the Acropolis, and of other classical motifs in his work, are listed by Alexander Grinstein, *Sigmund Freud's Dreams*, 5–6.

29 *Souvenirs*, 44. 'There is a place where perfection exists; there are not two of them: it is that one. I had never imagined anything like it. It was the ideal crystallised in pentelic marble that revealed itself to me.'

30 *Souvenirs*, 45. 'The surprising thing, indeed, is that the beautiful here is simply absolute honesty, reason, respect even towards the deity.'

31 Harold Bloom has commented in detail on this characteristic of Freud's thinking in his *Agon. Towards a Theory of Revisionism*, 91–118. The essay to which I refer is quoted above, 8.

32 See above, 30.

33 'The technique which I describe in the pages that follow differs in one essential respect from the ancient method: it imposes the task of interpretation upon the dreamer himself. It is not concerned with what occurs to the *interpreter* in connection with a particular element of the dream, but with what occurs to the dreamer' (IV, 98). Even in this retrospective footnote, Artemidorus seems still to be causing Freud problems – in that he here understates by far the complexity of the hermeneutic relationship between dreamer and interpreter that he himself had postulated in his main text. The *Oneirocritica* is now available in a modern English translation, bearing the title *The Interpretation of Dreams*, by Robert J. White (for Alexander's Tyrian dream, see 196).

34 Artemidorus's story appears also in Plutarch's *Life of Alexander* (*The Age of Alexander*, 279), although other early historians (notably Arrian and Curtius) report an entirely different dream at this point (see N. G. L. Hammond's *Three Historians of Alexander the Great*, 123–4). Hammond, in his synoptic reconstruction of the siege of Tyre, gives Aristander no role in Alexander's eventual success (*Alexander the Great*, 112–16).

35 Freud wrote to Jung on 6 March 1910: 'Just rest easy, dear son Alexander, I will leave you more to conquer than I myself have managed, all psychiatry and the approval of the civilized world, which regards me as a savage! That ought to lighten your heart' (*Freud/Jung Letters*, 300).

36 Leo Bersani has written with illuminating wit on the interplay between the 'upper body' of Freud's main text and the primitive libidinal material that often occupies the 'lower body' of his footnotes ('Theory and Violence', 60–5).

37 Much else in the psychoanalytic tradition also seeks to occlude politics, of course (see below 174–7), or to reduce it to a dim, locally varying 'background' to the central transhistorical dramas of the psyche, although in informal and off-centre ways Freud's writings have a complex political dimension that is now beginning to be studied coherently (by Carl E. Schorske, for example, in his seminal 'Politics and Patricide in Freud's *Interpretation of Dreams*').

38 The story of Freud's relationship with biology is very much more complex than this circular history makes it sound. As Frank Sulloway has shown – with superabundant supporting documentation – in his *Freud, Biologist of the Mind*, implicit explanatory models drawn from evolutionary biology were at work throughout the development of psychoanalytic theory: beneath the surface play of distance and proximity between psychoanalysis and biology that Freud's texts articulate, a tacit loyalty to the biological mode was helping to shape Freud's very notion of what a 'pure' non-biological psychodynamic system would have to be like in order to achieve coherence. For a penetrating survey of the many distinct 'models of rationality' that influenced Freud during the formative years of psychoanalytic theory, see Paul-Laurent Assoun, *Introduction à l'épistémologie freudienne*.

39 This passage is quoted at greater length below, 93.

40 This question is formulated in these terms by Carl E. Schorske ('Politics and Patricide', 192); this essay provides a detailed socio-political context for Freud's self-identification with Hannibal.

41 The translators of the Standard Edition hesitate over the term *Wißtrieb*. In certain cases (e.g. *Three Essays on the Theory of Sexuality* (VII, 194; *GW*, V, 95) or 'The Disposition to Obsessional Neurosis' (XII, 324; *GW*, VIII, 450)) 'instinct for knowledge' is given without apology; in others (e.g. 'Notes upon a Case of Obsessional Neurosis' (X, 245; *GW*, VII, 460) or *Introductory Lectures* (XVI, 327; *GW*, XI, 339)) the expression 'epistemophilic instinct' is also provided as an obfuscating gloss upon a readily accessible term. Freud's *Schautrieb* ('instinct for looking'), which often accompanies the *Wißtrieb* in his discussion of the 'component instincts', is sent on a similar detour through Greek on both the latter occasions – to return as the vaguely pathological-sounding 'scopophilic instinct'.

42 Leo Bersani has argued persuasively that Freud's study of the 'psycho-sexuality' of Leonardo 'enacts as a major crisis of psychoanalysis itself what it officially presents as nothing more or less than an exceptionally interesting case history'. The 'theoretical turbulence' of the essay has to do with the following factors, listed by Bersani: 'Freud's own inability to be theoretically conclusive (and even consistent), his divided feelings about conclusiveness and consistency, and . . . his unarticulated sense of the enormous theoretical consequences of what he has to say about both the origins and the value of the radically inconclusive mind' ('Representation and its Discontents', 10). Jack Spector is a lucid guide to the transformations of the Leonardo motif in Freud's writings (*The Aesthetics of Freud*, 53–60 and *passim*).

43 The occupational hazards of the model-builder and simile-user emerged as a theme in Freud's writing even before the doctrine of psychoanalysis had been formulated. In Freud's long final chapter to the Freud/Breuer *Studies on Hysteria* (1895), for example, he wrote: 'I am making use here of a number of similes, all of which have only a very limited resemblance to my subject and which, moreover, are incompatible with one another. I am aware that this is so, and I am in no danger of over-estimating their value. But my purpose in using them is to throw light from different directions on a highly complicated topic which has never yet been represented. I shall therefore venture to continue in the following pages to introduce similes in the same manner, though I know this is not free from objection' (II, 291) (see *The Interpretation of Dreams*, V, 536 for one of many later vigorous excursions on this theme). A fine brief discussion of the interplay between scientific and artistic procedures within Freud's theorising is to be found in Stuart Hampshire's *Modern Writers* (88–95).

2. PROUST, JEALOUSY, KNOWLEDGE

1 *Seven Types of Ambiguity*, 249.

2 'A work in which there are theories is like an object which still has its price-tag on it' (916).

3 'The lie, the perfect lie, about people we know, about the relations we have had with them, about our motive for some action, formulated in totally different terms, the lie as to what we are, whom we love, what we feel with

regard to people who love us and believe that they have fashioned us in their own image because they keep on kissing us morning, noon and night – that lie is one of the few things in the world that can open windows for us on to what is new and unknown, that can awaken in us sleeping senses for the contemplation of universes that otherwise we should never have known' (213).

4 On the development of this theme during Proust's post-1914 expansion of the novel, see Alison Finch's masterly *Proust's Additions. The Making of 'A la recherche du temps perdu'*. Finch writes: 'If the characters are now more inclined to pass on rumours, they also increasingly resort to lying. This particular expansion is one of the most striking in the post-1914 drafts. As in the case of the characters' language, it is perhaps those additions of simply a few lines which most arrest the attention: when, for example, in three-and-a-half pages of text, the only addition made is one introducing a consideration of lying not previously there, the sign of a powerful new intention is unmistakable' (264). Her entire chapter on 'Lies and Uncertainty' (254–96) provides a fascinating portrait of Proust's elaboration of the 'negative' elements within the book; the author pays particular attention to the presentation of the narrator's relationship with Albertine.

5 'a luminous section cut out of the unknown' (309).

6 'And perhaps the almost pleasurable sensation he felt at that moment was something more than the assuagement of a doubt, and of a pain: was an intellectual pleasure. If, since he had fallen in love, things had recovered a little of the delightful interest that they had had for him long ago – though only in so far as they were illuminated by the thought or the memory of Odette – now it was another of the faculties of his studious youth that his jealousy revived, the passion for truth, but for a truth which, too, was interposed between himself and his mistress, receiving its light from her alone, a private and personal truth the sole object of which (an infinitely precious object, and one almost disinterested in its beauty) was Odette's life, her actions, her environment, her plans, her past . . . the curiosity which he now felt stirring inside him with regard to the smallest details of a woman's daily life, was the same thirst for knowledge with which he had once studied history. And all manner of actions from which hitherto he would have recoiled in shame, such as spying, to-night, outside a window, to-morrow perhaps, for all he knew, putting adroitly provocative questions to casual witnesses, bribing servants, listening at doors, seemed to him now to be precisely on a level with the deciphering of manuscripts, the weighing of evidence, the interpretation of old monuments – so many different methods of scientific investigation with a genuine intellectual value and legitimately employable in the search for truth' (298–9). The reader of Proust in the new Scott Moncrieff/Kilmartin translation will find a key to the motif of jealousy in Terence Kilmartin's invaluable companion to the translation, *A Guide to Proust* (166–7).

7 The narrator gives his own summary list of these questions in *La Fugitive*: 'En son fond qu'était-elle? A quoi pensait-elle? Qu'aimait-elle? Me mentait-elle?' (516) ('In her heart of hearts what was she? What were her thoughts? What were her loves? Did she lie to me?', 527).

8 In *Sodome et Gomorrhe*, the narrator speaks ironically of the Montjouvain episode (I, 159–65) as having opened up within him 'la voie funeste et destinée

à être douloureuse du Savoir' (II, 1115) – 'the fatal and inevitably painful road of Knowledge' (1152). Leo Bersani writes, in *Marcel Proust. The Fictions of Life and Art*, that 'The need to become familiar with Albertine's desires is so intense that the activity of loving turns out to be something like a compulsive intellectual investigation' (61). Bersani discusses *La Prisonnière* and *La Fugitive* with great insight (see especially his chapters on 'The Anguish and Inspiration of Jealousy' and 'The Language of Love'), but shows signs of impatience with this 'intellectual investigation' and speaks, for example, of 'the heavy often oppressively dense analyses of *La Prisonnière*' (76).

9 Although the narrator is parsimonious while engaged in jealous calculation, he is elsewhere, of course, unashamedly prodigal in his attribution of causes. Newton's first rule for scientific reasoning, as formulated in the first edition of his *Principia*, was 'Causas rerum naturalium non plures admitti debere, quam quae et vera sunt et earum Phenomenis explicandis sufficiunt. Natura enim simplex est et rerum causis superfluis non luxuriat.' ('We ought to admit no more causes of natural things than such as are both true and sufficient to explain their appearances. For nature is simple and does not luxuriate in superfluous causes of things.') I quote text and translation from Alexandre Koyré's *Newtonian Studies*, 265.

10 'The evidence of the senses is also an operation of the mind in which conviction creates the facts' (188).

11 'The unknown element in the lives of other people is like that of nature, which each fresh scientific discovery merely reduces but does not abolish' (398–9).

12 'I had in the course of my life followed a progression which was the opposite of that adopted by peoples who make use of phonetic writing only after having considered the characters as a set of symbols; having, for so many years, looked for the real life and thought of other people only in the direct statements about them which they supplied me with of their own free will, in the absence of these I had come to attach importance, on the contrary, only to disclosures that are not a rational and analytical expression of the truth; the words themselves did not enlighten me unless they were interpreted in the same way as a rush of blood to the cheeks of a person who is embarrassed, or as a sudden silence. Such and such an adverb . . . bursting into flames through the involuntary, sometimes perilous contact of two ideas which the speaker has not expressed but which, by applying the appropriate methods of analysis or electrolysis, I was able to extract from it, told me more than a long speech. Albertine sometimes let fall in her conversation one or other of these precious amalgams which I made haste to "treat" so as to transform them into lucid ideas' (83).

13 Although it is unlikely that Proust had other than hearsay knowledge of psychoanalytic techniques, his interests as a psychological observer coincide with Freud's in numerous ways (see below, 68–97). His comments on the signifying power of verbal lapses are strikingly similar to Freud's in *The Psychopathology of Everyday Life* (see below, 71–6). For Freud on pathological jealousy, see (e.g.) 'Some Neurotic Mechanisms in Jealousy, Paranoia and Homosexuality' (1922) (XVIII, 223–32).

14 Throughout, in his comments on the speech and writing of others, the narrator is extraordinarily alert to idiosyncratic detail. The stylistic analysis that he practises is akin to that of Leo Spitzer (as R. A. Sayce has pointed out in his brilliant 'The Goncourt Pastiche in *Le Temps retrouvé*', 110). For Spitzer's

account of Proust as stylistician, see *Études de style*, 436–51. On the role of stylistic observation within *A la recherche du temps perdu*, see Jean-Yves Tadié's chapter on 'Le Monde du langage' in *Proust et le roman* (132–80).

15 'Which of these two hypotheses was the truth?' (367).

16 'There are thus certain mental states, and especially anxiety, which, offering us only two alternatives, are somehow as atrociously circumscribed as a simple physical pain' (409).

17 See, for example, the passage in *A l'ombre des jeunes filles en fleurs* on 'le système des fins multiples' (I, 938–40) ('this system of killing several birds with one stone' [literally: 'the system of multiple ends'], 1002).

18 'How many people, how many places (even places which did not concern her directly, vague haunts of pleasure where she might have enjoyed some pleasure, places where there are a great many people, where people brush against one) had Albertine – like a person who, shepherding all her escort, a whole crowd, past the barrier in front of her, secures their admission to the theatre – from the threshold of my imagination or of my memory, where I paid no attention to them, introduced into my heart! Now, the knowledge that I had of them was internal, immediate, spasmodic, painful. Love is space and time made perceptible to the heart' (392).

19 In most cases the phantasy is introduced or accompanied by a denial (for example: 'je ne pouvais pas occuper tous les points de l'espace et du temps qu'il eût fallu' (357)), although its power as an expression of desire is not, of course, thereby diminished. ('I could not occupy all the necessary points in space and time'; this passage, from one of Proust's late insertions, is not included in the Scott Moncrieff/Kilmartin translation.)

20 'How had I failed to observe long ago that Albertine's eyes belonged to the category which even in a quite ordinary person seem to be composed of a number of fragments because of all the places in which the person wishes to be – and to conceal the desire to be – on that particular day. Eyes mendaciously kept always immobile and passive, but none the less dynamic, measurable in the yards or miles to be traversed before they reach the desired, the implacably desired meeting-place, eyes that are not so much smiling at the pleasure which tempts them as shadowed with melancholy and discouragement because there may be a difficulty in their getting to the meeting-place. Even when you hold them in your hands, such persons are fugitives. To understand the emotions which they arouse, and which others, even better-looking, do not, we must realise that they are not immobile but in motion, and add to their person a sign corresponding to that which in physics denotes speed.

If you upset their plans for the day, they confess to you the pleasure they had concealed from you: "I did so want to go and have tea with so and so who I'm fond of." And then, six months later, if you come to know the person in question, you will learn that the girl whose plans you had upset, who, trapped, in order that you might set her free had confessed to you that she was thus in the habit of taking tea with a dear friend every day at the hour at which you did not see her, has never once been inside this person's house, that they have never had tea together, since the girl used to explain that her whole time was taken up by none other than yourself. And so the person with whom she confessed that she was going to tea, with whom she begged you to allow her to go to tea, that person was merely the excuse that necessity made her plead;

there was still something else, someone else! What else? Who else?

Alas, the kaleidoscopic eyes, far-ranging and melancholy, might enable us perhaps to measure distance, but do not indicate direction. The boundless field of possibilities extends before us, and if by any chance the reality presented itself to our eyes, it would be so far outside the limits of the possible that, knocking suddenly against this looming wall, we should fall over backwards in a daze. It is not even essential that we should have proof of her movement and flight, it is enough that we should guess them' (86–7). (This passage appears without paragraphing in Jean Milly's edition of *La Prisonnière*, 185–6.)

21 Writing of this kind is powerfully illuminated by George Craig in his 'Marcel Proust: the "petite phrase" and the sentence'. Craig writes: 'For as long as we think of the complex sentence. . . as the voluntary or involuntary elaboration of a simpler proto-sentence, we are caught in the toils of illusion: in this case the double illusion that the long sentences enact the errors and hesitations of Marcel, and herald the eventual and uncomplicated emergence of his truth . . . Quantity puts paid to the notion of local or temporary difficulty – there are not *some* unmanageable sentences: they are *all* unmanageable. Long or short, they do not, in their accumulation and variety, allow the conditions of manageability to arise' (273–4).

22 'Jealousy, which is blindfold, is not merely powerless to discover anything in the darkness that enshrouds it; it is also one of those tortures where the task must be incessantly repeated, like that of the Danaides, or of Ixion' (147–8). Jean-Louis Baudry has written of the intellectual and discursive consequences of Proustian jealousy in the following terms: 'la jalousie apparaît aux yeux de celui qui la subit comme la manifestation scandaleuse de ce corps de folie dont il est l'hôte et qui se sert des capacités de pensée, de rationalisation, de déduction, d'imagination, pour développer son organisme monstrueux et proliférant . . . La jalousie, qui est une folie, est d'abord un discours, et un discours interminable; elle accable celui qui en est la proie par les ressources d'une inspiration inépuisable, et, en même temps qu'elle s'offre comme un objet d'investigation infinie, elle présente, pour celui qui s'est placé dans la position d'écriture dont j'ai parlé, des analogies évidentes et comme une sorte de modèle. Parce que, par sa position, il lui permet de se manifester et qu'il y prête attention avec ce mouvement de main qui l'emporte, il sait qu'il est habité par une langue répétitive et obsédante' (*Proust, Freud et l'Autre*, 24–5).

23 'my reason moreover asked nothing better than to prove to me that I had been mistaken as to her evil plans, as I had perhaps been mistaken as to her vicious instincts' (374).

24 '[the Baron] felt himself tormented by an anxiety of the mind as well as of the heart, born of this twofold mystery which combined an extension of the field of his jealousy with the sudden inadequacy of a definition' (212).

25 'They – the spectacles – were in marvellous condition. But behind them I could see, minute, pallid, convulsive, expiring, a remote gaze placed under this powerful apparatus, as, in a laboratory too richly endowed for the work that is done in it, you may watch the last throes of some insignificant animalcule under the latest and most advanced type of microscope' (197).

26 'powerful and complicated . . . like astronomical instruments'.

27 'Thus he went on growing steadily colder, a tiny planet offering a prophetic image of the greater, when gradually heat will withdraw from the earth, then life itself' (182).

28 'They buried him, but all through that night of mourning, in the lighted shop-windows, his books, arranged three by three, kept vigil like angels with outspread wings and seemed, for him who was no more, the symbol of his resurrection' (186).

29 'If, on the contrary, she dispels with a tactful word, with loving caresses, the suspicions that have been torturing him for all his show of indifference, no doubt the lover does not feel that despairing increase of love to which jealousy drives him, but ceasing there and then to suffer, happy, mollified, relaxed as one is after a storm when the rain has stopped and one hears only at long intervals under the tall chestnut-trees the splash of the suspended raindrops which already the reappearing sun has dyed with colour, he does not know how to express his gratitude to her who has cured him' (190).

30 *Seven Types of Ambiguity*, 131.

31 'a joy which was like a certainty and which sufficed, without any other proof, to make death a matter of indifference to me' (900).

32 'Richard Wagner et *Tannhäuser* à Paris', *Œuvres complètes*, II, 785.

33 *Le plaisir du texte*, 39.

34 This complementarity between Proust's accounts of knowledge pursued and knowledge captured is reinforced by numerous verbal and conceptual overlappings. In the following passage, for example, the artist is praised in terms closely reminiscent of those used earlier of the liar (see above, 48–9): 'Des ailes, un autre appareil respiratoire, et qui nous permissent de traverser l'immensité, ne nous serviraient à rien, car si nous allions dans Mars et dans Vénus en gardant les mêmes sens, ils revêtiraient du même aspect que les choses de la Terre tout ce que nous pourrions voir. Le seul véritable voyage, le seul bain de Jouvence, ce ne serait pas d'aller vers de nouveaux paysages, mais d'avoir d'autres yeux, de voir l'univers avec les yeux d'un autre, de cent autres, de voir les cent univers que chacun d'eux voit, que chacun d'eux est; et cela nous le pouvons avec un Elstir, avec un Vinteuil, avec leurs pareils, nous volons vraiment d'étoiles en étoiles' (III, 258) ('A pair of wings, a different respiratory system, which enabled us to travel through space, would in no way help us, for if we visited Mars or Venus while keeping the same senses, they would clothe everything that we saw in the same aspect as the things of Earth. The only true voyage of discovery, the only really rejuvenating experience, would be not to visit strange lands but to possess other eyes, to see the universe through the eyes of another, of a hundred others, to see the hundred universes that each of them sees, that each of them is; and this we can do with an Elstir, with a Vinteuil; with men like these we do really fly from star to star', 259–60). This passage is discussed, and placed within its psychological and epistemological context in Proust's novel, by Roger Shattuck in his admirable *Proust* (102–10).

35 Proust wrote in *Le Temps retrouvé*, for example: 'Car les vérités que l'intelligence saisit directement à claire-voie dans le monde de la pleine lumière ont quelque chose de moins profond, de moins nécessaire que celles que la vie nous a malgré nous communiquées en une impression, matérielle parce qu'elle est entrée par nos sens, mais dont nous pouvons dégager l'esprit'

(878) ('For the truths which the intellect apprehends directly in the world of full and unimpeded light have something less profound, less necessary than those which life communicates to us against our will in an impression which is material because it enters us through the senses but yet has a spiritual meaning which it is possible for us to extract', 912). On Proust's complex account of human intelligence in this volume, see J. M. Cocking's indispensable 'The Coherence of *Le Temps retrouvé*' in *Proust. Collected Essays on the Writer and His Art* (164–77). Cocking discusses such apparent contradictions as that between 'l'instinct dicte le devoir et l'intelligence fournit les prétextes pour l'éluder' (879) ('instinct dictates our duty and the intellect supplies us with pretexts for evading it', 913–14) and 'Là où la vie emmure, l'intelligence perce une issue' (905) ('Where life immures, the intelligence cuts a way out', 943); he argues that the two accounts of intelligence are coherently interrelated, and motivated by the novel Proust wrote.

36 On Proust's revisions of *Du côté de chez Swann*, including the change from Vington to Vinteuil, see Alison Finch, 'Characterization in the Early *Du côté de chez Swann*'.

37 '"An audacity," he exclaimed to himself, "as inspired, perhaps, as that of a Lavoisier or an Ampère – the audacity of a Vinteuil experimenting, discovering the secret laws that govern an unknown force . . ."' (382).

3. FREUD AND PROUST

1 The first extended comparison between Proust and Freud was Milton L. Miller's *Nostalgia. A Psychoanalytic Study of Marcel Proust* (1957). Although this work has major limitations – it is based upon the Scott Moncrieff translation, the author regularly confuses Proust and the narrator of *A la recherche* (etc.) – Miller provides numerous valuable points of comparison between Proust and Freud (on phantasy, dream-interpretation, bisexuality and the Oedipus complex, for example) of which few have been fully developed in later criticism. Notable among more recent works are Serge Doubrovsky's *La Place de la madeleine* (1974), Jeffrey Mehlman's *A Structural Study of Autobiography* (1974), Randolph Splitter's *Proust's 'Recherche'. A Psychoanalytic Interpretation* (1981) and Jean-Louis Baudry's *Proust, Freud et l'Autre* (1984). Baudry considers the two writers separately (for the most part), but in doing so creates many new opportunities for comparative criticism.

2 See *The Interpretation of Dreams* (V, 538–9) for an earlier formulation of this idea, and editorial footnotes on V, 538 and XVIII, 25 for Freud's at least partial indebtedness to Breuer for the idea itself. Without mentioning any specific passage in *A la recherche* Walter Benjamin was already able in 1939 to translate this Freudian notion into convincing Proustian terms ('On Some Motifs in Baudelaire', *Illuminations*, 162–3).

3 *Politique et psychanalyse* (unpaginated).

4 'one is no more distressed at having become another person, after a lapse of years and in the natural sequence of time, than one is at any given moment by the fact of being, one after another, the incompatible persons, malicious, sensitive, refined, caddish, disinterested, ambitious which one can be, in turn, every day of one's life. And the reason why one is not distressed is the same,

namely that the self which has been eclipsed – momentarily in this latter case and when it is a question of character, permanently in the former case and when the passions are involved – is not there to deplore the other, the other which is for the moment, or from then onwards, one's whole self; the caddish self laughs at his caddishness because one is the cad, and the forgetful self does not grieve about his forgetfulness precisely because one has forgotten' (657).

5 'my mind was already accustomed to its new master – my new self'.

6 Frequenting the unconscious during the composition of *The Interpretation of Dreams* brought with it unsuspected literary hazards and problems of theoretical control. Freud evokes these in his letter to Fliess of 7 July 1898, speaking (we may assume) of a draft chapter: 'It completely follows the dictates of the unconscious, on the well-known principle of Itzig, the Sunday rider. "Itzig, where are you going?" "Do I know? Ask the horse." I did not start a single paragraph knowing where I would end up. It is of course not written for the reader; after the first two pages I gave up any attempt at stylization' (Freud/Fliess, 319; *Origins*, 258).

7 Bruno Bettelheim, in the course of a penetrating discussion of the term *Fehlleistung* and the unfortunate *parapraxis* which obscures it in the Standard Edition, suggests 'faulty achievement' as a preferable rendering (*Freud and Man's Soul*, 86–8).

8 'go and get myself [buggered]' (343). The expression is explained in translator's note 22 (1110).

9 '. . . the porter handed me a telegram which the messenger had already brought three times to the hotel, for owing to the inaccurate rendering of the addressee's name (which I recognised nevertheless, through the corruptions introduced by the Italian clerks, as my own) the post office required a signed receipt certifying that the telegram was indeed for me. I opened it as soon as I was in my room, and, glancing through the message which was filled with inaccurately transmitted words, managed nevertheless to make out: "My dear friend, you think me dead, forgive me, I am quite alive, I long to see you, talk about marriage, when do you return? Affectionately. Albertine"' (656).

10 This is the title of a collection of poems by Jules Supervielle. Blanchot, in his tribute to Supervielle (*L'Entretien infini*, 459–64), makes this title his central motif: 'La muse, ce n'est pas la Mémoire, c'est Oublieuse Mémoire' (460).

11 'The telegram that I had received a few days earlier, and had supposed to be from Albertine, was from Gilberte. As the somewhat laboured originality of Gilberte's handwriting consisted chiefly, when she wrote a line, in introducing into the line above it the strokes of her *t*'s which appeared to be underlining the words, or the dots over her *i*'s which appeared to be punctuating the sentence above them, and on the other hand in interspersing the line below with the tails and flourishes of the words immediately above, it was quite natural that the clerk who dispatched the telegram should have read the loops of *s*'s or *y*'s in the line above as an "-ine" attached to the word "Gilberte." The dot over the *i* of Gilberte had climbed up to make a full stop. As for her capital *G*, it resembled a Gothic *A*. The fact that, in addition to this, two or three words had been misread, had dovetailed into one another (some of them indeed had seemed to me incomprehensible), was sufficient to explain the details of my error and was not even necessary. How many letters are actually read into a word by a careless person who knows what to expect, who

sets out with the idea that the message is from a certain person? How many words into the sentence? We guess as we read, we create; everything starts from an initial error; those that follow (and this applies not only to the reading of letters and telegrams, not only to all reading), extraordinary as they may appear to a person who has not begun at the same starting-point, are all quite natural. A large part of what we believe to be true (and this applies even to our final conclusions) with an obstinacy equalled only by our good faith, springs from an original mistake in our premises' (671).

12 'Our love of life is only an old liaison of which we do not know how to rid ourselves. Its strength lies in its permanence' (660).

13 'the idea that the message is from a certain person'; 'everything starts from an initial error'; 'A large part of what we believe to be true . . . springs from an original mistake in our premises'.

14 'this applies not only to the reading of letters and telegrams, not only to all reading'.

15 This is Bayard Taylor's translation as given in the Standard Edition (VI, vii).

16 'Finally, inasmuch as inversion itself springs from the fact that the invert is too closely akin to woman to be capable of having any effective relations with her, it relates to a higher law which ordains that so many hermaphrodite flowers shall remain infertile, that is to say to the sterility of self-fertilisation. It is true that inverts, in their search for a male, often content themselves with other inverts as effeminate as themselves. But it is enough that they do not belong to the female sex, of which they have in them an embryo which they can put to no useful purpose, as happens with so many hermaphrodite flowers, and even with certain hermaphrodite animals, such as the snail, which cannot be fertilised by themselves, but can by other hermaphrodites. In this respect the race of inverts, who readily link themselves with the ancient East or the golden age of Greece, might be traced back further still, to those experimental epochs in which there existed neither dioecious plants nor monosexual animals, to that initial hermaphroditism of which certain rudiments of male organs in the anatomy of women and of female organs in that of men seem still to preserve the trace' (653).

17 The *Symposium* is a frequent reference-point both for Freud (see below, 80) and for Lacan. Among numerous discussions and allusions in the later pages of *Écrits*, see for example 825–6, 837, 845, 853. The eighth volume of Lacan's *Séminaire* (*Le Transfert* (1960–1), not yet published) is devoted in large part to a detailed reading of this dialogue (see Octave Mannoni, *Ça n'empêche pas d'exister*, 15–18). On the importance of the *Symposium* for psychoanalysis, with special reference to Lacan, see John Brenkman's 'The Other and the One: Psychoanalysis, Reading, *The Symposium*'.

18 On the charge of 'pan-sexualism', see above 40–1.

19 On the rhetoric of recantation and denial in *Civilization and its Discontents*, see above 28–9.

20 The epistemological function of such theoretical fictions thus resembles that of the 'primal phantasies' (*Urphantasien*) which psychoanalysis ascribes to the young child. Of these phantasies Laplanche and Pontalis write: 'If we consider the themes which can be recognised in primal phantasies (primal scene, castration, seduction), the striking thing is that they have one trait in common: they are all related to the origins. Like collective myths, they claim

to provide a representation of and a "solution" to whatever constitutes a major enigma for the child. Whatever appears to the subject as a reality of such a type as to require an explanation or "theory", these phantasies dramatise into the primal moment or original point of departure of a history' (*Language of Psycho-Analysis*, 332). On 'primal scenes', 'primal phantasies' and 'retrospective phantasies', see above, 181n. 13.

21 II, 630 (Proust); XVIII, 56 (Freud). The indispensable work on Darwin and the literary imagination, and on the interplay of theory and fiction in *The Origin of Species* itself, is now Gillian Beer's *Darwin's Plots*. On Darwin's own strain of bisexual phantasy in *The Descent of Man*, see Stanley Edgar Hyman's *The Tangled Bank*, 52–4.

22 Samuel Weber, who ends his consummately inventive and penetrating *The Legend of Freud* (146–64) upon an inter-reading of *Beyond the Pleasure Principle* and the *Symposium*, interprets Freud's playful and pleasure-seeking recourse to the poet-philosopher as having an outer edge of darkness and desperation – the sign of an unruly attempt both to woo and to resist the death instinct that *Beyond the Pleasure Principle* proclaims.

23 Thanks to Étienne Brunet's invaluable *Le Vocabulaire de Proust*, we are now able to confirm that *bissexuel* and its cognates are entirely absent from the text of Proust's novel.

24 'Besides it is usually to brutes that this role is assigned' (*Contre Sainte-Beuve* (etc), 633).

25 'Was it for this girl whom I saw in my mind's eye so bloated and who had certainly aged, as the girls whom she had loved had aged – was it for her that I must renounce the dazzling girl who was my memory of yesterday, my hope for to-morrow, to whom I could no longer give a sou, any more than to any other, if I married Albertine, that I must renounce this "new Albertine" whom I loved "not as hell had beheld her . . . but faithful, and proud, and even rather shy"' (659).

26 'I love King Theseus, not as once he was, / The fickle worshipper at countless shrines, / Dishonouring the couch of Hades' god; / But constant, proud, and even a little shy; / Enchanting, young, the darling of all hearts, / Fair as the gods; or fair as you are now' (trans. John Cairncross).

27 'like a princess in a tragedy oppressed by the weight of these vain ornaments, with no gratitude towards the importunate hand which, in curling all those ringlets, had been at pains to arrange my hair upon my forehead' (158). Antoine Compagnon, in his 'Proust sur Racine', has discussed the Racinian sub-text as an agent of sexual role-reversal and indetermination in *A la recherche*. This penetrating analysis dwells in particular on the presence of *Athalie* and *Esther* in *Sodome et Gomorrhe* (but on 'Que ces vains ornements . . .', see 49–50).

28 Freud's view that human beings at large are bisexually constituted (see above 77) was formed in the period 1896–1904 under the direct and continual influence of Wilhelm Fliess. In his letter to Fliess of 6 December 1896 Freud speaks of 'the bisexuality of all human beings' (I, 238; *Origins*, 179; Freud/Fliess, 212), and he alludes to this view on several later occasions in the same correspondence. The final Freud/Fliess letters (pp. 463–8) concern the question of Fliess's authorship of the view and the supposed plagiarism of Otto Weininger, who had made use of it in his *Sex and Character* (1903). On

July 27 1904, Freud wrote to Fliess: 'You must admit that a resourceful mind can on its own easily take the step from the bisexual disposition of some individuals to extending it to all of them, though this step is your *novum*. For me personally you have always (since 1901) been the author of the idea of bisexuality; I fear that in looking through the literature, you will find that many came at least close to you' (Freud/Fliess, 466–67). These letters do not appear in the selections from this correspondence published as *The Origins of Psycho-Analysis* (nor, of course, in the extracts from these selections given in the Standard Edition (I, 175–280)). Steven Marcus's 'The Origins of Psychoanalysis Revisited', though written before the complete text of the correspondence became available, contains by far the most perceptive brief account of the Freud/Fliess relationship (*Freud and the Culture of Psychoanalysis*, 6–21). For Freud's more *nuancé* history of the concept of 'bisexuality' in recent medical literature, see VII, 142–3.

29 The main Carpaccio episode was unavailable to the French reader until the publication of the Pléiade edition in 1954 and to the English reader until the publication of Terence Kilmartin's magnificent revised version of the Scott Moncrieff translation in 1981.

30 'A Carpaccio in Venice, Berma in *Phèdre*, masterpieces of pictorial or dramatic art which the glamour, the dignity attaching to them made so vividly alive for me . . .' (475).

31 'My mother and I would enter the baptistery, treading underfoot the marble and glass mosaics of the paving, in front of us the wide arcades whose curved pink surfaces have been slightly warped by time, thus giving the church, wherever the freshness of this colouring has been preserved, the appearance of having been built of a soft and malleable substance like the wax in a giant honeycomb, and, where time has shrivelled and hardened the material and artists have embellished it with gold tracery, of being the precious binding, in the finest Cordoba leather, of the colossal Gospel of Venice. Seeing that I needed to spend some time in front of the mosaics representing the Baptism of Christ, and feeling the icy coolness that pervaded the baptistery, my mother threw a shawl over my shoulders. When I was with Albertine at Balbec, I felt that she was revealing one of those insubstantial illusions which clutter the minds of so many people who do not think clearly, when she used to speak of the pleasure – to my mind baseless – that she would derive from seeing works of art with me. To-day I am sure that the pleasure does exist, if not of seeing, at least of having seen, a beautiful thing with a particular person. A time has now come when, remembering the baptistery of St Mark's – contemplating the waters of the Jordan in which St John immerses Christ, while the gondola awaited us at the landing-stage of the Piazzetta – it is no longer a matter of indifference to me that, beside me in that cool penumbra, there should have been a woman draped in her mourning with the respectful and enthusiastic fervour of the old woman in Carpaccio's *St Ursula* in the Accademia, and that that woman, with her red cheeks and sad eyes and in her black veils, whom nothing can ever remove from that softly lit sanctuary of St Mark's where I am always sure to find her because she has her place reserved there as immutably as a mosaic, should be my mother.

Carpaccio, as it happens, who was the painter we visited most readily when I was not working in St Mark's, almost succeeded one day in reviving my love for Albertine. I was seeing for the first time *The Patriarch of Grado exorcising a demoniac*. I looked at the marvellous rose-pink and violet sky and the tall encrusted chimneys silhouetted against it, their flared stacks, blossoming like red tulips, reminiscent of so many Whistlers of Venice. Then my eyes travelled from the old wooden Rialto to that fifteenth-century Ponte Vecchio with its marble palaces decorated with gilded capitals, and returned to the canal on which the boats are manoeuvred by adolescents in pink jackets and plumed toques, the spitting image of those avowedly inspired by Carpaccio in that dazzling *Legend of Joseph* by Sert, Strauss and Kessler. Finally, before leaving the picture, my eyes came back to the shore, swarming with the everyday Venetian life of the period. I looked at the barber wiping his razor, at the negro humping his barrel, at the Muslims conversing, at the noblemen in wide-sleeved brocade and damask robes and hats of cerise velvet, and suddenly I felt a slight gnawing at my heart. On the back of one of the *Compagni della Calza* identifiable from the emblem, embroidered in gold and pearls on their sleeves or their collars, of the merry confraternity to which they were affiliated, I had just recognised the cloak which Albertine had put on to come with me to Versailles in an open carriage on the evening when I so little suspected that scarcely fifteen hours separated me from the moment of her departure from my house. Always ready for anything, when I had asked her to come out with me on that melancholy evening which she was to describe in her last letter as "doubly crepuscular in that dusk was falling and we were about to part," she had flung over her shoulders a Fortuny cloak which she had taken away with her next day and which I had never thought of since. It was from this Carpaccio picture that that inspired son of Venice had taken it, it was from the shoulders of this *Compagno della Calza* that he had removed it in order to drape it over the shoulders of so many Parisian women who were certainly unaware, as I had been until then, that the model for it existed in a group of noblemen in the foreground of the *Patriarch of Grado* in a room in the Accademia in Venice. I had recognised it down to the last detail, and, that cloak having restored to me as I looked at it the eyes and the heart of him who had set out that evening with Albertine for Versailles, I was overcome for a few moments by a vague feeling of desire and melancholy' (660–2).

32 'still half Arab' (639).

33 'built of a soft and malleable substance like the wax in a giant honeycomb'.

34 'immutable as a mosaic'.

35 Carpaccio's main literary source (and that of earlier painters of Ursula cycles) is almost certain to have been *The Golden Legend* (see M. Cancogni and G. Perocco, *L'Opera completa del Carpaccio*, 88). The Ursula story that I summarise here is to be found in full on pp. 627–31 of the Ryan/Ripperger translation of Jacobus de Voragine's compilation.

36 'respectful and enthusiastic fervour'.

37 On the transmission of this figure, and on the tradition of Venetian narrative painting within which Carpaccio worked, see David Rosand's splendid *Painting in Cinquecento Venice*, 95ff.

38 I refer to the order of the panels in the narrative sequence rather than to their order of composition. On the latter question, see M. Cancogni and G. Perocco, *L'Opera completa del Carpaccio*, 88–92 and Terisio Pignatti, *Carpaccio*, 30.

39 For the first of these instances, see III, 625.
40 On Freud's archaeology, see above 17–27.
41 See, for example, 'Constructions in Analysis', XXIII, 260 (quoted above, 22).
42 On this 'curious reversal of commonplace opinions' in Freud, see John Forrester, *Language and the Origins of Psychoanalysis*, 209–10.
43 John Wisdom has written with extraordinary subtlety on the importance and the paradoxicalness, the 'logical confusion and logical penetration' (281) of such psychoanalytic statements as 'In your feelings your parents are inside you, watching every act you do, cognizant of every thought you think, and consequently hurt, pleased, angered not only by what you do but also by what you think of doing' or 'Unconsciously you think your parents are inside you' (*Philosophy and Psycho-Analysis*, 279).
44 'always ready for anything'.
45 On Proust's complex elaboration of the Fortuny motif in *A la recherche* during his revision of the novel, see Jean Milly's introduction to his edition of *La Prisonnière*, 28–36. Letters from Proust on Fortuny and Carpaccio are reprinted on pp. 47–50 of this volume.
46 'embellished with gold tracery'; 'encrusted chimneys'; 'curved pink surfaces'; 'flared stacks, blossoming like tulips'.
47 Gautier and Taine had both written with enthusiasm about Carpaccio's Ursula cycle. Gautier had pleaded the case for Carpaccio in these terms: 'Nous sommes étonné que le nom de Carpaccio ne soit pas plus généralement connu; il a toute la pureté adolescente, toute la séduction gracieuse du peintre d'Urbin dans sa première manière, et de plus cet admirable coloris vénitien qu'aucune école n'a pu atteindre' (*Italia*, 257–8). Taine had found in the cycle 'd'abord la maladresse de l'imagier féodal . . . D'autre part . . . les plus chastes figures du moyen âge et cet extrême fini, cette sincérité parfaite, cette fleur de conscience chrétienne que l'âge suivant . . . va fouler dans ses emportements' (*Voyage en Italie*, II, 328). Both writers are quoted at length in the Roudaut/Perocco *Carpaccio* (10).
48 'the negro humping his barrel'.
49 '. . . there was a march past of allied troops in the most variegated uniforms; and among them the Africans in their red divided skirts, the Indians in their white turbans were enough to transform for me this Paris through which I was walking into a whole imaginary exotic city, an oriental scene which was at once meticulously accurate with respect to the costumes and the colours of the faces and arbitrarily fanciful when it came to the background, just as out of the town in which he lived Carpaccio made a Jerusalem or a Constantinople by assembling in its streets a crowd whose marvellous motley was not more rich in colour than that of the crowd around me' (786).
50 For Proust, Carpaccio's art is one of measured and multi-focal transformation. The Carpaccio of *A la recherche* is thus very different both from the naïve narrator who appears, for instance, in Isaiah Berlin's cameo-portrait of Winston Churchill's historical imagination ('The whole is a series of symmetrically formed and somewhat stylised compositions, either suffused with bright light or cast in darkest shadow, like a legend by Carpaccio, with scarcely any nuance, painted in primary colours, with no half tones, nothing intangible, nothing impalpable, nothing half spoken or hinted or whispered:

the voice does not alter in pitch or timbre', *Personal Impressions*, 5) and from the producer of an endlessly mobile, bulging and shrinking, topography who appears in Michel Serres's *Esthétiques sur Carpaccio*.

51 On the contrast between 'plasticity' and 'adhesiveness', see above 41–4.

52 'my mother threw a shawl over my shoulders'; 'she had flung over her shoulders a Fortuny cloak'; 'it was from the shoulders of this *Compagno della Calza* that he had removed it in order to drape it over the shoulders of so many Parisian women'.

53 'marvellous motley'.

54 'a vague feeling of desire and melancholy'.

55 For Richard Terdiman, in his 'Narration in *La Fugitive*' (*The Dialectics of Isolation*, 199–225), Proust has, in this volume, 'simplified his hero to a recognizably fundamental form: the protagonist as *consciousness of loss*' (201). Terdiman analyses with unusual lucidity the new narrative techniques that propel and control Proust's exhaustive account of pained inwardness in *La Fugitive*.

56 'initial error on the part of society' (645). This reading of human history anticipates the systematic misreading discussed in *La Fugitive*: 'tout part d'une erreur initiale' (III, 656) (see above 74–6).

57 'initial hermaphroditism' (653).

4. LACAN

1 For a more literal English translation of the Hebrew translation of Maimonides's original Arabic letter (to Samuel Ibn Tibbon) see Shlomo Pines's introduction to his translation of *The Guide of the Perplexed*, lix.

2 'have these forms not led to a dispiriting formalism that discourages initiative by penalizing risk, and turns the reign of the opinion of the learned into a principle of docile prudence in which the authenticity of research is blunted before it finally dries up?' (31–2).

3 'As a substantive, it [the preconscious] denotes a system of the psychical apparatus that is quite distinct from the unconscious system; as an adjective, it qualifies the operations and contents of this preconscious system. As these are not currently present in the field of consciousness, they are unconscious in the "descriptive" sense of the term, but they differ from the contents of the unconscious system in that they are still in principle accessible to consciousness (e.g. knowledge and memories that are not presently conscious)' (J. Laplanche and J.-B. Pontalis, *The Language of Psycho-Analysis*, 325). In psychoanalysis, the preconscious and the conscious are commonly considered as one continuous system, sharply distinguishable from the unconscious system. (Laplanche's and Pontalis's invaluable reference work first appeared as *Vocabulaire de la psychanalyse* in 1967; the definitions quoted here and in subsequent notes are given in abridged form.)

4 In Book VII of *The Republic* Plato compares mankind caught within the world of appearance to a prisoner in an underground cave. The prisoner's attempt to escape from the cave corresponds to man's quest for enlightenment and wisdom.

5 'The locality in question is the entrance to the very cave in respect of which Plato is known to guide us towards the exit, whereas people imagine they see

the psychoanalyst going in. But things are less simple, because this is an entrance that you never reach until the moment they're closing (this locality will never attract the tourists), and because the only way of getting it to open a little is to call from the inside.'

6 Displacement: 'the fact that an idea's emphasis, interest or intensity is liable to be detached from it and to pass on to other ideas, which were originally of little intensity but which are related to the first idea by a chain of associations' (Laplanche and Pontalis, 121).

7 On Lacan's Actaeon, see below 167–73, 178.

8 'the immense genius of the master of psychoanalysis'.

9 For brief accounts of these concepts, see Laplanche and Pontalis, 169–70 and 43–5.

10 Jacques-Alain Miller, in his *Entretien sur le Séminaire*, describes his editorial responsibilities in preparing the *Séminaire* transcripts for publication and comments succinctly on such additional matters as: the senses in which he may be considered 'co-author' of the successive volumes; the relationship between obscurity and clarity in Lacan's writing and speech; the relationship between *Écrits* and the *Séminaire* as vehicles for Lacan's continuously self-transforming theory; the play between the improvisatory quality of Lacan's 'original' spoken text and Miller's own *logicisant* cast of mind as editor. For details of the contents of the individual *Séminaire* volumes (published and unpublished), and for the fullest publishing history to date of Lacan's writings, see Joël Dor's *Bibliographie des travaux de Jacques Lacan*.

11 'This jubilant assumption of his specular image by the child at the *infans* stage, still sunk in his motor incapacity and nursling dependence, would seem to exhibit in an exemplary situation the symbolic matrix in which the *I* is precipitated in a primordial form, before it is objectified in the dialectic of identification with the other, and before language restores to it, in the universal, its function as subject' (2).

12 For the distinctions between models of these three kinds, see Laplanche and Pontalis, 449–53; 126; 127–30.

13 Condensation: 'one of the essential modes of the functioning of the unconscious processes: a sole idea represents several associative chains at whose point of intersection it is located' (Laplanche and Pontalis, 82).

14 For a detailed account of Freud on Abel, see Émile Benveniste, *Problèmes de linguistique générale* [1], 75–87. Giulio Lespschy has convincingly demonstrated, in his 'Freud, Abel et gli opposti', that the 'Abel question' is a good deal more complex than those writing in the wake of Benveniste have been inclined to suggest, and that the ready espousal of Benveniste's critique by Lacan, Ricœur and others has drawn attention away from the fact that Abel was by no means alone within the history of philology in his speculations upon the 'antithetical meanings' of certain single words. Lepschy's argument here is summarised in English in his 'Linguistic Historiography'.

15 XI, 23 etc. 'The unconscious is structured like a language.'

16 Roman Jakobson and Morris Halle, *Fundamentals of Language*, 90–6.

17 This sentence and the two following now seem to me to mis-state the 'limitation' in question. Although there are few properly syntactic descriptions or models in Freud's metapsychological accounts of the unconscious, other writings of his – and notably his discussions of case-material – attend

closely to what John Forrester has called 'the propositional structure of neurosis'. My reader is referred to Forrester's admirable *Language and the Origins of Psychoanalysis* for a detailed analysis of such structures (131–65, in particular).

18 These papers, translated as 'The function and field of speech and language in psychoanalysis' and 'The agency of the letter in the unconscious or reason since Freud' are to be found on pp. 30–113 and 146–78 of *Écrits. A Selection.*

19 *Cours de linguistique générale*, 157. 'Again language is comparable to a sheet of paper: thought is the front and sound is the back; you cannot cut up the front without at the same time cutting up the back; similarly, in language you cannot isolate sound from thought, nor thought from sound; you could manage to do this only by a process of abstraction which would result in the creation of pure psychology or pure phonology'.

20 Metonymy: 'A figure in which the name of an attribute or adjunct is substituted for that of the thing meant'. Synecdoche: 'a figure by which a more comprehensive term is used for a less comprehensive or *vice versa*; as whole for part or part for whole, etc.' (Shorter OED)

21 *Fundamentals of Language*, 94–5.

22 Overdetermination: 'the fact that formations of the unconscious (symptoms, dreams, etc.) can be attributed to a plurality of determining factors' (Laplanche and Pontalis, 292).

23 'There is no metalanguage . . . no language can say the truth about the truth, since the truth founds itself on the fact that it speaks and that it has no other means of doing so.'

24 'Of Structure as an Inmixing of an Otherness Prerequisite to Any Subject Whatever', *The Structuralist Controversy* (ed. Macksey and Donato), 188. This paper was delivered in a mixture of English and French and published, in an edited and paraphrased form, in English.

25 'There is no structure except of [or from] language.' For a searching critique of the 'exorbitation of language' within structuralism and of Lacan's role in promoting a 'megalomania of the signifier', see Perry Anderson, *In the Tracks of Historical Materialism*, 40–55. The most ambitious attempt to produce a non-exorbitant philosophical account of language in psychoanalysis is to be found in Paul Ricœur's *De l'interprétation.*

26 On the concepts *Wortvorstellung* and *Sachvorstellung* (or *Dingvorstellung*), see the editorial note at XIV, 201, and Laplanche and Pontalis, 447–9. The indispensable discussion of this crucial area of complexity and terminological uncertainty within Freud's metapsychology is still Jean Laplanche and Serge Leclaire, 'L'Inconscient. Une étude psychanalytique' (translated by Patrick Coleman in *French Freud*, 118–75).

27 Qu. by Antoine Vergote, in *Interpreting Lacan* (ed. Smith and Kerrigan), 193.

28 'the supremacy of the signifier in the subject' (*French Freud*, 50); 'the pre-eminence of the signifier over the subject' (*French Freud*, 70); 'a signifier is that which represents the subject for another signifier' (316). On the logocentric metaphysics and the 'reversed' Cartesianism underlying the last of these formulations, see Anthony Wilden, *System and Structure*, 460–1.

29 'the displacement of the signifier determines the subjects in their acts, in their destiny, in their refusals, in their blindnesses, in their end and in their fate, their innate gifts and social acquisitions notwithstanding, without regard for

character or sex, and . . . willingly or not, everything that might be considered the stuff of psychology, kit and caboodle, will follow the path of the signifier' (*French Freud*, 60).

30 '*The real is that which always comes back to the same place*' (*Four Fundamental Concepts*, 42).

31 'Don't you feel there's something derisory and laughable in the fact that the dice have already been cast?'

32 'It is the world of words that creates the world of things – the things originally confused in the *hic et nunc* of the all in the process of coming-into-being' (65).

33 'It is in the *name of the father* that we must recognise the support of the symbolic function which, from the dawn of history, has identified his person with the figure of the law' (67). Lacan's vigorously anti-biologistic encyclopaedia article on the family (1938), which contains his fullest account of the determining force exerted by the family on the human individual and a sketch of many theoretical positions that were to be developed only much later in his career, has now been reprinted as *Les complexes familiaux dans la formation de l'individu* (1984).

34 The main mediators between Lacan (in common with many prominent members of his generation in France) and Hegel were Alexandre Kojève and Jean Hyppolite, the French translator of *Phänomenologie des Geistes*. Hegel's chapter on Master and Slave, as translated and discussed by Kojève in his *Introduction à la lecture de Hegel* (11–34), provides an essential background to the philosophical tone and diction of Lacan's many discussions of 'the Other'. (This passage occurs on pp. 111–19 of A. V. Miller's English translation of the *Phenomenology*.) After 1943, Sartre's *L'Etre et le néant* is likely to have reinforced the Hegelianism of Lacan's thinking on 'the Other', 'Master and Slave' and related concepts (for numerous striking parallels, see *L'Etre et le néant*, 288–364). An early acknowledgement of Lacan's indebtedness to Hegel via Kojève and Hyppolite is to be found in 'Propos sur la causalité psychique' (172). For further remarks on Lacan and Hegel, see below 146–9, 155–7.

35 'What I seek in speech is the response of the other. What constitutes me as subject is my question. In order to be recognised by the other, I utter what was only in view of what will be. In order to find him, I call him by a name that he must assume or refuse in order to reply to me' (86).

36 '. . . it is from the Other that the subject receives even the message that he emits' (305).

37 'The Other is, therefore, the locus in which is constituted the I who speaks to him who hears, that which is said by the one being already the reply, the other deciding to hear it whether the one has or has not spoken' (141).

38 '. . . man's desire finds its meaning in the desire of the other, not so much because the other holds the key to the object desired, as because the first object of desire is to be recognised by the other' (58).

39 'Indeed, it is quite simply . . . as desire of the Other that man's desire finds form' (311).

40 '. . . man's desire is the desire of the Other in which the 'of' provides what grammarians call the "subjective determination", namely that it is *qua* Other that he desires (which is what provides the true compass of human passion)' (312).

41 'radical ex-centricity of one to himself' (171, trans. modified). Freud himself was the author of many pungent phrases on this theme. The main discoveries of psychoanalysis, he said in 1917, 'amount to a statement that *the ego is not master in its own house*' (XVII, 143).

42 'the unconscious is the discourse of the Other'. This dictum appears in a variety of forms in *Écrits*. The essay from which my present quotation is drawn does not figure in the current English translation, but a minimally different version of the dictum is to be found on p. 172 of *Écrits. A Selection*.

43 'The unconscious is that discourse of the Other where the subject receives, in the inverted form which is appropriate to the promise, his own forgotten message'.

44 'the other which is not an other at all, since it is essentially coupled with the ego'.

45 'the *objet a* is no being at all. The *objet a* is that which a demand presupposes by way of emptiness'. Lacan's account of the *objet a* as a point of failed juncture between the body and language skirts, but never actually reproduces, Bossuet's celebrated description of human flesh *post mortem*: 'il devient un je ne sais quoi qui n'a plus de nom dans aucune langue' (*Oraisons funèbres*, 173–4). For references in *Écrits* to the *objet a* see Jacques-Alain Miller's 'Index raisonné des concepts majeurs' (900). Lacan's account of the concept in his 'Remarque sur le rapport de Daniel Lagache' (682) offers one useful point of departure for further exploration, as do such remarks in discussion as those in *Les quatre concepts fondamentaux de la psychanalyse* (XI, 95–6) (*Four Fundamental Concepts*, 103–4).

46 The most ambitious attempt to consider Lacan's work in this way is to be found in Alain Juranville's *Lacan et la philosophie*, which is an indispensable guide to the philosophical background and content of Lacan's writings. On 'the Other', see in particular 128–40.

47 'rhetoric, dialectic in the technical sense that this word assumes in the *Topics* of Aristotle, grammar, and, that supreme pinnacle of the aesthetics of language, poetics, which would include the neglected technique of the witticism' (76).

48 'Periphrasis, hyperbaton, ellipsis, suspension, anticipation, retraction, negation, digression, irony, these are the figures of style (Quintilian's *figurae sententiarum*); as catachresis, litotes, antonomasia, hypotyposis are the tropes, whose terms suggest themselves as the most proper for the labelling of these mechanisms. Can one really see these as mere figures of speech when it is the figures themselves that are the active principle of the rhetoric of the discourse that the analysand in fact utters?' (169).

49 I return to the question of Lacan and rhetoric on pp. 142–3, 148–50, 159–62 below.

50 'The ego must unseat the id.'

51 '[that] of an imperative which urges me to assume my own causality'.

52 The first, third and fifth of these versions may be found, re-retranslated, on pp. 171, 129 and 314 of *Écrits. A Selection* and the fourth on p. 44 of *Four Fundamental Concepts*. The second might be rendered 'There where it was, there as subject must I arrive.'

53 Lionel Trilling, in his 'Freud: Within and Beyond Culture' – an essay which speaks with approval of the conservative strain in Freud's cultural criticism –

called attention to the final cadence of Freud's lecture as a possible point of moral ambiguity: 'The aim of all his effort is the service of culture – he speaks of the work of psychoanalysis as "the draining of the Zuyder Zee", the building of the dyke, the seeing to it that where id was ego should be. Yet at the same time his adverse attitude to culture is very strong, his indignation is very intense' (*Beyond Culture*, 101).

54 'Our fable is so constructed as to show that it is the letter and its diversion which governs their [the subjects'] entries and roles. If *it* be "in sufferance" *they* shall endure the pain. Should they pass beneath its shadow, they become its reflection. Falling in possession of the letter – admirable ambiguity of language – its meaning possesses them' (*French Freud*, 60).

55 A brilliant debate was initiated by Derrida (when he made this charge against Lacan's analysis) in 'Le Facteur de la vérité' (*La Carte postale*, 441–524). See in particular Barbara Johnson's 'The Frame of Reference: Poe, Lacan, Derrida' (*The Critical Difference*, 110–46) and Marian Hobson's 'Deconstruction, Empiricism and the Postal Services' (especially 303–7).

56 For a more detailed discussion of literature as a model for the unconscious, see below 136–43, 158–9.

57 'But one has only to listen to poetry . . . for a polyphony to be heard, for it to become clear that all discourse is aligned along the several staves of a score.

There is in effect no signifying chain that does not have, as if attached to the punctuation of each of its units, a whole articulation of relevant contexts suspended "vertically", as it were, from that point' (154). I return to this passage below, 158.

58 'the master of the signifier' (81).

59 See above 124.

60 'For the signifier is a unit in its very uniqueness, being by nature symbol only of an absence' (*French Freud*, 54).

61 'Man's freedom is entirely inscribed within the constituting triangle of the renunciation that he imposes on the desire of the other by the menace of death for the enjoyment of the fruits of his serfdom – of the consented-to sacrifice of his life for the reasons that give to human life its measure – and of the suicidal renunciation of the vanquished partner, depriving of his victory the master whom he abandons to his inhuman solitude' (104).

62 A useful but impatient preliminary account is to be found in Georges Mounin's *Introduction à la sémiologie*, 181–8.

63 'the domain of the senseless'.

64 'I wander about in what you regard as being the least true in essence: in the dream, in the way the most far-fetched conceit, the most grotesque nonsense of the joke defies sense, in chance, not in its law, but in its contingence, and I never do more to change the face of the world than when I give it the profile of Cleopatra's nose' (122).

65 'say always an Other-thing'. On this phrase, see also below 150 and 207–8 n. 27 (where its original context is supplied).

66 The main differences between Freud and Lacan as *stylists* are well described by Patrick Mahony, *Freud as a Writer*, 74–7.

67 *The Freudian Slip*, 58.

68 Lacan has found, particularly in the United States, a number of devoted readers and explicators who have succeeded in preserving a tangible sense of

this 'unreadability' even while elucidating the detail of his texts. Distinctive and valuable works of this kind include: Anthony Wilden, *The Language of the Self*; Jeffrey Mehlman, *A Structural Study of Autobiography* [pp. 229–38 are a reader's guide to Lacan's 'Radiophonie', *Scilicet*, 2/3, 55–99]; John P. Muller and William J. Richardson, *Lacan and Language*; Jane Gallop, *Reading Lacan*. The last two works listed appeared after the publication of Alan Sheridan's translation *Écrits. A Selection* and provide important annotation to that work.

69 A vigorous beginning has been made by Sherry Turkle in her *Psychoanalytic Politics* (1978). Among numerous *post mortem* accounts of Lacan's impact on French culture, Catherine Clément's *Vies et légendes de Jacques Lacan* and Bernard Sichère's *Le moment lacanien* are both remarkable for their theoretically self-aware portrayals of Lacan as a charismatic *maître-à-penser* and of the recent French transformation of psychoanalytic theory into public passion.

70 It is unfortunate that most published accounts of the institutional repercussions have been written by lay observers and memorialists rather than by members of the French analytic community. A notable exception is Moustapha Safouan's *Jacques Lacan et la question de la formation des analystes*, which sets out clearly the theoretical background to a number of Lacan's major innovations in psychoanalytic technique. I am not competent to describe or assess Lacan's achievement as a clinician and am conscious that no 'introduction to Lacan' can be complete without taking this area of his professional activity into account. Those wishing to explore case-material from the Lacanian sphere could begin with Stuart Schneiderman's collection *Returning to Freud* and Rosine Lefort's *Naissance de l'Autre*. On the split (in the public perception of Lacan) between the 'thinker' and the 'practitioner', see pp. 9–16 of Schneiderman's introduction.

71 '[It] will provide scientific bases for its theory or for its technique only by formalising in an adequate fashion the essential dimensions of its experience which, together with the historical theory of the symbol, are: intersubjective logic and the temporality of the subject' (77).

72 'Analysis can have for its goal only the advent of a true speech and the realisation by the subject of his history in his relation to a future' (88).

73 For Stuart Schneiderman in *Jacques Lacan. The Death of an Intellectual Hero* (see especially 52ff.), Lacan was remarkable, within a psychoanalytic tradition that is often pre-eminently concerned with sex and sexual relations, for his willingness to confront and symbolise death – both in his theoretical writings and in his clinical practice.

74 This does not mean of course that the rhetoric of Lacan's rhetorical talk is not itself in urgent need of analysis. For the rhetoric of this talk inflects the psychoanalytic field in new and controversial ways. We may hope that in due course Lacanian psychoanalysis will acquire a 'metahistorian' as acute as Hayden White, who in his pioneering *Metahistory* has analysed what he calls the 'prefigurative' capacity of the rhetorical modes underlying nineteenth-century historiography.

75 'intangible but radical' (174).

5. LACAN AND LITERATURE

1 On the context of high literacy in which Freud grew up and worked, see Jack Spector's 'Vienna and Freud's Education' (*The Aesthetics of Freud*, 3–32) and George Steiner's penetrating 'A Remark on Language and Psychoanalysis'

(*On Difficulty*, 48–9). For an example of this literacy in action during dreams, see n.3 below; for Freud's 1907 listings of 'great', 'good' and 'favourite' books, see *Letters*, 278. An invaluable overview of Freud on the arts is to be found in Richard Wollheim's *On Art and the Mind* (202–19).

2 I quote Heine's quatrain from Pierre Grappin's edition of the *Buch der Lieder*, 293, and the translation from Hal Draper's *The Complete Poems*, 107.

3 'Schön', like its English equivalents, has of course a common ironic usage. In giving a sub-subsection of *The Interpretation of Dreams* the title 'Ein schöner Traum' (*GW*, II/III, 290–91; IV, 284–5), Freud made it plain that the dreamer concerned was being congratulated not only on the aesthetic and intellectual qualities of his 'exceptionally clever dream-production' (these qualities being enhanced by a 'lovely dream' of Faust's that appears among his associations) but on his ingenuity in turning disreputable dream-materials to gratifying effect. The same ironic tinge has been well caught by the English translators in the present case. In a reported conversation, Wittgenstein defended another of these 'lovely dreams' against Freud's irony, holding Freud responsible for destroying the genuine beauty of the dream with the 'coarsest sexual stuff, bawdy of the worst kind' (*Lectures and Conversations*, 23) (Wittgenstein seems to have transposed the title 'Ein schöner Traum' to the 'flowery' dream reported later in the same work and also described as 'schöne': *GW*, II/III, 352; V, 347).

4 The pattern of these references and allusions in the '*Non vixit*' dream has been traced by Alexander Grinstein, *Sigmund Freud's Dreams*, 282–316. *Faust*, which appears only incidentally in this dream, has quite special prominence elsewhere in *The Interpretation of Dreams*. During an earlier discussion of nodal points, for example, poetry had been called upon to collaborate in its own undoing: Mephistopheles's 'weaver's masterpiece' speech on the fabric of thought (*Faust*, Part I, Scene 4) is quoted to reinforce Freud's claim that 'nodal points' are characteristic of the mental life at large (IV, 283). Freud quoted the speech again in 1930, in the final paragraph of the address he gave on receiving the Goethe Prize (XXI, 212).

5 In a further reference to Heine's 'Die Heimkehr', Freud wrote of 'secondary revision' in dreams: 'This function behaves in the manner which the poet maliciously ascribes to philosophers: it fills up the gaps in the dream-structure with shreds and patches' (V, 490). The poem to which Freud alludes here (LVIII: see Grappin's edition of the *Buch der Lieder*, 271 and Draper's translation, 99) is quoted in the *New Introductory Lectures* (XXII, 161).

6 'Freud and Literature', *The Liberal Imagination*, 52.

7 Throughout Freud's writings *Hamlet* was a stable reference-point. The first extended account is to be found in a letter to Fliess of 15 October 1897 (I, 265–6; Freud/Fliess, 272–73; *Origins*, 223–4), although the discussion that has been most discussed in its turn is undoubtedly *The Interpretation of Dreams*, IV, 261–6. Landmarks in the later psychoanalytic and para-psychoanalytic literature on the play include Ernest Jones's *Hamlet and Oedipus* (1949); Jean Starobinski's 'Hamlet et Œdipe' (1967), in *La relation critique*, 286–319 (originally written as an introduction to the French translation of Jones's work); and André Green's *Un œil en trop* (1969) (although Green's main discussion of Shakespeare concerns *Othello*).

8 'The word is not a sign but a signifying knot. And if I say the word "curtain", for example, it's not just by convention to indicate the use of an object that may be diversified in myriad ways by the intentions through which it is

perceived by the worker, the tradesman, the painter or the Gestalt psychologist, as work, exchange value, coloured physiognomy or spatial structure. By metaphor, it's a curtain of trees; by punning the ripples and the laughter of water and my friend Leiris controlling these glossolalic games better than I do. By decree it's the limit of my realm or by chance the screen of my meditation in the room that I share. By a miracle it's space opening out on the infinite, the unknown [person] on the threshold or the morning departure of the solitary. By obsession it's the movement that betrays the presence of Agrippina in the Council of the Empire or Madame de Chasteller's gaze as Lucien Leuwen goes past. By mistake it's Polonius that I strike: "A rat! a rat! a huge rat!" By an interjection, at the interval of a play, it's the cry of my impatience or the word of my weariness. Curtain! It's an image, finally, of meaning as meaning, which in order to be discovered has to be unveiled.'

9 Lacan's main account of *Hamlet* was given as part of the 1958–59 seminar on *Le désir et son interprétation* (as yet unpublished in its entirety). Transcripts of the seven sections devoted to Hamlet are to be found in *Ornicar?*, 24 (pp. 5–31), 25 (pp. 11–36) and 26–27 (pp. 5–44). (These have been translated in part by James Hulbert in *Literature and Psychoanalysis* (*Yale French Studies*, 55/56, 11–52.)

10 Lacan's allusion here is to Michel Leiris's *Glossaire j'y serre mes gloses* (1939). In the preface to this work (reprinted in *Brisées*) Leiris had written: 'En disséquant les mots que nous aimons, sans nous soucier de suivre ni l'étymologie, ni la signification admise, nous découvrons leurs vertus les plus cachées et les ramifications secrètes qui se propagent à travers tout le langage, canalisées par les associations de sons, de formes et d'idées' (11). As if in anticipation of Lacan's tribute, two successive items in Leiris's glossolalic glossary are: 'PSYCHANALYSE – lapsus canalisés au moyen d'un canapé-lit. PSYCHOSE – les hypostases sont mises en cause' (*Mots sans mémoire*, 105).

11 'No, no, the time is past when Nero young / Passed the court's adoration on to me, / When he relied on me to run the state, / When my command convoked the senate here, / When I, behind a veil, invisible, / Was that great body's all-deciding soul' (trans. John Cairncross).

12 Derrida has written with his customary wit and trenchancy about the 'unveiling' of truth in psychoanalysis: 'A vouloir distinguer la science de la fiction, on aura finalement recours au critère de vérité. Et à se demander "qu'est-ce que la vérité?" on reviendra très vite, au-delà des relais de l'adéquation ou de l'*homoiosis*, à la valeur de dévoilement, de révélation, de mise à nu de ce qui est, tel qu'il est, dans son être' (*La Carte postale*, 447).

13 *Romans et Nouvelles*, I, ed. Henri Martineau, 794. 'The young woman closed her casement and watched, half-hidden by the curtain of embroidered muslin at her window. She was perhaps twenty-four or twenty-five years old. Lucien found a singular expression in her eyes; was it irony, hatred, or quite simply youth and a certain tendency to find everything amusing?'

14 'an irony, no doubt rather risky'.

15 On Quintilian, see *Écrits*, 466, 467, 521 etc. The literature on psychoanalysis and rhetoric is now extensive. Distinguished contributions are to be found in Émile Benveniste, *Problèmes* [I], 86–7, Francesco Orlando, *Toward a Freudian Theory of Literature*, 161–75 and Tzvetan Todorov, 'La Rhétorique de Freud' *Théories du symbole*, 285–321. Useful commentary upon Lacan's handling of rhetorical terms, and upon the rhetorical structure of his own prose, is

provided by A. Kremer-Marietti in *Lacan ou la rhétorique de l'inconscient* and J.-B. Fages in *Comprendre Jacques Lacan* (see in particular, 74–92).

16 'Men are so necessarily mad that it would be being mad by another kind of madness *not* to be mad' (tr. Anthony Wilden, *The Language of the Self*, 135). This *pensée* appears as 414 in the Brunschvicg edition.

17 'Es como hidra bocal una dicción, pues a más de su propia y directa significación, si la cortan o la trastruecan, de cada sílaba renace una sutileza ingeniosa y de cada acento un concepto' (*Obras completas*, 386). My translation is taken from Monroe Z. Hafter's *Gracián and Perfection*, 115. The *Agudeza*, having waited almost 350 years for a French translator, burst as a two-headed hydra upon the Parisian scene in 1983, translated by Benito Pelegrín and Michèle Gendreau-Massaloux/Pierre Laurens (see 211 and 229 respectively for the 'vocal hydra' (or the 'mouth hydra') in French).

18 'irritating from the start'. 'Quelques traits du style de Jacques Lacan', *Introduction à la sémiologie*, 181.

19 On Lacan's discussion of this phrase in *Écrits* and the *Séminaire*, see above 122–3.

20 'An enunciation that denounces itself, a statement that renounces itself, ignorance that dissipates itself, an opportunity that loses itself, what remains here if not the trace of what *must* be in order to fall from being?

A dream described by Freud in his article, 'Formulations on the Two Principles of Mental Functioning', gives us, with all the pathos that the figure of a dead father returning as a ghost would be invested, the sentence: 'He did not know that he was dead.'

I have already taken the pretext of this sentence to illustrate the relation of the subject to the signifier – a relation that is embodied in an enunciation (*énonciation*) whose being trembles with the vacillation that comes back to it from its own statement (*énoncé*).

If the figure of the dead father survives only by virtue of the fact that one does not tell him the truth of which he is unaware, what, then, is to be said of the *I*, on which this survival depends?

He did not know . . . A little more and he'd have known. Oh! let's hope that never happens! Rather than have him know, *I*'d die. Yes, that's how *I* get there, there where it was: who knew, then, that *I* was dead?

Being of non-being, that is how *I* as subject comes on the scene, conjugated with the double aporia of a true survival that is abolished by knowledge of itself, and by a discourse in which it is death that sustains existence' (300).

21 This paper dates from 1911. In the same year Freud added to *The Interpretation of Dreams* (v, 430–1) an account of the dream-narrative from which the proposition is taken.

22 *Phenomenology of Spirit*, trans. A. V. Miller, 19. All subsequent references to the *Phenomenology* (*Phen.*) in English are to this translation.

23 *Phen.*, 66.

24 For a brief introductory account of Lacan's distinction between *moi* ('ego') and *sujet* ('subject'), see above 114–15.

25 *Phen.*, 309. The German text is quoted from the Bonsiepen/Heede edition of *Phänomenologie des Geistes* (276).

26 'Always, at every hour, thus without ceasing / my life must end, and begin / Within this death that is uselessly alive'.

27 One of Lacan's clearest statements on the limits of his debt to Hegel, and on

his refusal of Hegel's idealist programme, is to be found in 'Position de l'inconscient': 'notre usage de la phénoménologie de Hegel ne comportait aucune allégeance au système, mais prêchait d'exemple à contrer les évidences de l'identification . . .

Au-delà, les énoncés hégéliens, même à s'en tenir à leur texte, sont propices à dire toujours Autre-chose. Autre-chose qui en corrige le lien de synthèse fantasmatique, tout en conservant leur effet de dénoncer les identifications dans leurs leurres.

C'est notre *Aufhebung* à nous, qui transforme celle de Hegel, son leurre à lui, en une occasion de relever, au lieu et place des sauts d'un progrès idéal, les avatars d'un manque' (837). ('the use we made of Hegel's phenomenology involved no allegiance to the system, but preached by example in order to counter the obvious facts of identification . . .

Beyond that, the Hegelian utterances, even if one confines oneself to the text of them, are propitious for saying always an Other-thing. An Other-thing that corrects their linkage by phantasmatic synthesis, while at the same time preserving the effect they have of exposing identifications in their illusoriness.

This is our personal *Aufhebung*, which transforms that of Hegel, which was his personal illusion, into an opportunity to pick out, instead and in place of the leaps of an ideal progress, the avatars of a lack'.) See also Alain Juranville, *Lacan et la philosophie*, 120–28.

28 *Style, Rhetoric and Rhythm*, 207–8. A useful review of more recent scholarly work on baroque prose is to be found in Marc Fumaroli's monumental *L'Age de l'éloquence*, 1–34.

29 *Style, Rhetoric and Rhythm*, 218–19.

30 Patrick Mahony, also citing Croll, has drawn attention to the presence of 'baroque' elements in the writing of Freud himself (*Freud as a Writer*, 163–5). A brief guide to work in German, English and French on Freud's style is to be found in François Roustang's 'Du Chapitre VII' (*Écrire la psychanalyse*, 65–95).

31 For Lacan on Góngora, see *Écrits*, 410, 467, *Ornicar?*, 26–7 (p. 25), etc. *Culteranismo*, whose outstanding representative Góngora was, has been defined by R. O. Jones: 'a term coined early in the seventeenth century . . . connotes a style of extreme artificiality, which in practice meant Latinisation of syntax and vocabulary, constant use of classical allusion, and the creation of a distinctive poetic diction as far removed as possible from the language of everyday discourse' (*A Literary History of Spain. The Golden Age: Prose and Poetry*, 142). *Conceptismo* (or *agudeza*) involved the use of conceits, and found its supreme theoretical and practical exponent in Gracián, whose *Agudeza* is described by Jones as a 'rhetoric of wit' (201). The 'clash' between the two traditions, vigorous as it was, should not be exaggerated: in his search for examples of *agudeza* Gracián turned more often to Góngora than to any other writer, with the possible exception of Martial.

32 Lacan in 'Ciceronian' mood is to be observed elsewhere in 'Subversion du sujet': see, for example, the second paragraph on p. 812. On the phrase 'dire toujours Autre-chose', see above 128 and 207–8n.27 (where its original context is supplied).

33 Definitions and descriptions of these and other vices are to be found in Lee A. Sonnino's *A Handbook to Sixteenth-Century Rhetoric*.

34 On *vérité*, see for example the brief, clear statements in 'Fonction et champ' (255–6) and the entire paper entitled 'La science et la vérité' (855–77).

35 'The unconscious is that chapter of my history that is marked by a blank or occupied by a falsehood: it is the censored chapter. But the truth can be rediscovered; usually it has already been written down elsewhere. Namely:

— in monuments: this is my body. That is to say, the hysterical nucleus of the neurosis in which the hysterical symptom reveals the structure of a language, and is deciphered like an inscription which, once recovered, can without serious loss be destroyed;

— in archival documents: these are my childhood memories, just as impenetrable as are such documents when I do not know their provenance;

— in semantic evolution: this corresponds to the stock of words and acceptations of my own particular vocabulary, as it does to my style of life and to my character;

— in traditions, too, and even in the legends which, in a heroicized form, bear my history;

— and, lastly, in the traces that are inevitably preserved by the distortions necessitated by the linking of the adulterated chapter to the chapters surrounding it, and whose meaning will be re-established by my exegesis' (50).

36 Anthony Wilden has sketched the pattern of Lacan's allusions to Freud in this passage (*The Language of the Self*, 108–9). For more detailed accounts of the two metaphorical orders, see above 18–27 (archaeological) and Anthony Wilden, *System and Structure*, 43–6 (semiotic).

37 For Freud on the decipherment of hieroglyphics, see XIII, 177 (qu. above, 120).

38 'Freud et la scène de l'écriture', *L'Ecriture et la différence*, 334–5.

39 For Freud's account of this imaginary educational establishment and Lacan's suggested additions to its curriculum, see above 119–20.

40 'Literary inflation'. *Scilicet*, I, 1968, 192. Stuart Schneiderman's *Jacques Lacan. The Death of an Intellectual Hero* begins with an autobiographical reminiscence that contains a salutary lesson for anyone who is persuaded that literary criticism offers a privileged point of entry to psychoanalysis: 'My previous exploration of literature, especially Shakespeare, had prepared me well to appreciate Lacan. His writings are finely wrought, even overwrought, and they do not easily make sense. In this they resemble poetry, and like poetry they yield to critical thinking. Yet this resemblance is a ploy, a rhetorical ploy. This was my thought when I decided that it would be contradictory for me to continue explicating texts when I knew nothing of the experience from which the texts were drawn. Thus I left Buffalo and a career as a professor of English to become a Lacanian psychoanalyst' (v–vi). Comparable reservations about the literary route to Lacan are forcibly expressed by Jane Gallop in her *Reading Lacan* – expressed in the teeth, as it were, of her own expertise as a critical reader.

41 A compelling outline of what such a criticism might comprise was provided by Fredric Jameson in 1977 in his 'Imaginary and Symbolic in Lacan', although in the interval since then little detailed work of this kind having a specifically Lacanian focus has appeared.

42 For Hegel's main discussion of the *schöne Seele*, see *Phen.*, 397–409 (352–62 in the Bonsiepen/Heede edition of the German text and II, 186–200 in the Hyppolite translation to which Lacan was indebted).

43 *Phen.*, 221–8, 406–7.
44 *Phen.*, 225–6, 407.
45 'Alceste is mad and . . . Molière shows him to be such – very rightly in this: that in his beautiful soul he does not recognise that he is himself conducing to the very disorder against which he is in rebellion.' In the course of a brilliant alternative Freudian reading of *Le Misanthrope*, Francesco Orlando takes Lacan to task for his 'Molière le montre comme tel': 'now Alceste is *nothing* apart from the way in which Molière shows him to be, and in which the complications of what Lacan defines as madness are not those of the psychological functioning of a person but a small part of those complications of the semiological functioning of a literary work. In the compromise-formation proper to a literary work, Alceste's "madness" is inseparable both from a comic dimension that distances it from us and from a complicity that draws it closer to us. Fortunately, in these pages by Lacan [172–6] the potential reification of the utterance and the corresponding indifference to the specificity of the enunciation do not have time to develop into an arbitrary reading' (*Lettura freudiana del 'Misanthrope'* (218–19, trans. Ann Caesar). Lacan returns to the theme of the 'beautiful soul' in 'La Chose freudienne' (415).
46 'To be more precise, he is mad not because he loves a woman who is a coquette or betrays him, which a recent generation of learned fellows would no doubt relate to his vital maladaptation, but because he's caught, beneath the flag of Love, by the very feeling that leads the dance of that art of the mirage in which the beautiful Célimène triumphs: namely that narcissism of the idle which provides the psychological structure of 'society' at all periods, here doubled by that other narcissism which manifests itself more especially at certain periods in the collective idealisation of the emotion of love'.
47 'the suicidal aggression of narcissism'.
48 'I could, instead of Alceste, have sought the game played by the law of the heart in the fate that leads the old revolutionary of 1917 into the dock at the Moscow trials. But what is demonstrated in the poet's imaginary space is metaphysically equivalent to the bloodiest things that happen in the world, for it is that which, in the world, makes blood flow'.
49 Jean Hyppolite has traced the pattern of these allusions in his notes to pp. 302–9 of his translation of the *Phenomenology* (vol. 1) and on pp. 275–8 of his *Genèse et Structure* (the main passage referred to by Hyppolite is to be found on pp. 221–6 of the English and pp. 202–6 of the German texts that I have used). Diderot fares rather better than Schiller in the *Phenomenology* in that his *Le Neveu de Rameau* is quoted at least twice in Hegel's text and named in footnotes (*Phen.*, 318, 332).
50 This passage is discussed on p. 125 above and translated on p. 203n.57. For an earlier and less vacillatory formulation of this analogy, see 'Fonction et champ' (291).
51 'Of Structure as an Inmixing of an Otherness Prerequisite to Any Subject Whatever', in *The Structuralist Controversy*, ed. Richard Macksey and Eugenio Donato, 189. This paper was given in a mixture of English and French and published in English.
52 'Any return to Freud that provides subject-matter for a teaching worthy of the name will be produced only by the path by which the most hidden truth reveals itself in the revolutions of culture. That path is the only formation that

we can claim to transmit to those who follow us. It is called: a style.' This passage closes 'La psychanalyse et son enseignement' (437–58), which was first presented – to a philosophical audience – in 1957.

53 On the crucial Freudian concept of *Nachträglichkeit* ('deferred action', 'retroaction', 'l'après-coup'), see Laplanche and Pontalis, 111–14.

54 'The author of these lines has attempted to demonstrate in the logic of a sophism the temporal sources through which human action, in so far as it orders itself according to the action of the other, finds in the scansion of its hesitations the advent of its certainty; and in the decision that concludes it, this action given to that of the other – which it includes from that point on – together with its consequences deriving from the past, its meaning-to-come.

In this article it is demonstrated that it is the certainty anticipated by the subject in the '*time for understanding*' which, by the haste which precipitates the '*moment of concluding*', determines in the other the decision that makes of the subject's own movement error or truth' (75).

55 *Figures* III, 82.

56 Few general statements on the relationship between literature and psychoanalysis are more compellingly topical – if one assumes the relationship to have a future – than the 'Polemical Epilogue' to C. Barry Chabot's *Freud on Schreber*: 'One might say that the problem with most extant efforts to align psychoanalysis and literary studies is that they perceive the benefits that accrue from the enterprise as falling solely in one direction: literary studies apparently bring no dowry . . . if psychoanalysis can contribute to literary studies the substantial benefits of its psychological theory, literary studies can reciprocate by lending the former the benefits of their recognition of the linguistic nature of their evidence . . . Only in such a cooperative spirit can either discipline flourish; only once joined can they achieve their separate ends' (152–3). Outstanding among works that have embarked on the programme outlined here is Peter Brooks's *Reading for the Plot. Design and Intention in Narrative* (1984): Brooks's discussion of *Beyond the Pleasure Principle* in particular (90–112) sets entirely new standards for the close critical reading of Freud's texts.

57 See, for example, *The Interpretation of Dreams*, IV, 48–9, V, 535–6, *Introductory Lectures*, XV, 90, *An Autobiographical Study*, XX, 59.

58 Freud paraphrases Fechner as saying that 'der *Schauplatz der Träume ein anderer ist als der des wachen Vorstellungslebens*' ('the scene of action of dreams is different from that of waking ideational life') (*GW*, II/III, 51; IV, 48). On Freud's debt to Fechner, see Paul-Laurent Assoun, *Introduction à l'épistémologie freudienne*, 150–8.

EPILOGUE

1 Above, 103.

2 'But if a more serious metaphor befits the protagonist, it is that which shows us in Freud an Actaeon perpetually slipped by dogs that have been tracked down from the beginning, and which he strives to draw back into pursuit, without being able to slacken the chase in which only his passion for the goddess leads him on. Leads him on so far that he cannot stop until he reaches the grottoes in which the chtonian Diana in the damp shade, which makes

them appear as the emblematic seat of truth, offers to his thirst, with the smooth surface of death, the quasi-mystical limit of the most rational discourse in the world, so that we might recognize the place in which the symbol is substituted for death in order to take possession of the first swelling of life.

As we know, this limit and this place are still well outside the reach of his disciples, if indeed they make any attempt at all to seek it, and so the Actaeon who is dismembered here is not Freud, but every analyst who can measure up to the passion that consumed him and which has made him, according to the signification that Giordano Bruno gave this myth in his *Furori eroici*, the prey of the dogs of his thoughts' (124).

3 On the mythopoeic dimension of Freud's 'three blows', see Gillian Beer, *Darwin's Plots*, 12–13.

4 This passage from Part I, Dialogue 4 of *De gl' Heroici Furori* (1585) is one of several that employ Actaeon imagery. The Italian text is quoted from Paul-Henri Michel's edition, and the translation from Paul Eugene Memmo's. Michel's edition, which includes a complete French translation, was published two years before the composition of 'La Chose freudienne'. A still more topical reminder of Actaeon is likely to have been provided by Pierre Klossowski's *Le Bain de Diane*, which was published in the year of composition of Lacan's paper (1956). Lacan's paragraphs on Diana also provide a gloss (of sorts) on Freud's enigmatic short paper 'Great is Diana of the Ephesians' (1911) (XII, 342–4), and a response to Sartre's *complexe d'Actéon* ('Le savant est le chasseur qui surprend une nudité blanche et qui la viole de son regard', *L'Etre et le néant*, 667): Sartre's Actaeon, unlike Ovid's and Lacan's, goes unpunished for the violence of his gaze.

5 *Rime sparse*, 23 (p. 67 in Robert M. Durling's bilingual edition, from which text and translation are here quoted). This poem dates from *c.* 1350. Durling discusses penetratingly Petrarch's handling of the Actaeon myth and other Ovidian materials in the Introduction to his edition (27–33). The myth is retold by Boccaccio in his *Genealogie deorum gentilium libri* (Book V, Chapter 14) (*Opere*, X, 249).

6 *Either/Or*, Vol. 1, 431.

7 Jean Starobinski, declaring his debt to Klossowski's *Le Bain de Diane* (see n. 4 above), ends his essay 'Psychanalyse et connaissance littéraire' (1964) upon a more temperate invocation to Actaeon in his role as patron of psychoanalysis: 'Critiques, analystes, gardez allumée la lampe de Psyché, mais songez au destin d'Actéon!' (*La relation critique*, 285).

8 The ellipses here are Lacan's. 'For truth proves to be complex in essence, humble in its offices and alien to reality, stubborn to the choice of sex, akin to death and, all in all, rather inhuman, Diana perhaps . . . Actaeon, too guilty to hunt the goddess, the prey in which is caught, O huntsman, the shadow that you become, let the pack pass by without hastening your step, Diana will recognise the hounds for what they are . . .' (145).

9 'Every drive is virtually (a/the) death drive.'

10 See, for example, *Five Lectures on Psycho-Analysis* (1910) (XI, 39), 'A Difficulty in the Path of Psycho-Analysis' (1917) (XVII, 137–44) and 'The Resistances to Psycho-Analysis' (1925) (XIX, 213–22).

11 See above 129–31.

12 I am unacquainted with the publishing history of this work in translation; it is quite possible that the work, originally written in Russian and published in the Soviet Union, was unavailable until recently to the majority of those Freudians who could have read it with profit.

13 Among the most searching of recent Marxist critiques of psychoanalysis is Richard Lichtman's *The Production of Desire* (1982). The disparate strands of Freud's own reflection on the relationship between psychoanalysis and politics are surveyed by Philip Rieff in his still remarkable and still pertinent *Freud. The Mind of the Moralist* ('Politics and the Individual', 220–56).

14 'One of the room waiters was known to me, and I pointed out to him an interesting little page who opened carriage doors and who remained recalcitrant to my proposals. Finally, in my exasperation, in order to prove to him that my intentions were pure, I made him an offer of a ridiculously high sum simply to come upstairs and talk to me for five minutes in my room. I waited for him in vain. I then took such a dislike to him that I used to go out by the service door so as not to see his villainous little mug at the other. I learned afterwards that he had never had any of my notes, which had been intercepted, the first by the room waiter who was jealous, the next by the day porter who was virtuous, the third by the night porter who was in love with the little page, and used to couch with him at the hour when Dian rose. But my disgust persisted none the less, and were they to bring me the page like a dish of venison on a silver platter, I should thrust him away with a retching stomach' (635).

List of works cited

Anderson, Perry, *In the Tracks of Historical Materialism*, Verso, 1983.

Artemidorus [of Daldis], *The Interpretation of Dreams* [*Oneirocritica*]. Translation and commentary by Robert J. White, Park Ridge, New Jersey, Noyes Press, 1975.

Assoun, Paul-Laurent, *Introduction à l'épistémologie freudienne*, Payot, 1981.

Badcock, C. R., *The Psychoanalysis of Culture*, Basil Blackwell, 1980.

Barthes, Roland, *Le plaisir du texte*, Seuil, 1973.

Baudelaire, Charles, *Œuvres complètes*, ed. Claude Pichois, II, Bibliothèque de la Pléiade, Gallimard, 1976.

Baudry, Jean-Louis, *Proust, Freud et l'Autre*, Minuit, 1984.

Beer, Gillian, *Darwin's Plots. Evolutionary Narrative in Darwin, George Eliot and Nineteenth-Century Fiction*, Routledge and Kegan Paul, 1983.

Benjamin, Walter, *Illuminations*, ed. Hannah Arendt, trans. Harry Zohn, Collins/Fontana, 1973.

Benveniste, Émile, *Problèmes de linguistique générale* [I], Gallimard, 1966.

Berlin, Isaiah, *Personal Impressions*, The Hogarth Press, 1980.

Bersani, Leo, *Marcel Proust. The Fictions of Life and Art*, Oxford University Press, 1965.

Bersani, Leo, 'Representation and its Discontents', *Raritan*, Summer 1981, 3–17.

Bersani, Leo, 'Theory and Violence', *Raritan*, Summer 1983, 54–73.

Bersani, Leo, *Théorie et violence*, Seuil, 1984 [in English: *The Freudian Body. Psychoanalysis and Art*, New York, Columbia University Press, 1986].

Bettelheim, Bruno, *Freud and Man's Soul*, Chatto and Windus/Hogarth Press, 1983.

Blanchot, Maurice, *L'Entretien infini*, Gallimard, 1969.

Bloom, Harold, *Agon. Towards a Theory of Revisionism*, New York and Oxford, Oxford University Press, 1982 ['Freud and the Sublime', 91–118].

Boccaccio, Giovanni, *Genealogie deorum gentilium libri* (1350–75), ed. Vincenzo Romano (*Opere*, X and XI), Bari, Laterza, 1951.

Bossuet, Jacques-Bénigne, *Oraisons funèbres*, ed. Jacques Truchet, Garnier, 1961.

Brenkman, John, 'The Other and the One: Psychoanalysis, Reading, *The Symposium*', *Yale French Studies* 55/56, 1977 (*Literature and Psychoanalysis*), 396–456.

Brooks, Peter, *Reading for the Plot. Design and Intention in Narrative*, Oxford, Clarendon Press, 1984.

Brunet, Étienne, *Le Vocabulaire de Proust*, 3 vols, Genève–Paris, Slatkine–Champion, 1983.

Bruno, Giordano, *Des Fureurs héroïques (De gl'Heroici Furori)*. Texte établi et traduit par Paul-Henri Michel, Les Belles Lettres, 1954.

Bruno, Giordano, *The Heroic Frenzies*. A Translation with Introduction and Notes by Paul Eugene Memmo, Jr. (Studies in the Romance Languages and Literatures, 50), Chapel Hill, University of North Carolina Press, 1964.

List of works cited

Cancogni, Manlio and Perocco, Guido, *L'Opera completa del Carpaccio* (Classici dell'Arte, 13), Milan, Rizzoli, 1967.

Chabot, C. Barry, *Freud on Schreber. Psychoanalytic Theory and the Critical Act*, Amherst, University of Massachusetts Press, 1982.

Clément, Catherine, *Vies et légendes de Jacques Lacan*, Grasset, 1981.

Cocking, J. M., *Proust. Collected Essays on the Writer and his Art*, Cambridge, Cambridge University Press, 1982.

Compagnon, Antoine, 'Proust sur Racine', *Revue des sciences humaines*, No. 196, 1984/4, 39–64.

Craig, George, 'Marcel Proust: the "petite phrase" and the sentence', *History of European Ideas*, Vol. 1, No. 3, 259–76.

Croll, Morris W., *Style, Rhetoric, and Rhythm*. Essays edited by J. Max Patrick and Robert O. Evans, Princeton, New Jersey, Princeton University Press, 1966.

Deleuze, Gilles and Guattari, Félix, *L'Anti-Œdipe* (*Capitalisme et schizophrénie*, I), Minuit, 1972.

Deleuze, Gilles and Guattari, Félix, *Mille Plateaux* (*Capitalisme et schizophrénie*, II), Minuit, 1980.

Deleuze, Gilles and Guattari, Félix, *Politique et psychanalyse*, Éditions des Mots Perdus, 1977.

Derrida, Jacques, *L'Écriture et la différence*, Seuil, 1967.

Derrida, Jacques, *La Carte postale, de Socrate à Freud et au-delà*, Aubier-Flammarion, 1980 ['Le Facteur de la vérité', 441–524].

Donato, Eugenio and Macksey, Richard (eds), *The Structuralist Controversy*, Baltimore and London, Johns Hopkins University Press, 1970.

Dor, Joël, *Bibliographie des travaux de Jacques Lacan*, InterEditions, 1983.

Doubrovsky, Serge, *La Place de la madeleine*, Mercure de France, 1974.

Écrire la psychanalyse, Nouvelle revue de psychanalyse [Gallimard], No. 16, automne 1977.

Empson, William, *Seven Types of Ambiguity* (1930), Third Edition, Chatto and Windus, 1953.

Engelman, Edmund, *Berggasse 19. Sigmund Freud's Home and Offices, Vienna 1938*. The Photographs of Edmund Engelman. With an Introduction by Peter Gay, Chicago and London, University of Chicago Press, 1976.

Fages, Jean-Baptiste, *Comprendre Jacques Lacan*, Privat, 1971.

Finch [Winton], Alison, *Proust's Additions. The Making of 'A la recherche du temps perdu'*, Cambridge University Press, 1977.

Finch [Winton], Alison, 'Characterization in the Early *Du côté de chez Swann*', *Modern Language Review*, Vol. 74, January 1979, 49–61.

Forrester, John, *Language and the Origins of Psychoanalysis*, Macmillan, 1980.

Foucault, Michel, *Histoire de la sexualité*, Gallimard, I: *La volonté de savoir*, 1976. II: *L'usage des plaisirs*, 1984. III: *Le souci de soi*, 1984.

Freud, Ernst (with Lucie Freud and Ilse Grubrich-Simitis), ed., *Sigmund Freud. His Life in Pictures and Words*. With a Biographical Sketch by K. R. Eissler, André Deutsch, 1978.

Freud, Sigmund, *The Complete Letters of Sigmund Freud to Wilhelm Fliess, 1887–1904*. Translated and Edited by Jeffrey Moussaieff Masson, Cambridge, Mass. and London, Harvard University Press, 1985.

Freud, Sigmund, *Letters, 1873–1939*, ed. Ernst L. Freud, trans. Tania and James Stern, The Hogarth Press, 1970.

Freud, Sigmund, *The Letters of Sigmund Freud and Arnold Zweig*, ed. Ernst L. Freud, trans. Prof. and Mrs W. D. Robson-Scott, The Hogarth Press and the Institute of Psycho-Analysis, 1970.

Freud, Sigmund, *Gesammelte Werke*, edited by Anna Freud and others, 18 vols, London, Imago, 1940–52 (Vols 1–17) and Frankfurt am Main, Fischer Verlag, 1968 (Vol. 18).

Freud, Sigmund, *The Origins of Psycho-Analysis. Letters to Wilhelm Fliess, Drafts and Notes, 1887–1902*, ed. Marie Bonaparte, Anna Freud and Ernst Kris, trans. Erich Mosbacher and James Strachey, London and New York, Imago, 1954.

Freud, Sigmund, *The Standard Edition of the Complete Psychological Works*, translated from the German under the general editorship of James Strachey, 24 vols, The Hogarth Press and the Institute of Psycho-Analysis, 1953–74.

Freud, Sigmund and Jung, C. G., *The Freud/Jung Letters*, edited by William McGuire, trans. Ralph Manheim and R. F. C. Hull, The Hogarth Press and Routledge and Kegan Paul, 1974.

Fromm, Erich, *The Crisis of Psychoanalysis*, Jonathan Cape, 1970 ['The Method and Function of an Analytic Social Psychology' (1932), 135–62].

Fumaroli, Marc, *L'Age de l'éloquence. Rhétorique et 'res literaria' de la Renaissance au seuil de l'époque classique*, Genève, Droz, 1980.

Gallop, Jane, *Reading Lacan*, Ithaca and London, Cornell University Press, 1985.

Gallop, Jane, *Feminism and Psychoanalysis. The Daughter's Seduction*, Macmillan, 1982.

Gautier, Théophile, *Italia*, Victor Lecou, 1852 [repr. 'Les Introuvables', Éditions d'Aujourd'hui, 1976].

Gay, Peter, *Freud, Jews and Other Germans. Masters and Victims in Modernist Culture*, New York, Oxford University Press, 1978.

Gay, Peter, *Freud for Historians*, New York, Oxford University Press, 1985.

Genette, Gérard, *Figures* III, Seuil, 1972.

Gracián, Baltasar, *Obras completas*, ed. Arturo del Hoyo, Madrid, Aguilar, 1960 [*Agudeza y arte de ingenio*, 229–514].

Gracián, Baltasar, *Art et figures de l'esprit*. Traduction, introdution et notes de Benito Pelegrín, Seuil, 1983.

Gracián, Baltasar, *La Pointe ou l'Art du Génie*. Traduction intégrale par Michèle Gendreau-Massaloux et Pierre Laurens, préface de Marc Fumaroli, L'Age d'Homme, 1983.

Green, André, *Un œil en trop. Le complexe d'Œdipe dans la tragédie*, Minuit, 1969.

Green, André, 'Transcription d'origine inconnue', *Écrire la psychanalyse*, 27–63 [see above, 215].

Grinstein, Alexander, *Sigmund Freud's Dreams*, Second Edition, New York, International Universities Press, 1980.

Grünbaum, Adolf, *The Foundations of Psychoanalysis. A Philosophical Critique*, Berkeley, Los Angeles and London, University of California Press, 1984.

Hafter, Monroe Z., *Gracián and Perfection. Spanish Moralists of the Seventeenth Century*, Cambridge, Mass., Harvard University Press, 1966.

Hammond, N. G. L., *Alexander the Great. King, Commander and Statesman*, Chatto and Windus, 1981.

Hammond, N. G. L., *Three Historians of Alexander the Great*, Cambridge, Cambridge University Press, 1983.

Hampshire, Stuart, *Modern Writers and Other Essays*, Chatto and Windus, 1969.

List of works cited

Hegel, G. W. F., *Phänomenologie des Geistes* [*Gesammelte Werke*, 9]. Herausgegeben von Wolfgang Bonsiepen und Reinhard Heede, Hamburg, Felix Meiner, 1980.

Hegel, G. W. F., *Phenomenology of Spirit*. Trans. A. V. Miller, with Analysis of the Text and Foreword by J. N. Findlay, Oxford, Clarendon Press, 1977.

Hegel, G. W. F., *La Phénoménologie de l'Esprit*. Traduction de Jean Hyppolite, 2 vols, Aubier Montaigne, [1939–41].

Heine, Heinrich, *Buch der Lieder* (*Historisch-kritische Gesamtausgabe der Werke*, Band I/i), bearbeitet von Pierre Grappin, Hamburg, Hoffmann und Campe, 1975.

Heine, Heinrich, *The Complete Poems*. A Modern English Version by Hal Draper, Boston, Suhrkamp/Insel, 1982.

Hobson, Marian, 'Deconstruction, Empiricism and the Postal Services', *French Studies*, XXXVI, July 1982, 290–314.

Hyman, Stanley Edgar, *The Tangled Bank. Darwin, Marx, Frazer and Freud as Imaginative Writers*, New York, Atheneum, 1962.

Hyppolite, Jean, *Genèse et Structure de la 'Phénoménologie de l'Esprit' de Hegel*, Aubier Montaigne, 1946.

Irigaray, Luce, *Ce sexe qui n'en est pas un*, Minuit, 1977.

Irigaray, Luce, *Éthique de la différence sexuelle*, Minuit, 1984.

Irigaray, Luce, *Parler n'est jamais neutre*, Minuit, 1985.

Jakobson, Roman and Halle, Morris, *Fundamentals of Language*, The Hague, Mouton, 1956.

Jameson, Fredric, 'Imaginary and Symbolic in Lacan: Marxism, Psychoanalytic Criticism, and the Problem of the Subject', *Yale French Studies*, 55/56, 1977 (*Literature and Psychoanalysis*), 338–95.

Johnson, Barbara, *The Critical Difference. Essays in the Contemporary Rhetoric of Reading*, Baltimore and London, Johns Hopkins University Press, 1980.

Jones, Ernest, *Hamlet and Oedipus*, Gollancz, 1949.

Jones, Ernest, *Sigmund Freud. Life and Work*, The Hogarth Press, Vol. I (new ed.), 1954; Vol. II (new ed.), 1958; Vol. III, 1957.

Jones, R. O., *A Literary History of Spain. The Golden Age: Prose and Poetry*, Ernest Benn, 1971.

Juranville, Alain, *Lacan et la philosophie*, Presses universitaires de France, 1984.

Kerrigan, William and Smith, Joseph H., *Interpreting Lacan* (Psychiatry and the Humanities, 6), New Haven and London, Yale University Press, 1983.

Kierkegaard, Søren, *Either/Or* (1843), Vol. 1, trans. David F. Swenson and Lillian Marvin Swenson (with revisions and a foreword by Howard A. Johnson), Princeton, Princeton University Press, 1959.

Kilmartin, Terence, *A Guide to Proust*, Chatto and Windus/Hogarth Press, 1983.

Klossowski, Pierre, *Le Bain de Diane* (1956), Gallimard, 1980.

Kojève, Alexandre, *Introduction à la lecture de Hegel*, Gallimard, 1947.

Koyre, Alexandre, *Newtonian Studies* (1965), Phoenix Books, Chicago, University of Chicago Press, 1968.

Kremer-Marietti, Angèle, *Lacan ou la rhétorique de l'inconscient*, Aubier Montaigne, 1978.

Lacan, Jacques, *Les complexes familiaux dans la formation de l'individu. Essai d'analyse d'une fonction en psychologie*, Navarin, 1984 [reprints 'La Famille', *Encyclopédie française*, VIII, 1938].

Lacan, Jacques, *De la psychose paranoïaque dans ses rapports avec la personnalité* (1932) suivi de *Premiers écrits sur la paranoïa*, Seuil, 1975.
Lacan, Jacques, *Écrits*, Seuil, 1966.
Lacan, Jacques, *Écrits. A Selection*, trans. Alan Sheridan, Tavistock Publications, 1977.
Lacan, Jacques, *The Four Fundamental Concepts of Psycho-Analysis*, ed. Jacques-Alain Miller, trans. Alan Sheridan, The Hogarth Press and the Institute of Psycho-Analysis, 1977.
Lacan, Jacques, *Le Séminaire*, Seuil, 1973– [Livre I: *Les écrits techniques de Freud* (1975); Livre II: *Le moi dans la théorie de Freud et dans la technique de la psychanalyse* (1978); Livre III: *Les psychoses* (1981); Livre XI: *Les quatre concepts fondamentaux de la psychanalyse* (1973); Livre XX: *Encore* (1975)].
Lacan, Jacques, *Télévision*, Seuil, 1973.
Lacan, Jacques, 'Hamlet', *Ornicar?*, 24, automne 1981, 5–31; 25, rentrée 1982, 11–36; 26/27, été 1983, 5–44 [trans. in part by James Hulbert in *Literature and Psychoanalysis* (*Yale French Studies*, 55/56), 11–52].
Lacan, Jacques, ['Note de lecture'], *Scilicet*, 1, 1968, 192.
Lacan, Jacques, 'Of Structure as an Inmixing of an Otherness Prerequisite to Any Subject Whatever', *The Structuralist Controversy*, ed. Richard Macksey and Eugenio Donato, Baltimore and London, Johns Hopkins University Press, 1970, 186–200.
Lacan, Jacques, 'Radiophonie', *Scilicet*, 2/3, 1970, 55–99.
Laplanche, Jean, *Vie et mort en psychanalyse*, Flammarion, 1970 [trans. Jeffrey Mehlman as *Life and Death in Psychoanalysis*, Baltimore and London, Johns Hopkins University Press, 1976].
Laplanche, Jean and Pontalis, J.-B., 'Fantasme originaire, fantasmes des origines, origine du fantasme', *Les Temps modernes*, No. 215, avril 1964, 1833–68.
Laplanche, Jean and Pontalis, J.-B., *Vocabulaire de la psychanalyse*, Presses universitaires de France, 1967 [trans. Donald Nicholson-Smith as *The Language of Psycho-Analysis*, The Hogarth Press and the Institute of Psycho-Analysis, 1973].
Leclaire, Serge and Laplanche, Jean, 'L'Inconscient. Une étude psychanalytique', in *L'Inconscient*, Desclée de Brouwer, 1966, 95–130 and 170–7 [trans. Patrick Coleman in *French Freud*, ed. Mehlman, 118–75].
Lefort, Rosine (en collaboration avec Robert Lefort), *Naissance de l'Autre. Deux psychanalyses: Nadia (13 mois) et Marie-Françoise (30 mois)*, Seuil, 1980.
Leiris, Michel, *Brisées*, Mercure de France, 1966.
Leiris, Michel, *Mots sans mémoire* [includes, pp. 71–116, *Glossaire j'y serre mes gloses* (1939)], Gallimard, 1969.
Lepschy, Giulio, 'Freud, Abel et gli opposti', in *Mutamenti di prospettiva nella linguistica*, Bologna, Il Mulino, 1981 [173–98].
Lepschy, Giulio, 'Linguistic Historiography', in *Linguistic Controversies. Essays in Linguistic Theory and Practice in Honour of F. R. Palmer*, ed. David Crystal, Edward Arnold, 1982 [25–31].
Lichtman, Richard, *The Production of Desire. The Integration of Psychoanalysis into Marxist Theory*, New York and London, The Free Press, 1982.
Macksey, Richard and Donato, Eugenio (eds), *The Structuralist Controversy*, Baltimore and London, Johns Hopkins University Press, 1970.

Mahony, Patrick, *Freud as a Writer*, New York, International Universities Press, 1982.
Maimonides, Moses, *The Guide of the Perplexed*. Two vols. Trans. Shlomo Pines, Chicago and London, Chicago University Press, 1963.
Mannoni, Maud, *La théorie comme fiction. Freud, Groddeck, Winnicott, Lacan*, Seuil, 1979.
Mannoni, Octave, *Ça n'empêche pas d'exister*, Seuil, 1982.
Mannoni, Octave, *Fictions freudiennes*, Seuil, 1978.
Marcus, Steven, *Freud and the Culture of Psychoanalysis. Studies in the Transition from Victorian Humanism to Modernity*, Allen and Unwin, 1984.
Mehlman, Jeffrey, ed., *French Freud. Structural Studies in Psychoanalysis, Yale French Studies*, 48, 1972.
Mehlman, Jeffrey, *A Structural Study of Autobiography. Proust, Leiris, Sartre, Lévi-Strauss*, Ithaca and London, Cornell University Press, 1974.
Miller, Jacques-Alain, *Entretien sur le Séminaire, avec François Ansermet*, Navarin, 1985.
Miller, Milton L., *Nostalgia. A Psychoanalytic Study of Marcel Proust*, Gollancz, 1957.
Milner, Max, *Freud et l'interprétation de la littérature*, Société d'Édition d'Enseignement Supérieur, 1980.
Mitchell, Juliet, *Psychoanalysis and Feminism*, Harmondsworth, Penguin, 1975.
Mitchell, Juliet and Rose, Jacqueline (eds.), *Feminine Sexuality. Jacques Lacan and the 'École freudienne'*, Macmillan, 1982.
Mounin, Georges, *Introduction à la sémiologie*, Minuit, 1970.
Muller, John P. and Richardson, William J., *Lacan and Language. A Reader's Guide to 'Écrits'*, New York, International Universities Press, 1982.
Orlando, Francesco, *Lettura freudiana del 'Misanthrope', e due scritti teorici*, Torino, Giulio Einaudi, 1979.
Orlando, Francesco, *Toward a Freudian Theory of Literature, with an analysis of Racine's 'Phèdre'*, trans. Charmaine Lee, Baltimore and London, Johns Hopkins University Press, 1978.
Pascal, Blaise, *Pensées et opuscules*, ed. Léon Brunschvicg, Hachette [1961].
Petrarch's Lyric Poems. The 'Rime sparse' and Other Lyrics, trans. and ed. Robert M. Durling, Cambridge, Mass., and London, Harvard University Press, 1976.
Pignatti, Terisio, *Carpaccio*, Lausanne, Skira, 1958.
Plutarch, *The Age of Alexander* [*Nine Greek Lives*], trans. Ian Scott-Kilvert, Harmondsworth, Penguin, 1973.
Politzer, Georges, *Critique des fondements de la psychologie* (1928), Presses universitaires de France, 1974.
Pontalis, J.-B., *Entre le rêve et la douleur*, Gallimard, 1977.
Pontalis, J.-B. and Laplanche, Jean, *Vocabulaire de la psychanalyse*, Presses universitaires de France, 1967 [trans. Donald Nicholson-Smith as *The Language of Psycho-Analysis*, The Hogarth Press and the Institute of Psycho-Analysis, 1973].
Pontalis, J.-B. and Laplanche, Jean, 'Fantasme originaire, fantasmes des origines, origine du fantasme', *Les Temps modernes*, No. 215, avril 1964, 1833–68.
Proust, Marcel, *A la recherche du temps perdu*, 3 vols, ed. Pierre Clarac and André Ferré, Bibliothèque de la Pléiade, Gallimard, 1954.

Proust, Marcel, *Contre Sainte-Beuve*, précédé de *Pastiches et mélanges* et suivi de *Essais et articles*, ed. Pierre Clarac, Bibliothèque de la Pléiade, Gallimard, 1971.
Proust, Marcel, *La Prisonnière*, ed. Jean Milly, Flammarion, 1984.
Proust, Marcel, *Remembrance of Things Past*, 3 vols, trans. C. K. Scott Moncrieff and Terence Kilmartin, Chatto and Windus, 1981.
Racine, Jean, *Andromache, Britannicus, Berenice*. Translated and Introduced by John Cairncross, Harmondsworth, Penguin, 1967.
Racine, Jean, *Iphigenia, Phaedra, Athaliah*. Translated and Introduced by John Cairncross, Harmondsworth, Penguin, 1963.
Racine, Jean, *Œuvres complètes*, t.1, ed. Raymond Picard, Bibliothèque de la Pléiade, Gallimard, 1950.
Rank, Otto, *The Myth of the Birth of the Hero. A Psychological Interpretation of Mythology* (1909), trans. F. Robbins and Smith Ely Jelliffe, New York, Robert Brunner, 1952.
Renan, Ernest, *Souvenirs d'enfance et de jeunesse* (1883), Édition de Jean Pommier (1959), 'Folio', Gallimard, 1983.
Richardson, William J. and Muller, John P., *Lacan and Language. A Reader's Guide to 'Écrits'*, New York, International Universities Press, 1982.
Ricœur, Paul, *De l'interprétation. Essai sur Freud*, Seuil, 1965.
Rieff, Philip, *Freud. The Mind of the Moralist*, Gollancz, 1959.
Robert, Marthe, *D'Œdipe à Moïse. Freud et la conscience juive*, Calmann-Lévy, 1974.
Rosand, David, *Painting in Cinquecento Venice. Titian, Veronese, Tintoretto*, Yale University Press, 1982.
Rose, Jacqueline and Mitchell, Juliet (eds.), *Feminine Sexuality. Jacques Lacan and the 'École freudienne'*, Macmillan, 1982.
Roudaut, Jean and Perocco, Guido, *Tout l'œuvre peint de Carpaccio* (Les Classiques de l'art), Flammarion, 1981 [French version of the Cancogni/Perocco *Carpaccio* – see above].
Roustang, François, 'Du Chapitre VII', *Écrire la psychanalyse*, 65–95 [see above].
Safouan, Moustapha, *Jacques Lacan et la question de la formation des analystes*, Seuil, 1983.
Said, Edward W., *Beginnings. Intention and Method*, Baltimore and London, Johns Hopkins University Press, 1975.
Sartre, Jean-Paul, *L'Etre et le néant*, Gallimard, 1943.
Saussure, Ferdinand de, *Cours de linguistique générale*, ed. Tullio de Mauro, Payot, 1978.
Sayce, R. A., 'The Goncourt Pastiche in *Le Temps retrouvé*' in *Marcel Proust. A Critical Panorama*, ed. Larkin B. Price, Urbana, Chicago and London, University of Illinois Press, 1973, 102–23.
Schneiderman, Stuart, *Jacques Lacan. The Death of an Intellectual Hero*, Cambridge, Mass., Harvard University Press, 1983.
Schneiderman, Stuart (editor and translator), *Returning to Freud. Clinical Psychoanalysis in the School of Lacan*, New Haven and London, Yale University Press, 1980.
Schorske, Carl E., *Fin-de-siècle Vienna. Politics and Culture*, Cambridge University Press, 1981 ['Politics and Patricide in Freud's *Interpretation of Dreams*', 181–207].
Schur, Max, *Freud. Living and Dying*, The Hogarth Press and the Institute of Psycho-Analysis, 1972.
Serres, Michel, *Esthétiques sur Carpaccio* (Collection Savoir), Hermann, 1975.

Shattuck, Roger, *Proust*, Fontana/Collins, 1974.
Sichère, Bernard, *Le moment lacanien*, Grasset, 1983.
Smith, Joseph H. and Kerrigan, William, *Interpreting Lacan* (Psychiatry and the Humanities, 6), New Haven and London, Yale University Press, 1983.
Sonnino, Lee A., *A Handbook to Sixteenth-Century Rhetoric*, Routledge and Kegan Paul, 1968.
Spector, Jack J., *The Aesthetics of Freud. A Study in Psychoanalysis and Art* (1972), New York, McGraw-Hill, 1974.
Spitzer, Leo, *Études de style*, Gallimard, 1970.
Splitter, Randolph, *Proust's 'Recherche'. A Psychoanalytic Interpretation*, Routledge and Kegan Paul, 1981.
Starobinski, Jean, *La relation critique* (*L'Œil vivant*, II), Gallimard, 1970.
Steiner, George, *On Difficulty and Other Essays*, Oxford University Press, 1978.
Stendhal, *Romans et Nouvelles*, I, ed. Henri Martineau, (Pléiade), Gallimard, 1952.
Sulloway, Frank J., *Freud, Biologist of the Mind. Beyond the Psychoanalytic Legend*, Burnett Books, 1979.
Tadié, Jean-Yves, *Proust et le roman*, Gallimard, 1971.
Taine, Hippolyte, *Voyage en Italie* (1866), t.I: *Naples et Rome*, t.II: *Florence et Venise*, Hachette, 1897–8.
Terdiman, Richard, *The Dialectics of Isolation. Self and Society in the French Novel from the Realists to Proust*, New Haven, Yale University Press, 1976.
Timpanaro, Sebastiano, *The Freudian Slip. Psychoanalysis and Textual Criticism* (1974), trans. Kate Soper, New Left Books, 1976.
Timpanaro, Sebastiano, 'Freud's "Roman Phobia"', *New Left Review*, 147, September–October, 1984, 4–31.
Todorov, Tzvetan, *Théories du symbole*, Seuil, 1977.
Trilling, Lionel, *Beyond Culture. Essays on Literature and Learning*, Secker and Warburg, 1966 ['Freud: Within and Beyond Culture', 87–110].
Trilling, Lionel, *The Liberal Imagination*, Secker and Warburg, 1951.
Turkle, Sherry, *Psychoanalytic Politics. Freud's French Revolution*, Burnett Books/André Deutsch, 1979.
Vološinov, V. N., *Freudianism. A Marxist Critique*, trans. I. R. Titunik and edited in collaboration with Neal H. Bruss, New York, Academic Press, 1976.
Voragine, Jacobus de, *The Golden Legend*, trans. and adapted from the Latin by Granger Ryan and Helmut Ripperger, New York, Longmans, Green, 1941.
Weber, Samuel, *The Legend of Freud*, Minneapolis, University of Minnesota Press, 1982.
White, Hayden, *Metahistory. The Historical Imagination in Nineteenth-Century Europe*, Baltimore and London, Johns Hopkins University Press, 1973.
Wilden, Anthony, ed., *The Language of the Self. The Function of Language in Psychoanalysis* ['Fonction et champ' by Jacques Lacan]. Translated with notes and commentary by A. W., Baltimore, Johns Hopkins University Press, 1968.
Wilden, Anthony, *System and Structure. Essays in Communication and Exchange*, Tavistock Publications, 1972.
Wisdom, John, *Philosophy and Psycho-Analysis*, Oxford, Basil Blackwell, 1953.
Wittgenstein, Ludwig, *Lectures and Conversations on Aesthetics, Psychology and Religious Belief*, ed. Cyril Barrett, Oxford, Basil Blackwell, 1966.
Wollheim, Richard, *On Art and the Mind. Essays and Lectures*, Allen Lane, 1973.
Wollheim, Richard, *The Thread of Life*, Cambridge University Press, 1984.
Wright, Elizabeth, *Psychoanalytic Criticism. Theory in Practice*, Methuen, 1984.

Index

Index